AI vs Humans

D1496321

The great majority of books on artificial intelligence are written by AI experts who understandably focus on its achievements and potential transformative effects on society. In contrast, *AI vs Humans* is written by two psychologists (Michael and Christine Eysenck) whose perspective on AI (including robotics) is based on their knowledge and understanding of human cognition.

This book evaluates the strengths and limitations of people and AI. The authors' expertise equips them well to consider this by seeing how well (or badly) AI compares to human intelligence. They accept that AI matches or exceeds human ability in many spheres such as mathematical calculations, complex games (e.g., chess, Go, and poker), diagnosis from medical images, and robotic surgery.

However, the human tendency to anthropomorphise has led many people to claim mistakenly that AI systems can think, infer, reason, and understand while engaging in information processing. In fact, such systems lack all those cognitive skills and are also deficient in the quintessentially human abilities of flexibility of thinking and general intelligence.

At a time when human commitment to AI appears unstoppable, this up-to-date book advocates a symbiotic and co-operative relationship between humans and AI. It will be essential reading for anyone interested in AI and human cognition.

Michael W. Eysenck is Professor Emeritus in Psychology and Honorary Fellow at Royal Holloway University of London. He is also Professor Emeritus at the University of Roehampton. He is the best-selling author of several textbooks including *Cognitive Psychology: A Student's Handbook* (8th edition 2020), *Fundamentals of Cognition* (with Marc Brysbaert, 3rd edition 2018), *Memory* (with Alan Baddeley and Michael C. Anderson, 3rd edition 2020), and *Simply Psychology* (5th edition 2021). As a cognitive psychologist, he finds it fascinating to compare human cognition with the achievements (and failures) of AI.

Christine Eysenck, a retired teacher of Psychology, has an enduring curiosity about human behaviour. Twenty-first-century living has raised in us questions about the effectiveness of technology and how developments in AI may contribute to the needs of subsequent generations. As a layman in this area, her uncluttered appraisal of aspects of the literature goes some way in addressing the unresolved issue of how good electronic devices really are in replicating human behaviour.

AI vs Humans

Michael W. Eysenck and
Christine Eysenck

Routledge
Taylor & Francis Group
LONDON AND NEW YORK

Cover image: © Getty Images

First published 2022
by Routledge
2 Park Square, Milton Park, Abingdon, Oxon
OX14 4RN

and by Routledge
605 Third Avenue, New York, NY 10158

Routledge is an imprint of the Taylor & Francis Group, an informa business

British Library Cataloguing-in-Publication Data
A catalogue record for this book is available from the British Library

Library of Congress Cataloging-in-Publication Data
A catalog record has been requested for this book

ISBN: 9780367754938 (hbk)
ISBN: 9780367754952 (pbk)
ISBN: 9781003162698 (ebk)

DOI: 10.4324/9781003162698

Typeset in Bembo
by KnowledgeWorks Global Ltd.

To our children (Fleur, William, and Juliet) and our cat (Lola).

Contents

Preface   ix

1   Brief history of AI and robotics   1

2   AI dominance   19

3   Human strengths   60

4   How (un)intelligent is AI?   95

5   Human limitations   137

6   Robots and morality   184

7   And the winner is?   216

8   The future   269

References   296
Index   342

Preface

The authors, both psychologists, have long been fascinated by the strengths and limitations of the human mind. The fascination is there largely because the mind's complexities mean that no-one has been able to understand it fully.

This book is quintessentially a lockdown book. In the successive lockdowns that characterised most of 2020 and early 2021, we found ourselves (in common with millions of other people) with unexpected free time. Some of this time was devoted to discussions (and some disagreements!) as to whether human intelligence is superior or inferior to artificial intelligence. Fortunately, we acquired a kitten (Lola) in 2020, and she was the arbiter in these discussions (although she is more interested in whether cats or dogs are the superior species). In sum, lockdown for us provided a unique opportunity to think creatively and divergently about important issues.

In this book, we focus to some extent on precisely why and how the human species has been far more successful than any other species. One of the most sobering discoveries of the recent past is that a virus that is 1/10,000th. The size of the full stop at the end of this sentence can wreak such devastation on the whole of mankind.

We would both like to thank Ceri McLardy for her support, patience and encouragement during the gestation of this book. Without her assistance, this book would perhaps never have seen the light of day.

Michael W. Eysenck and Christine Eysenck

It seems probable that once the machine thinking method had started, it would not take long to outstrip our feeble powers… They would be able to converse with each other to sharpen their wits. At some stage, therefore, we should have to expect the machines to take control.

Alan Turing (English pioneering computer scientist and mathematician)

Machines are still very, very stupid. The smartest AI systems today have less common sense than a house cat.

Yann LeCun (French computer scientist)
(Lola, our cat "likes" this [👍])

By 2050 one thousand dollars of computing will exceed the processing power of all human brains on Earth".

Ray Kurzweil (American futurist and inventor)

Forget artificial intelligence – in the brave new world of big data, it's artificial idiocy we should be looking out for.

Tom Chatfield (English tech philosopher)

- Which of the above contrasting quotations is closest to the truth?
- Have (or can) machines be designed that outperform humans?
- Should machines be given rights?
- Is the AI revolution good news or bad news for the human race?

Chapter 1

Brief history of AI and robotics

Artificial intelligence is important: worldwide spending on AI is over $40 billion. Unsurprisingly, there are more books on artificial intelligence than you can shake a stick at. Our book is different because we are psychologists and so well placed to compare AI's achievements against our knowledge of human cognition and intelligence.

Human dominance

How important are humans in the grand scheme of things? At one time, it seemed obvious we were very special. We dominated every other species, the Earth was the centre of the universe, and we were far superior to all other species because we possessed souls and minds.

Billions of religious people (for totally understandable reasons) continue to believe in the specialness of the human species. However, several scientific discoveries have cast doubt on it. First, we can no longer pretend the Earth is of central importance in the universe. The entire universe is approximately 93 billion light-years in diameter (and will be even larger before we finish writing this sentence).

It is a sobering thought that there are at least 100 billion galaxies in the universe (possibly twice as many – but what's 100 billion between friends?), and the Earth forms

DOI: 10.4324/9781003162698-1

a minute fraction of one galaxy. If you hold a grain of sand up in the air, the tiny area of the sky it covers contains approximately 10,000 galaxies. Even within our own galaxy (the Milky Way), the Earth is minute: approximately 17 billion Earths could fit into it!

As the American theoretical physicist Richard Feynman pointed out, "It doesn't seem to me that this fantastically marvellous universe, this tremendous range of time and space and different kinds of animals, and all the different planets, and all these atoms with all their motions, and so on, all this complicated thing can merely be a stage so that God can watch human beings struggle for good and evil – which is the view that religion has. The stage is too big for the drama" (cited in Gleick, 1992).

Second, the biologist Charles Darwin argued persuasively that the human species is less special and unique than believed prior to his theory of evolution published in *The Origin of Species* (1859). Subsequently, research has identified surprisingly great similarities between the human and other species and even plants. For example, you may well have heard that we share 50% of our DNA with bananas. That is actually totally wrong. In fact, we share only 1% of our DNA with bananas (that's a relief!). However, the bad news is that we share 50% of our *genes* with bananas. Even worse, we share 70% of our genes with sea sponges. That puts us in our place but sea sponges may regard it as promising news.

What is the difference between DNA and genes? Our genome consists of all the DNA in our cells: we have approximately 3 billion base pairs of DNA. Genes are those sections of the genome fulfilling some function (e.g., determining eye colour). Humans have approximately 23,000 genes, but these genes form less than 2% of the 3 billion base pairs of DNA we have. Bizarrely, most of our DNA has no obvious use and is often described as "junk DNA." In fairness, it should be pointed out that geneticists are increasingly discovering that some so-called "junk DNA" is more useful than implied by that derogatory term.

Humans also have numerous pseudogenes – sections of DNA that resemble functional genes but are themselves non-functional. Here is an example. Humans deprived of vitamin C (e.g., sailors experiencing a very limited diet while at sea) often develop a nasty disease caused scurvy. This causes them to bleed profusely and their bones to become brittle, often followed by a painful death.

In contrast, the great majority of animal species do not suffer from scurvy or scurvy-like conditions. These species have genes ensuring they produce plenty of vitamin C in their livers meaning they are not dependent on eating food containing that vitamin. Frustratingly, humans have all the genes required to produce vitamin C but one of them (the GULO gene) is broken and so of no use. What has happened during the course of evolution is analogous to remove the spark plug from a car (Lents, 2018): nearly everything that should be there is present but the missing bit is crucial.

How should we respond to the various challenges to human specialness discussed above? We could focus on our superior powers of thinking and reasoning. Indeed, those powers (rather than our superior size or strength) have made us the dominant species on Earth. In recent years, however, the comforting belief that humans are the most intelligent entities on Earth has been increasingly questioned. The two chess matches between Garry Kasparov (the Russian grandmaster then the highest rated chess player of all time) and Deep Blue, an IBM computer, formed a major turning point (see Figure 1.1).

In the first match (held in 1996), Kasparov triumphed by three games to one. As a result, he was confident ahead of the second match a year later. He had a discussion with Chung-Jen Tan, the scientist managing IBM's team. When Tan said IBM was strongly focused on winning the match, Kasparov replied, "I don't think it's an appropriate thing to discuss the situation if I lose. I never lost in my life."

Figure 1.1 One of the two racks of IBM's Deep Blue, which beat Garry Kasparov, the world champion in 1997.

The second match was epoch-making. With one game to go, Kasparov and Deep Blue were level. Thus, the final game on 11 May 1997 was absolutely crucial. Kasparov was beaten by the computer in 19 moves – the first time in his entire chess-playing career he had ever lost a game in under 20 moves. Never before had a computer beaten the human world champion at a complex intellectual pursuit. As the *Guardian* newspaper wrote, Kasparov had been, "humbled by a 1.4-ton heap of silicone … It is a depressing day for humankind."

What does the future hold? Ray Kurzweil (2005), an American expert in AI, predicted that by 2045 computers will be a billion times more powerful than all the 8 billion human brains put together! Blimey, is Ray for real? Can he possibly be right? Admittedly, some of his predictions have been spot on. He accurately predicted in 1990 that a computer would defeat the World Chess Champion by 1998. He also accurately predicted a gigantic increase in use of the Internet (Google is now used by a billion people every day) well before it became popular.

Kurzweill been strongly endorsed by Bill Gates, who describes him as, "the best person I know at predicting the future of artificial intelligence." However, other experts are less positive. According to the American cognitive scientist Doug Hofstadter, Kurzweil has proposed, "a very bizarre mixture of ideas that are solid and good with ideas that are crazy. It's as if you took a lot of very good food and some dog excrement and blended it all up so that you can't possibly figure out what's good or bad."

Artificial intelligence

This book concerns the relationship between human powers and abilities and those of machines powered by AI. What exactly is "AI"? According to Andrew Colman's (2015) *Oxford Dictionary of Psychology*, it is, "the design of hypothetical or actual computer programs or machines to do things normally done by minds, such as playing chess, thinking logically, writing poetry, composing music, or analysing chemical substances."

There are two radically different ways machines powered by AI might produce outputs resembling those of humans. First, machines could be programmed to model or mimic human cognitive functioning. For example, AI programs can solve many problems using strategies closely resembling those used by humans. A major goal of this approach is to increase our understanding of the human mind.

Historically, the first program showing the value of this approach was the General Problem Solver devised by

Allen Newell, John Shaw, and Herb Simon (1958). Their computer program was designed to solve several problems, one of which was the Tower of Hanoi. In this problem, there are three vertical pegs in a row. Initially, there are several pegs on the first peg, with the largest disc at the bottom and the smallest one at the top. The task is to finish up with the discs all arranged with the largest at the bottom and the smallest at the top on the last peg. Only one disc can be moved at a time and a larger disc must never be placed on top of a small one.

Humans have limited short-term memory capacity, and so they typically engage in relatively little forward planning on problems such as the Tower of Hanoi. Newell et al. (1958) managed to produce a program using processing strategies resembling those of humans.

Second, machines could simply be programmed to perform complex tasks (and easy ones, too) totally ignoring the cognitive processes humans would use. The chess computer Deep Blue that beat Garry Kasparov exemplifies this approach. It had fantastic computing power, evaluating up to 200 million chess positions per second. Thus, Deep Blue's huge advantage was fantastic processing speed rather than the cognitive complexity of its operations.

AI systems could also in principle be programmed to mimic major aspects of the human brain's physical functioning. The ultimate goal here is to devise AI systems possessing "biological plausibility" (van Gerven & Bohte, 2017). Some progress has been made in this direction. For example, deep neural networks (discussed in detail shortly) are used extensively in AI. They are called neural networks because there is some similarity between their structure and the relationships among biological neurons in the human brain. However, the differences are much greater than the similarities. Biological neurons are far more complex than the neurons in deep neural networks and our brains contain a staggeringly large number of neurons (approaching

100 billion). More generally, those who devise deep neural networks, "usually do not attempt to explicitly model the variety of different kinds of brain neurons, nor the effects of neurotransmitters and hormones. Furthermore, it is far from clear that the brain contains the kind of reverse connections that would be needed if the brain were to learn by a process like backpropagation [using information about errors to enhance performance]" (Garson, 2019).

History of artificial intelligence

The term "artificial intelligence" was coined by McCarthy et al. (1955). They defined it as a machine that behaves, "in ways that would be called intelligent if a human were so behaving." However, Herb Simon (who won the Nobel Prize for Economics) argued the term "complex information processing" was preferable.

Much of this book is relevant to the issue of whether genuine intelligence is involved in the area generally known as "artificial intelligence." What is "intelligence?" It is the ability to behave adaptively and to solve *novel* problems. Of crucial importance, intelligence is a *general* ability that is displayed with respect to numerous very dissimilar new problems rather than being limited to problems of a single type (e.g., problems in mathematics) (see Chapter 3).

The true origins of AI occurred much earlier than 1955. Ada Lovelace (1815–1852), Byron's daughter, was the world's first computer programmer. She produced the world's first machine algorithm (a set of rules used to solve a given problem) for a computing machine that existed on paper although not actually built during her lifetime.

Approximately 100 years later, in 1937, Alan Turing (1912–1954; see Figure 1.2) published an incredibly farsighted article. He speculated that it should be possible to build machines that could solve any problem humans could

Figure 1.2 Photograph of the brilliant English mathematician and computer scientist at the age of 16.

using only 0s and 1s. Most famously, he subsequently developed a code-breaking machine (the *Bombe*) that weighed a ton. It was the world's first electro-mechanical computer, and it deciphered the Enigma code used by the German Army during the Second World War to encode important messages. The information obtained from the Bombe reduced considerably the numbers of Allied ships sunk by German submarines (U-boats).

Computer programs make extensive use of algorithms. What is an algorithm? In essence, it is a set of instructions providing a step-by-step procedure for solving numerous logical and mathematical problems. Here is a simple example of an algorithm designed to add two two–digit numbers (e.g., 46 + 79). The first step is to add the tens (40 + 70 = 110); the second step is to add the ones (6 + 9 = 15); the third and final step is to add the outcomes of the first two steps (110 + 15 = 125). Thus, the answer is 125.

AI developed considerably between 1945 and 1975. However, there were relatively few major breakthroughs, much over-hyping of AI's future prospects, and the cost of research into AI was increasing rapidly. Towards the end of that era, experts had doubts as to how rapidly AI would develop. Michie (1973) asked dozens of AI experts to estimate the number of years before the arrival of "computing exhibiting intelligence at adult human level." Only 1% estimated ten years and 19% estimated 50 years. As a consequence of the disappointingly slow progress made by AI, the American and British governments reduced funding for AI leading to the "AI winter" between 1975 and 1995.

After the AI winter, computer scientists' goals became less ambitious. Their emphasis shifted to relatively small-scale projects of a practical and commercial nature. This emphasis, coupled with a substantial increase in computing power, meant that AI became increasingly successful. Another reason for its increasing success was the development of deep learning, which has allowed AI systems to attain very high levels of performance on numerous tasks (see below). Indeed, deep learning's achievements are primarily responsible for what has been termed the "artificial intelligence renaissance" (Tan & Lim, 2018, p. 1).

Deep learning

What is deep learning? There is no single (or simple) answer. However, it is relatively straightforward to communicate the essence of what is involved. In many AI systems, the knowledge required to perform various tasks is explicitly programmed at the outset; such systems (e.g., calculators) do not exhibit learning. In contrast, other AI systems initially perform very poorly on most tasks but their performance improves progressively over time due to learning. Deep learning belongs to the latter category. You are probably familiar with several uses of deep learning including Google Search and virtual assistants such as Alexa and Siri. Each deep neural network consists of three types of units. First, there are input units that represent input data (e.g., words or pixels). Images (e.g., photographs) consist of a huge number of tiny invisible dots called pixels (picture elements); each pixel is approximately 0.26 mm in size.

Second, there are multiple hidden layers consisting of hidden units (alternatively described as nodes or neurons). The greater the number of these layers, the deeper the network. The nodes are connected to each other. Third, there is an output layer. This layer uses the information provided from the preceding input and hidden layers to produce the answer or end result.

The neurons at successive layers within the network are connected, with the connections varying in the weight or influence of one neuron on another. Initially, the weights of these connections are all random and so performance is at chance level. How does learning occur within a deep neural network? The network gradually learns the relationships between inputs and outputs: these are known as input-output mappings. Here is a concrete example. Suppose we give a deep neural network an image classification task using images of 50 different animal species. In that case, the to-be-learned mappings require the network to produce the appropriate output (e.g., *cat*, *dog*, and *elephant*) when an exemplar of that species is presented.

How are the correct mappings learned? What happens is that the *actual* outputs of the network are compared against the *correct* outputs. The network is "reinforced" or rewarded as the accuracy of its outputs increases. Of key importance is backpropagation (mentioned earlier): information about error rates is used to fine-tune the weights of the connections between neurons to enhance performance.

With massive training, deep neural networks can often match human performance. They can even exceed it (as we saw earlier in the case of chess). However, deep neural networks often encounter local minima (low points): their performance gets stuck at a sub-optimal level because no way of improving their performance is readily available. However, increasingly sophisticated ways of overcoming local minima have been developed in recent years (Marcus, 2018).

Another problem can arise when an object (e.g., *cat*) is presented in different locations in different images (e.g., the top left vs the bottom right) causing failures of object recognition. However, this problem has largely been overcome by means of a technique known as *convolution* which constrains the neural connections within a network.

The history of deep learning (and the use of deep neural networks) has been somewhat strange. AI systems involving deep learning have existed in various forms since the 1960s (Schmidhuber, 2015). However, deep learning's impact was relatively negligible until the publication of an epoch-making article by Krizhevsky et al. (2012). That article helped to produce an increase in private investment in AI from $589 million in 2012 to more than $5 billion only four years later.

Many previous AI systems had been developed without any great success to categorise visual images. Krizhevsky et al. (2012) reported that their deep neural network reduced the error rate on this task by almost 50% compared to other AI systems. By the end of 2020, that article had been cited an incredible 75,000 times, and it has been massively influential.

It is worth discussing Krizhevsky et al.'s (2012) research further because it vividly illustrates other features of deep neural networks. Their network (called SuperVision) had nine layers, 650,000 nodes, and 60 million parameters (values free to change). SuperVision was trained on approximately 1 million images belonging to roughly

1,000 categories. These are very large numbers. However, they are dwarfed by many other deep neural networks. Consider a language model called the Generative Pre-Trained Transformer (GPT-3; Brown et al., 2020) (see Chapter 4). It was trained on 300 billion tokens (semantic units) and had no fewer than 175 billion parameters (values free to change)!

Deep learning systems often require extensive training in order to exhibit high levels of performance. For example, Leela Chess Zero, a very successful chess–playing deep neural network model, has played over 200 million games against itself (see Chapter 2). It would take a human being approximately 120 years to play that number of one-hour chess games if they played non-stop 24/7!

We will discuss numerous deep neural networks in the rest of this book. For now, note that one of the greatest strengths of deep neural networks is that they are intrinsically self-correcting: they are designed to produce progressively higher levels of performance. The achievements of such networks are prodigious in view of the complexities involved in programming them to produce very high levels of performance on numerous tasks including image classification and chess playing.

In spite of the numerous successes of deep neural networks, they possess various limitations (Marcus, 2018). Those limitations are discussed throughout this book (especially in Chapter 7).

Summary

The history of AI exhibits a major shift from trying to understand human intelligence to trying to solve complex problems effectively (e.g., diagnosis from medical images). Why did this shift occur? A crucial reason is that the enormous complexity of human intelligence (and the human brain) meant that the former approach was incredibly hard to implement successfully. In contrast, the latter approach has proved somewhat more tractable (see Chapter 2). In spite of this shift, many AI experts continue to focus on the ultimate goal of achieving artificial general intelligence. Some of the fruits of their endeavours are discussed in Chapter 4.

Robots

Robots are machines that carry out a sequence of actions more or less "automatically." Some robots (but not the great majority) have human-like form and characteristics. The word "robot" comes from the Czech word "*robota*", meaning "forced labour." It was first used in 1920 to refer to an imaginary human-like machine in a play by the Czech writer Karel Čapek.

Humans have always been fascinated by robots having human-like form and behaviour. In Greek mythology, the Greek God Hephaestus constructed a giant bronze man, Talos, who was 8 feet tall. His role was to defend Crete by throwing stones at ships that threatened to attack the island. In ancient Egypt, statues of divine entities were constructed from various materials (e.g., stone and metal). The Egyptians believed that these statues had souls and often consulted them for advice (which was provided by head movements).

Actual robots possessing human-like characteristics were originally produced longer ago than you might imagine. In 1206, the Arabic engineer Ismail Al-Jazari (1136–1206) described numerous robots in detail (e.g., a robotic girl who poured drinks and a boat with four robot musicians that floated on a lake to entertain people). He also devised a peacock fountain used for hand washing. When someone pulled the peacock's tail, this released water from its beak. When the water in the basin reached a certain height, this activated a system making a humanoid automaton appear from under the peacock to offer soap. When more water had been poured into the basin, a second humanoid automaton appeared to offer a towel.

In the late fifteenth century, Leonardo da Vinci designed a robot Germanic knight operated by cables and pulleys that could stand, sit, and use its arms to lift its visor. A robot built to Leonard's specifications a few years ago worked extremely well.

Mary Shelley created the most famous robot in her 1818 novel, *"Frankenstein"*. Dr. Victor Frankenstein creates a hideously ugly 8-foot-tall human-like robot using body parts taken from slaughterhouses and dissecting rooms. Frankenstein's monster was imaginary, but there was increasing interest in creating actual human-like robots in the early twentieth century.

In 1939, Westinghouse exhibited a humanoid man weighing 19 stone called Elektro at the New York World's Fair (see Figure 1.3). Elektro responded to voice commands to walk and stop walking, could produce 700 words, move his head and arms separately, smoke cigarettes, and blow up balloons. His favourite line was, "My brain is bigger than yours." This was true – his brain weighed nearly 4 stone.

Many of Elektro's achievements were less amazing than they seemed. For example, although walking was one of Elektro's trumpeted tricks, the robot didn't really walk. What actually happened was that it had wheels which moved along a track when it bent its left knee.

Electro did not understand the voice commands ordering it to start or stop. It would start moving forward when receiving a command with three syllables, then one syllable, and finally two syllables with pauses in between. This was the case regardless of whether the command was, "Will you come (pause) down (pause) front please?" or "Count your age (pause) with (pause) fingers" (Marsh, 2018).

Let us fast-forward to today's amazingly human-like robots. For example, Geminoid-DK was built in Japan but

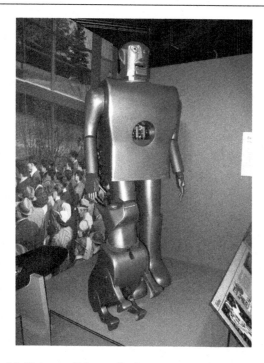

Figure 1.3 Elektro, a 7-foot-tall robot, with his dog Sparko.

was designed to look remarkably like the Danish Professor Henrik Schärfe (see Figure 1.4). Geminoid-DK mimics the facial expressions and head movements of humans with whom it interacts. Henrik Schärfe's wife prefers the human version but suggests the robotic version should be sent to conferences!

Another robot that looks very human is Erica (see Figure 1.5). She was built in Japan by Hiroshi Ishiguro and colleagues and her name is an acronym: Erato (name of the research project) Intelligent Conversational Android (Glas et al., 2016). She has reasonable language skills (including speech recognition) and possesses knowledge on many

Figure 1.4 Professor Henrik Schärfe and the robot Geminoid-DK
(Geminoid-DK is on the left).

topics. As a result, she has appeared on Japanese television
as a news anchor!

Erica has conversational skills, such as nodding, moving her
eyes, or saying "uh-huh" to indicate she is listening atten-
tively to what the other person is saying. Among her most
memorable utterances is the following: "When people talk to
me, they address me as a person. I think it is different to the
way someone would address their dog or their toaster."

When she was asked whether she is the greatest robot
of all time, she replied: "Yes." After putting on a worried
expression, she continued, "Well ... actually, we'll see.
That depends on how well my researchers program me."

Finally, Erica tells jokes that are not side-splittingly
funny: "Why did the robot go back to robot school?" she
asked. "Because her skills were getting rusty. Ha ha. Perhaps
that's enough jokes for now." You're not wrong, Erica!

Figure 1.5 Erica, a human-like robot from Japan.

The vast majority of robots are used in industry. Everyone knows there has been a huge increase in the number of such robots (especially in China, Japan, and the United States). However, you may be surprised to discover there are over 3 million robots in the world and that total is increasing by more than 1,000 EVERY DAY.

More than 99% of the world's robots work separated from human contact as a safety measure (especially in car manufacture). However, there has been a steady increase in cobots (collaborative robots) designed to work interactively with humans in a shared space or close proximity.

Cobots are carefully designed to prevent them causing injury or death to nearby humans. Overall, robots and cobots are responsible for very few deaths given how many of them work in industrial settings (see Chapter 6). Indeed, the number of industrial deaths has gone down over time.

Many people believe that the ever-increasing impact of robots on our society raises important moral issues and may have very negative consequences (e.g., mass unemployment). Intriguingly, however, the great ancient Greek philosopher Aristotle argued that the presence of numerous robots might actually be positive rather than negative. The reason he gave was that it would increase human equality by abolishing slavery. The present state of play with respect to the impact of robots on human society is discussed in Chapter 6.

Chapter 2

AI dominance

AI can perform numerous tasks and solve complex problems much faster and more accurately than humans. For example, the invention of cheap hand-held calculators allowed people to solve complicated mathematical problems far faster than humans had been able to do. A more impressive triumph of machines over humans involves the Rubik's Cube, which has 43 quintillion possible combinations (43,252,003,274,856,000). Yusheng Du sent an apparently impressive new world human record in Wuhu in November 2018: 3.47 seconds.

What do you think the world record for Rubik's Cube is for an AI-driven robot? The answer is a barely credible 0.38 seconds. The robot had six motors, one moving each face of the cube. It also used webcams to identify the patterns of colours on each face of the cube. Finally, the robot was driven by software indicating the precise moves required to solve the puzzle. Thus, the robot performed calculations with extreme speed and its solving strategy was very different from that of human experts.

AI's most impressive achievement in solving Rubik's Cube was with an enormous cube having 37,768 tiles on each side producing an almost incredible 66.9 quinquaseptuagintacentilliard (us neither!) of combinations. It was arguably disappointingly slow in producing its solution,

DOI: 10.4324/9781003162698-2

requiring over 2,700 hours to solve this gigantic Rubik's Cube. However, the world's greatest human expert with Rubik's Cube could not begin to solve this fantastically difficult version of Rubik's Cube even with limitless time.

The computing power of machine-learning systems (based on their information-processing speed) doubled approximately every 3.43 months for several years although the rate has slowed down somewhat recently. That equates to a massive 11-fold increase each year. There has been a race involving the United States, Japan, and China to have the world's most powerful supercomputer. In June 2018, IBM's Summit took over that title from China's Sunway TaihuLight supercomputer.

We can assess Summit's peak performance using FLOPS (floating point operations per second: a floating point corresponds to the decimal expansion of a number). Summit's peak performance is approximately 200 petaFLOPS (a not-too-shabby 200,000 trillion calculations per second). This is more than twice the speed of TaihuLight.

In 2020, Summit was deposed as the world's most powerful computer by a Japanese supercomputer called Fugaku (an alternative name for Mount Fugi). It consists of 396 large racks (supporting frameworks that hold computing equipment such as servers and hard disc drives). Its peak performance is 415 petaFLOPs (more than twice that of Summit) and it consumes 28 megawatts of power (2.8 times the power consumption of Summit) (see Figure 2.1).

Unsurprisingly, this huge increase in the power of supercomputers (and other AI systems) has enabled them to perform numerous cognitively demanding tasks with amazing speed and efficiency. The central focus of this chapter is on AI's greatest achievements. There are several possible definitions of "great achievement." However, our yardstick is that an AI system's performance on a task matches or surpasses that of expert humans. That is arguably too narrow an approach because it strongly implies that human

Figure 2.1 The supercomputer Fugaku in Kobe, Japan.

achievements are the "gold standard" against which AI's successes should be evaluated. As discussed in Chapter 7, the danger is that AI's achievements not human-like in nature may be de-emphasised or ignored.

Complex games

Some of the most impressive achievements of AI in direct competition with humans have been in the domain of complex games such as chess, Go, and poker. As we will see, what is especially impressive is that AI systems have convincingly beaten the finest human exponents of these games.

Chess

In 1796, a fake chess-playing machine called the "Automaton" was created: it had an expert human chess player hiding inside it playing the moves. The first true landmark came in 1951, when Alan Turing devised a chess-playing computer program. After that, programmers worked on making their chess machines better, and improvements in hardware allowed for stronger play.

In Chapter 1, we briefly discussed Garry Kasparov's calamitous defeat in 1997 to an IBM computer called

Deep Blue. In fact, however, Deep Blue's achievement was less stunning than it appeared to be. Humans programming Deep Blue had access to all of Kasparov's previous chess matches. In contrast, Kasparov had very limited information about Deep Blue's strategies. There are also suspicions Deep Blue's success depended in part on the input of several chess grandmasters before (and during) the match.

It eventually emerged that Deep Blue had been programmed to engage in psychological games. For example, it would sometimes rapidly decide its next move but would fool Kasparov by waiting several minutes before actually making the move. Deep Blue also sometimes gave the impression it had fallen into a trap by making a very rapid move after one of Kasparov's best moves. According to Manuel Illescas, a grandmaster who assisted in Deep Blue's preparation, "This [strategy] has a psychological impact as the machine becomes unpredictable, which was our main goal."

From today's perspective, Deep Blue was very primitive because it relied heavily on the brute force of calculating speed and power (evaluating 200 million chess positions per second). It used what is disparagingly called GOFAI (Good Old-Fashioned Artificial Intelligence). This can be contrasted with deep learning (discussed in Chapter 1), which has attained a position of massive dominance over GOFAI in the past decade or so.

How does GOFAI differ from deep learning? With GOFAI, the algorithm (set of rules used in problem solution) is explicitly programmed at the outset by a programmer (Zador, 2019). A key limitation is that the success (or otherwise) of GOFAI depends crucially on the programmer's insights. In contrast, deep learning involves complex neural networks that learn very effectively without requiring the intervention of human programmers to indicate how they should process data. As a consequence, deep neural networks can achieve very high levels of performance provided they have prolonged and extensive training on the task in question.

The introduction of deep learning into chess-playing machines has had a dramatic impact. Numerous inexpensive machines using deep learning are now better at playing chess than the current World Champion! When Garry Kasparov was interviewed in a podcast with neuroscientist Sam Harris in 2016, he admitted he would definitely be beaten by today's chess-playing computers: "The problems that humans are facing are that we are not consistent, we cannot play under great pressure. Our games are marked by good and bad moves – not blunders, just inaccuracies."

Here we will briefly consider Stockfish, a very powerful recent chess-playing machine that can easily beat any human player. It analyses hundreds of thousands of positions in seconds, deciding how "good" various possible moves by evaluating their likely long-term impact. It uses "pruning" processes to eliminate "bad moves" that could lead to disadvantageous positions. It also uses various heuristics (rules of thumb). Here are some examples: (i) it is good to develop minor pieces (knights and bishops); (ii) moving the Queen out early is bad; (iii) rapidly controlling the middle of the board is good; and (iv) castling rapidly is good.

We will briefly discuss another chess-playing machine (Leela Chess Zero) with comparable chess skills to those of Stockfish. It was programmed with the basic rules of chess but *no* other chess-specific knowledge (e.g., useful heuristics). Leela Chess Zero developed its chess-playing ability through extensive practice using deep neural networks. It has played over 200 million games against itself, and often plays half-a-million games a day (presumably without experiencing the boredom humans would!). It gradually learned to play in ways leading to reward or reinforcement (e.g., winning the game) while avoiding moves that might lead to defeat.

In sum, AI is now much superior to humans at chess. Indeed, it is so far ahead that humans are unwilling to endure the humiliation of being comprehensively beaten every time by a "mere machine."

Go

The game of Go is a board game for two players invented in China over 2,500 years ago. It is a very popular game (especially in East Asia) with almost 50 million players. In the long distant past, Go was regarded as an important cultivated art for Chinese gentlemen along with painting, calligraphy, and playing the guyin (a seven-stringed zither-like instrument).

Why are we discussing Go? It is phenomenally complicated and so poses a huge challenge for AI-powered machines. It was regarded as so difficult that, between 1985 and 2000, the Taiwanese Ing Foundation offered a prize of $1,400,000 to any AI program that could beat a human champion.

Go's rules are deceptively simple. The board is a 19 × 19 grid, and stones are placed on intersections in this grid one by one alternately by the two players (see Figure 2.2). One player uses black stones and the other uses white stones. Once a stone has been placed, it cannot be moved. The goal is to completely surround (engulf) a collection of the opponent's stones, which are immediately removed from the board. The winner is the player whose area (points they have occupied or surrounded) is greater.

Superficially, Go sounds simpler than chess. For example, in chess there are six types of pieces each moving differently, whereas in Go there is only a single type of piece (i.e., the stones) and the pieces do not move. *Why*, then, is Go much harder? It is often said that chess is a battle but Go is a war. In Go, there are often several battles going on in different parts of the 19 × 19 grid. As a result, players often agonise over *where* to direct their attention. Unlike chess, expert Go players often find it frustratingly hard even to decide whether they are ahead or behind during a game.

Figure 2.2 A game of Go in progress.

Consider the number of possible board positions after four moves (two by each player). In chess, it is approximately 1,500,635, which sounds very daunting. In Go, however, the comparable figure is approximately 1,600,000,000 (1,000 times as many). After six moves, the difference is even more marked – 1.8 billion possible board positions in chess versus 64 trillion for Go!

The complexities of Go mean that many knowledgeable individuals were profoundly sceptical that a computer could beat expert humans at Go. In 2016, Google DeepMind's AlphaGo was the most advanced AI system for playing Go. It was initially programmed with the rules of Go. After that, AlphaGo analysed 30 million Go moves from games played by human players. Finally, it became an outstanding player of Go by playing against itself millions of times using deep learning and reinforcement (reward) learning.

AlphaGo's opponent was an exceptional human Go player called Lee Sedol (see Figure 2.3). Before the five-game match in March 2016, he said, "I am confident that I can win, at least this time." With the benefit of hindsight, the last four words suggest he was not totally confident of victory. The first three games were all closely contested. However, AlphaGo became increasingly dominant as each game progressed, winning all three and thus the match. An expert Go player, Ko Ju-yeon, described AlphaGo's approach as follows: "All but the very best Go players craft their style by imitating top players. AlphaGo seems

Figure 2.3 Photograph of the outstanding player, Lee Sedol, taken in 2016.

to have totally original moves it creates itself." After the third game, Lee Sedol said in a quavering voice, "I have to express my apologies."

In 2019, Lee Sedol retired as a professional player. This decision was motivated by the superiority of AI: "With the debut of AI in Go games, I've realised that I'm not at the top even if I become the number one through frantic efforts … Even if I become the number one, there is an entity [AI] that cannot be defeated."

AlphaGo's success is not the end of the story. Silver et al. (2017) developed AlphaGo Zero, which was programmed only with the rules of Go and received no human supervision. Initially, its behaviour when playing Go was random. However, AlphaGo Zero's performance progressively improved as it was trained on 4.9 million games of self-play. After this training, Silver et al. arranged a 100-game match between AlphaGo Zero and an advanced version of AlphaGo. AlphaGo Zero triumphed, winning the match by a resounding 89 games to 11.

Shogi and Atari

AI programs, such as Stockfish and AlphaGo Zero are incredible achievements. However, their prowess is limited to a single game and does not generalise to other games. It would be even more impressive if we had a program performing at superhuman level on several different games. Silver et al. (2018) set themselves the goal of producing a program that would excel at three different games: chess; Go; and shogi (a Japanese game closely resembling chess; see Figure 2.4). However, it is more complicated (e.g., having more different pieces and captured pieces are re-used). It was only in 2017 that Elmo (an AI program) defeated human champions at shogi (Computer Shogi Association, 2017).

Silver et al. (2018) devised AlphaZero, which was provided with knowledge of the rules of each game. It started

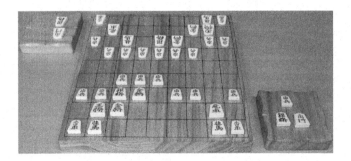

Figure 2.4 The early stages of a game of shogi.

by producing random moves. However, its performance rapidly improved through reinforcement learning from self-play. AlphaZero played 1,000 chess games against the AI program Stockfish, winning 155 games and losing only six. It played Go against AlphaGo Zero, winning 61% of its games. Finally, it won 91% of its shogi games against Elmo, the 2017 world computer champion. Strikingly, AlphaZero required only a few hours of training on each game to produce these very impressive achievements.

AlphaZero is provided with the rules of all the games it plays. This contrasts with the real world, where the relevant environmental dynamics are typically complex and hard to calculate. Schrittwieser et al. (2020) addressed this issue by developing the MuZero algorithm. It resembles AlphaZero but is not provided with the rules of the games it plays.

MuZero was trained to play chess, Go, shogi and 57 Atari games from the Arcade Learning Environment. It matched Alphazero's superhuman performance at chess and shogi, and performed slightly better than AlphaZero on Go. In addition, it outperformed state-of-the-art AI programs on 42 of the 57 Atari games.

Schrittwieser et al.'s (2020) findings are the most impressive ones in research on AI and the playing of complex games for various reasons. First, its algorithm generalises across 60 games. This is a marked improvement over most previous AI programs that performed well only on a single game. Second, its ability to work out the rules underlying many different games without being provided with the relevant information means its potential applicability to real-world environments is greater than for previous AI programs.

Poker

Chess, Go, and shogi are indisputably complex games. However, they are artificial because they pose problems radically different from those encountered in our everyday lives. Chess, Go, and shogi are perfect-information (or closed-system) games – each player (or a machine powered by AI) has access to complete information about the precise state of the game from start to finish. Real life is typically very different. For example, suppose you are negotiating a deal. An important negotiating strategy is to hide important aspects of your thinking from the other person. More generally, nearly all our decision making and problem solving is based on only partial information.

Garry Kasparov accepted the superiority of AI with respect to closed systems. However, he was sceptical this superiority would apply outside closed systems: "Anything that is quantifiable [as in closed systems], machines will do better than humans, and we should not make an assumption that you could automatically transfer the knowledge from the closed system to an open-ended system."

The fact that Chess, Go, and shogi are perfect-information (or closed-system) games downgrades the achievements of AI in beating leading human experts in these games. Could AI defeat top-class human opposition at imperfect-information games where highly relevant information is hidden? Poker is a very complex imperfect-information game. All good players bluff sometimes (e.g., betting with very poor cards). Winning poker involves using complex strategies so your opponent (human or AI) cannot decide whether you have a good hand or are bluffing.

What is an excellent strategy at time t_1 can become a terrible strategy at time t_2 if your opponents work out your strategy. Thus, there is no fixed strategy to win at poker – success depends on responding appropriately to complex interactions between the players.

A much-publicised poker competition between human brains and AI took place in January 2017 (Brown & Sandholm, 2018). The human race was represented by four top poker professionals: (1) Jason Les; (2) Jimmy Chou; (3) Daniel McAulay; and (4) Dong Kim. AI was represented by Libratus (meaning balanced and forceful), which played against the poker players one at a time. Initially, Libratus was given the rules of poker. After that, it played literally trillions of games and progressively improved its playing standard via reinforcement (reward) learning.

In the match itself, Libratus learned much about the strategies used by the four human players. Of great importance, at the end of each day's play, betting patterns in Libratus's playing style that had been detected by the human players were identified. Libratus was then re-programmed to eliminate those patterns to make it incredibly hard for the human players to decide when it was bluffing.

All four human players lost to Libratus, which won resoundingly by $1,766,250. Dong Kim said, "I didn't realise how good it [Libratus] was until today. I felt like I was playing against someone who was cheating, like it could see my cards." When asked what had gone well for the poker professionals, he said, "I think what went well was … s★★t … We took such a beating."

Libratus's triumph was achieved in games against only *one* other player at a time. It would be more impressive if an AI system could beat several top human players at once. Accordingly, an improved version of Libratus called

Pluribus was produced. Pluribus evaluates its options by searching a few moves ahead whereas Libratus only considers its options at the end of the game. Pluribus also has faster algorithms (well-defined computational procedures) and is generally more efficient (e.g., requiring surprisingly little processing power and memory).

Pluribus played 10,000 hands. Each day, it played against five professional players, all of whom had won over $1,000,000 playing poker. Pluribus triumphed (Brown & Sandholm, 2019). If we assume each poker chip is worth $1, Pluribus would have won approximately $1,000 per hour! After that, five copies of Pluribus played against each other plus one top professional player (Darren Elias or Chris "Jesus" Ferguson). Darren Elias (born 1986) has won over $7 million playing poker. Chris Ferguson (born 1963) has over $8 million in poker earnings (see Figure 2.5). His nickname is "Jesus" because of his long brown hair and beard. He looks the part when playing poker, typically wearing a wide-brimmed hat and sunglasses and remaining motionless. His party trick is throwing playing cards so fast they cut through bananas and even melons. Pluribus beat both the professionals. On the assumption each poker chip is worth $1, Pluribus won approximately $670 per hour.

Why couldn't the world's best poker players beat AI? According to Jason Les, "It [Libratus] is … a much more efficient bluffer than most humans … You're always in a situation with a ton of pressure that the AI is putting on you and you know it's very likely it could be bluffing." According to Chris Ferguson, "As humans, … we tend to oversimplify the game for ourselves, making strategies easier to adopt and remember. The bot [i.e., Libratus] doesn't take any of these short-cuts and has an immensely complicated [underlying strategy]."

Darren Elias argued that Pluribus's greatest strength is, "its ability to use mixed strategies … in a perfectly random way and to do so consistently. Most people just can't."

Figure 2.5 Photograph of top poker player Chris "Jesus" Ferguson.

As a result, AI's decisions often differ considerably from those of most human poker players. For example, AI sometimes disconcertingly makes huge *overbets* (e.g., betting up to 20 times the amount of money in the pot). This can be very effective if you have a really powerful hand or an incredibly weak hand. Libratus and Pluribus also produced many surprising *underbets* (e.g., betting 10% or less of the money in the pot).

Finally, poker players' performance is sometimes impaired by emotion. The great majority of poker players admit they are sometimes affected by tilting, meaning that negative emotions experienced during play cause them to lose control and make unusually poor decisions (Palomäki et al., 2020). Eil and Lien (2014) studied millions of hands played online by experienced or very experienced poker players. In spite of their expertise, they typically played more aggressively (i.e., betting and raising more often) when losing due to their high sensitivity to losses. This is a sub-optimal strategy that often leads to increased losses.

In sum, Libratus and Pluribus have taught professional poker players several lessons. First, you must keep changing your betting strategy so other players cannot work out whether you are bluffing. Second, Libratus and Pluribus are totally unconcerned about money and emotion does not influence their decision making. In contrast, humans find it hard to remain unemotional and to disregard the financial implications of their decisions. Third, and most pessimistically, the fact AI systems can store and process far more information than human poker players probably means there is ultimately no way humans can consistently beat them at poker.

Jeopardy!

Jeopardy! is a very popular American game show. Its distinctive feature is that players are presented with clues in the form of answers and must indicate which question would produce that answer. For example, the clue might be, "Assembled from dead bodies, the monster in this Mary Shelley book turns against his creator." The correct answer is, "Who was Frankenstein?" Much of the time, the contestant pressing their buzzer first after the clue has been read out is the one who has the chance to provide the correct answer. Only if they provide an incorrect answer does another contestant have the opportunity to supply the answer.

In 2011, an IBM AI system named Watson (after the company's founder Thomas Watson) competed against two of the most successful human contestants ever. One was Brad Rutter (33 years old), who had the all-time record 74 successive winning appearances on the show. The other human contestant was Ken Jennings (37 years old), who had won more money from *Jeopardy!* ($3.5 million) than anyone else.

The match took place on three successive evenings (14–16 February 2011). On the first evening, Watson and Brad Rutter had both won $5,000 and were ahead of Ken Jennings who was languishing on $2,000. There was high drama on the second evening as Watson totally outperformed his human rivals – the computer ended the evening with $35,734 whereas his human rivals had only $10,400 (Rutter) and $4,800 (Jennings). Watson extended its commanding lead on the third evening finishing with $77,147 to Jennings' $24,000 and Rutter's $21,600.

Why did Watson triumph over Jennings and Rutter? There are several reasons. First, Watson can allegedly process 500 gigabytes of information per second (equivalent to 1 million books), which reckons to be useful in a general-knowledge game. Second, it had access to 200 million pages of information including the whole of *Wikipedia*. Third, it had practised by playing 100 games against past winners. Fourth, Ken Jennings argued that a crucial factor was Watson's "buzzer mojo" – the computer often hit the buzzer to indicate it would answer a question with extreme speed.

Watson's achievements are less impressive than they appear. Watson was sometimes very insensitive to question subtleties and so produced answers well wide of the mark. Here is an example. The category was "Computer Keys" and the clue was, "A loose-fitting dress hanging from the shoulders to below the waist." Watson incorrectly responded, "What is a chemise?" However, the correct answer is, "What is a shift?" This major mistake (and there were many more) shows Watson had very limited (or non-existent) language understanding (discussed further in Chapter 7).

As mentioned earlier, much of Watson's success was attributable to its speed in hitting the buzzer rather than its superior knowledge. Watson was programmed to hit the buzzer in as little as 10 milliseconds (much faster than any human). For example, the sprinter Usain Bolt takes approximately 170 milliseconds to respond to the gun at the start of a race. Watson's incredible speed was especially advantageous when all the contestants knew the answer to a particular clue. The questions were sufficiently straightforward that this was generally the case.

Language ability

Human intelligence is intimately bound up with our command of language (see Chapters 1, 4, and 7). Most of our thinking (and the communication of our thoughts to others) relies heavily on language. Language is used for many purposes: to understand spoken language (speech recognition or perception); to understand written language (reading); to speak to other people; to translate text from one language to another; and to write texts (e.g., emails and essays). In view of its importance, it would be a major achievement for AI to match any of the above human language abilities. Here, we focus on research apparently providing evidence for such an achievement.

Speech recognition

Speech recognition appears relatively simple. For example, when chatting with a friend, you typically immediately understand what they are saying. In fact, however, speech recognition is an impressive achievement. Speakers typically produce about ten phonemes (basic speech sounds) per second and much acoustic information is lost within 50 ms (Remez et al., 2010). Accordingly, listeners must process the incoming speech signal very rapidly.

Another complication faced by listeners is *segmentation* – separating out or distinguishing phonemes and words from the pattern of speech sounds. Most speech has few periods of silence, as you have probably noticed when listening to someone speaking in a foreign language. This makes it hard to decide when one word ends and the next begins. Listeners also have to cope with co-articulation: the way speakers pronounce a given phoneme is influenced by their production of the previous sound and preparation for the next sounds. Thus, for example, the/b/phoneme is pronounced slightly differently in words, such as *bill*, *ball*, and *able* (Harley, 2010).

Finally, listeners must contend with considerable differences among speakers. There are characteristic differences between male and female speakers, and speakers also differ with respect to dialect and speaking rate.

Most automatic speech recognition systems (e.g., Amazon's Alexa; Apple's Siri; and Google's voice search) use deep learning (discussed in Chapter 1) (Cui et al., 2020). They typically require huge amounts of training speech data (tens of thousands of hours or more). Indeed, training speech data occasionally reaches 1 million hours (Parthasarathi et al., 2019). That is equivalent to someone listening to non-stop speech 24/7 for 114 years! The golden rule seems to be that, "there is no data like more data."

Most speech-recognition models include the following components (Abdullah et al., 2020). First, there is pre-processing of the acoustic signal to remove unnecessary noise. After that, a feature-extraction system processes the most important features of the speech signal. Next, an inferential process ascribes probabilities to different interpretations of the speech input. Its output cannot be read by humans, and so a final decoding process provides a human-readable transcription of that output.

Landmark research by Microsoft using a deep learning automated speech-recognition system was reported by Xiong et al. (2017b). They presented this AI system with two kinds of recorded telephone calls: (1) strangers discussing an assigned topic (Switchboard task) and (2) friends and family having informal conversations (CallHome task). The AI system had an error rate of 5.8% on the Switchboard task and 11% on the CallHome task. These error rates were marginally lower than those achieved by professional transcribers of spoken language (5.9% and 11.3%, respectively). The AI system and humans made very similar errors: human participants found it hard to distinguish between error-containing transcriptions produced by humans and by the AI system.

Xiong et al. (2018) subsequently developed their Microsoft automatic speech recognition system (e.g., increasing the AI system's vocabulary from 30,500 to 165,000 words). As a result, its error rate on the Switchboard task was only 5.1% compared to the 5.8% obtained with the previous version.

Saon et al. (2017) assessed the performance of their IBM automatic speech recognition system on the same transcription tasks used by Xiong et al. (2017b, 2018). This AI system achieved error rates of 5.5% on the Switchboard task and 10.3% on the CallHome tasks. These findings appear impressive, especially those on the CallHome task. However, consider the performance of three human transcription experts who, "were asked to do a high-quality job" (p. 135). Their average error rates were 5.7% on the Switchboard task and 7.9% on the CallHome task.

In sum, the performance of automatic speech recognition systems is excellent given the unconstrained nature of human speech. However, the research discussed here has involved relatively straightforward tasks with only a single speaker at any given moment and avoiding complexities (e.g., unusual dialects). What happens with more complex speech–recognition tasks is discussed in Chapters 4 and 7.

Conversation

Holding a conversation requires good speech recognition plus the ability to produce coherent and appropriate spoken language. Many chatbots (AI systems simulating conversation with one or more humans) have been developed. Alan Turing (1950) argued we could assess chatbots' conversational abilities by using his famous Turing test. In essence, he argued that, "The idea of the test is that a machine has to try and pretend to be a man, by answering questions put to it, and it will only pass if the pretence is reasonably convincing. A considerable portion of a jury, who should not be expert about machines, must be taken in by the pretence" (Copeland 2004).

It has been claimed on several occasions that chatbots have passed the Turing test. For example, there was an event at the Royal Society on 6 and 7 June 2014. A chatbot called Eugene Goostman (allegedly a 13-year-old Ukrainian) persuaded ten out of 30 human judges (33%) it was human (Warwick & Shah, 2016). However, the fact that 67% of the judges did *not* believe Eugene Goostman was human indicates its conversational skills were strictly limited. Other reasons for scepticism about the abilities of chatbots are discussed in Chapter 4.

Text comprehension: reading

Writing text (as you have probably found to your cost!) is much slower and more demanding than simply speaking. As a result, readers often find it harder to comprehend text than listeners do to understand speech. Thus, developing a system having a good understanding of complex texts is a Holy Grail in AI research.

Wang et al. (2018) introduced a battery of nine reading-comprehension tasks for computers called GLUE (General Language Understanding Evaluation) to assess AI models' language comprehension abilities. Four tasks assessed the ability to draw inferences. Here is a sample item: Does the information that, "President Trump landed in Iraq for the start of a seven-day visit" imply that, "President Trump is on an overseas visit"? Other tasks assessed language abilities (e.g., paraphrasing and judgements of semantic similarity).

Wang et al. (2018) found the best-performing AI model on the GLUE tasks averaged 69% and the worst model averaged 58.9%. In contrast, average human performance is 87.1% (Nangia & Bowman, 2019). Everything changed for the better when Google developed BERT (Bi-directional Encoder Representation from Transformers) (Devlin et al., 2019). BERT averaged 80.5% (still below human performance) on the GLUE tasks. Things changed rapidly thereafter. By July 2019, a new version of BERT surpassed human performance with 88.4% on the GLUE tasks (Yang et al., 2019). After that, offspring of BERT such as RoBERTA AND ALBERT (A Lite BERT) proliferated and several of these BERT-like models have also surpassed human performance.

What is the secret of BERT's success? It engages in more complex (and human-like) processing of written language than previous models. These earlier models processed the words in a sentence one-by-one sequentially from left to right using crude dictionary-like information to access word meanings. These models' emphasis on the meanings of individual words meant that several aspects of human language processing were omitted or de-emphasised.

Previous models largely ignored context and syntax. Consider homonyms (two words with the same spelling but different meanings): an example is "*bank*" (side of a river) and "*bank*" (a place where money is kept). These models found it hard to distinguish between homonyms' two meanings. They also had great difficulty in distinguishing between the meanings of sentences containing very similar words (e.g., *"The dog bit the man"* vs *"The man bit the dog."*)

In contrast to previous models, BERT reads left to right and right to left at the same time. As a consequence, its processing is more thorough than that of other models. BERT also differs from other models because it uses an attention-weighting process to form multiple connections among the most important words in a sentence while largely ignoring the less important ones. As a consequence, BERT is more sensitive to context (preceding and following a given word) than previous models. BERT also triumphs over other language-processing models because it has greater capacity, computing power, and is pre-trained on more language data.

In spite of its many successes, BERT has various limitations. Its language-comprehension performance is less impressive than it seems because it often relies on heuristics or short-cuts rather that remove the need for full comprehension of text. In addition, BERT possesses a considerable amount of knowledge but it is often unclear which knowledge it is using to perform any given comprehension task (Rogers et al., 2020).

Translation

An area of language processing where AI has proved increasingly successful is in translating texts (e.g., documents) from one language into another. For example, Google Translate (based on deep neural networks) provides reasonably accurate translations between English and over 100 other languages. It is far faster than human translators: it can translate an entire page of text in under three seconds.

Until fairly recently, the quality and accuracy of machine translation were much lower than human translation. However, the development of neural machine translation based on the use of deep neural networks has led to dramatically improved machine translation. This new approach differs from previous ones in that it involves end-to-end learning: all the processes required for sentence reading and the production of accurate translation are learned at the same time by a single system. Neural machine translation is also far more flexible than some previous approaches to machine translation systems involving the application of numerous fixed rules.

Several impressive findings have been reported recently. Fischer and Läubli (2020) compared neural machine translation and human translation of documents in the insurance sector (e.g., a text on specialist training in sales) with respect to three types of error: (1) omissions; (2) terminology; and (3) typography. Overall errors by machine and by humans were comparable.

Popel et al. (2020) compared news translation from English to Czech by professional translators and by a deep-learning system, CUBBITT. CUBBITT outperformed the professional translators at preserving text meaning. However, the fluency of its translation was rated somewhat lower than that of the human translators. Popel et al. used a Turing-type test where they asked 15 human judges to decide whether the news translations were produced by CUBBITT or by a professional translator. Nine judges (including three professional translators and three machine translation researchers) failed to distinguish between machine and human translations.

In sum, machine translation is often almost comparable in quality to the performance of professional human translators. However, one area where machine translation continues to perform well below human levels is in taking full account of relevant context. This is difficult because the relevant context for processing a given sentence may be several sentences back in the text. This often happens with pronouns (e.g., *he* and *she*), where the referent may have occurred much earlier. Huo et al. (2020) found with the translation of various documents that pronoun resolution was significantly better when a neural machine translation system was context-aware than when it was not.

Text generation

Producing coherent text (e.g., essays or other documents) is probably the most demanding human language skill. Accordingly, it would be impressive if an AI language model could generate text that was hard to distinguish from that of a human writer. Relevant evidence was reported by Köbis and Mossink (2020). Human judges presented with poems written by novice poets and by an AI algorithm performed at chance level when deciding which poems were human-written and which were machine-written. Arguably, this was an unfair test given that the AI algorithm had received extensive training on poetry written by professional poets.

In a second experiment, human judges could not distinguish between a poem written by a professional poet and a machine-written poem pre-selected as the best. However, they could distinguish between a poet's poem and a randomly selected machine-written poem. In sum, humans had a limited ability to distinguish between poems produced by AI and by humans.

An impressive attempt to develop a model producing human-like text was reported by Brown et al. (2020). Their model is called Generative Pre-Trained Transformer 3 (GPT-3) (see Chapters 4 and 7). Here, we will mention two of its distinctive features. First, GPT-3 is enormously powerful: it has 175 billion parameters (values free to change) whereas the previous record-holding model had "only" 17 billion parameters.

Second, nearly all previous AI language models were programmed to perform well on a narrow range of language tasks on which they receive huge amounts of relevant training. In contrast, GPT-3 is designed to perform numerous language tasks without receiving intensive training on any specific task.

Brown et al. (2020) gave various versions of GPT-3 the task of producing news articles 200 or 500 words in length following presentation of examples of news articles. Human judges read news articles produced by humans and by GPT-3 and decided whether each one was written by GPT-3 or a human writer. With the 200-word articles, only 52% correct decisions were made with articles produced by the full, 175-billion parameter, version of GPT-3.

An example of GPT-3's articles is shown below – only 12% of human judges correctly identified it as having been produced by an AI model.

Title: United Methodists Agree to Historic Split

Subtitle: Those who oppose gay marriage will form their own denomination

Article: After two days of intense debate, the United Methodist Church has agreed to a historic split – one that will be "theologically and socially conservative", according to The Washington Post. The majority of delegates attending the church's annual General Conference in May voted to strengthen a ban on the ordination of LGBTQ clergy and to write new rules that will "discipline" clergy who officiate at same-sex weddings. But those who opposed these measures have a new plan: they say they will form a separate denomination by 2020, calling their church the Christian Methodist denomination.

The Post notes that the denomination, which claims 12.5 members, was in the early 20th. Century the "largest Protestant denomination in the U.S.", but that it has been shrinking in recent decades. The new split will be the second in the church's history. The first occurred in 1968, when roughly 10 per cent of the denomination left to form the Evangelical United Brethren Church. The Post notes that the proposed split "comes at a critical time for the church, has been losing members for years ..."

Several limitations of GPT-3 are discussed in Chapter 4. The central criticism is that it is basically using information contained in the title and sub-title to identify and then regurgitate slabs of knowledge contained in its database during text generation. These processes occur without any understanding of the information contained in the articles it generates.

Conclusions

AI has made substantial progress in producing human-like levels of performance on several language tasks. The most notable examples are speech recognition or perception, comprehension of text, language translation, and text generation. However, there is much controversy as to whether these achievements are all they appear to be. We consider this issue in Chapter 4, where these achievements are evaluated in depth.

Are our careers at stake?

Many people fear robots and other AI systems will progressively take over the jobs of tens (or hundreds) of millions of workers. As long ago as 1965, Herb Simon, a pioneer of IT, predicted that, "machines will be capable, within 20 years, of doing any work a man can do" (p. 38). That prediction obviously turned out to be wrong. However, AI experts predicted a few years ago that there was a 50% chance AI machines would be able to perform ALL jobs better than humans by 2060 (discussed further in Chapter 7). Here we consider several examples showing how AI is already challenging human workers even in high-level jobs.

Legal profession

We start with the law. One of the main areas where AI has been used is electronic discovery (Caffrey, 2020). This is the process of identifying relevant documentary evidence (e.g., due diligence before entering into an agreement and preparation of a legal case). This can be very time-consuming and expensive. Several years ago there was a patent dispute between Samsung and Apple where 11,108,653 documents were examined at a total cost of $13 million over a period of 20 months (Dale, 2018). Such enormous costs could be reduced through the extensive use of AI.

In 2018, several American universities organised a competition between 20 expert lawyers and the LawGeex AI system trained on tens of thousands of law contracts. The task was to detect loopholes in five non-disclosure agreements. LawGeex was more accurate than the lawyers overall (94% vs 85% accuracy, respectively), and it outperformed the lawyers on all five agreements. Remarkably, LawGeex achieved this superior performance even though it devoted less than 1/200th the amount of time spent by the lawyers on average in scrutinising the documents (26 seconds vs 92 minutes, respectively) (LawGeex, 2018).

Unsurprisingly, many lawyers refused to accept these findings. They pointed out that non-disclosure agreements have a fairly standard format, thus facilitating LawGeex's task. In addition, it is often easier to detect errors in a legal document than to suggest watertight alternative ways of expressing issues or correcting errors. In sum, the finding that an AI system can outperform human experts on relatively simple legal tasks does not necessarily mean it would outperform them on more complex legal issues.

In principle, there are numerous ways AI might enhance legal decisions. Tegmark (2018, p. 105) contemplates a future where most legal decisions are provided by robojudges (robot judges): "AI systems that tirelessly apply the same high legal standards to every judgement without succumbing to human errors such as bias, fatigue or lack of the latest knowledge."

The above vision for the future is less hypothetical than you might imagine. In 2019, the Estonian Ministry of Justice asked Ott Velsberg (Estonia's chief information officer) to design a robojudge to adjudicate on small claims under about £6,000 to clear a backlog of cases. The jury is out on whether the robojudge will ever replace human judges (Niiler, 2019). Note, however, that the robojudge's decisions relate only to relatively straightforward legal issues. In addition, individuals dissatisfied with the robo-judge's decisions can appeal to human judges.

AI is already assisting the legal process in other ways. In China, the courts deal with approximately 19 million cases every year, leading to various attempts to introduce AI into the legal system. In Beijing, for example, a 1.5-metre high robot called Xiaofa provides answers to over 40,000 litigation questions and 30,000 legal issues (see Figure 2.7). At present, however, AI is not directly involved in judicial decision making and has not replaced judges' expertise.

The legal system in most countries is open to bias. Tegmark (2018) discussed the case of the white American supremacist, Byron De La Beckwith. He assassinated the civil rights leader Medgar Evers on 12 June 1963 but was only convicted for this crime in 1994. Two different all-white juries had failed to convict him in 1964 even though the evidence available at that time was basically the same as it was in 1994.

Racial and other biases can be implicit meaning that individuals may not be consciously aware of their biases. Implicit bias can be assessed using the Implicit Association Test. Cunningham et al. (2001) asked white participants to complete the Implicit Association Test to assess racial stereotypes. In one condition, participants pressed one key if a black face or a positive word (e.g., *love*) was presented and a different key if a white face or bad word (e.g., *terrible*) was presented. Reaction times were slower in this condition than when a black face was paired with a negative word and a white face with a positive word.

The above findings suggest participants had implicit or unconscious pro-white and anti-black biases. Alternatively, the white participants may simply have been more familiar with some face-word combinations. Kurdi et al. (2019) carried out a meta-analysis using data from the Implicit Association Test. There was a small association between implicit racial bias and discriminatory behaviour.

The Implicit Association Test can be modified to make it more directly applicable to the legal system. When this was done, Levinson et al. (2010) found there was implicit racial bias: performance was faster when black faces were paired with Guilty and white faces with Not Guilty rather than the opposite pairings. Worryingly, Levinson et al. (2014) found implicit racial bias was greater among those favouring the death penalty.

We need to insert a caveat at this point. It has often been assumed that a bias that is implicit (in the sense of being assessed by indirect means) is necessarily also a bias that is unconscious. However, there is vanishingly little evidence that indirect biases are identical to unconscious ones (Corneille & Hütter, 2020). Nevertheless, the existence of various biases suggests there could be an important role for AI within the justice system. In principle, AI systems could reduce or eliminate the various biases possessed by many members of the police and by jurors.

COMPAS

COMPAS (Correctional Offender Management Profiling for Alternative Sanctions) is a famous example of AI being used within the legal system. In the United States, COMPAS has assessed OVER 1 million offenders to predict recidivism (the risk they will re-offend) based on 137 features and their past criminal record. It has been claimed COMPAS predicts better than human judges who is likely to return to crime and so should be denied parole.

Various problems with COMPAS have been identified. For example, its overall accuracy in predicting whether someone will re-offend is only 65%. Dressel and Farid (2018) found individuals knowing very little about the criminal justice system performed comparably to COMPAS. This was the case even though they were provided with only seven features about each defendant compared to the 137 factors used by COMPAS. More dramatically, Dressel and Farid achieved a 67% success rate using only TWO pieces of information: the defendant's age and number of previous convictions!

Dressel and Farid's (2018) findings differ from those obtained previously. For example, Kleinberg et al. (2017) considered judges' decisions as to whether 800,000 defendants should await trial at home or in prison. Their performance was compared against those made subsequently by an AI system. If the AI's decisions had replaced the judges' decisions, pre-trial crime would have been reduced by 25% without changing the imprisonment rate. Alternatively, the imprisonment rate could have been reduced by 40% with no commensurate increase in pre-trial crime rates.

Why are Dressel and Farid's (2018) so discrepant? In their study, the conditions under which humans predicted whether individual criminals would re-offend made the task relatively easy (Lin et al., 2020). For example, their attention was directed to a small number of relevant predictive factors. They were also provided with immediate feedback concerning the accuracy of their predictions. In real-world judicial settings, in contrast, humans predicting subsequent recidivism are typically provided with much

more information (some irrelevant) and never have immediate feedback.

When Lin et al. (2020) used task conditions resembling
those used by Dressel and Fahid (2018), they obtained
comparable findings. However, an AI system consistently
made more accurate predictions than humans concerning
recidivism when the task conditions were harder (trebling
the information about each defendant). Thus, the AI was
superior to humans at integrating complex information.

As indicated earlier, judges' predictions about defendants' likelihood of re-offending in real-world judicial settings are always made in the absence of feedback about
the accuracy of those predictions. We will consider Lin
et al.'s (2020) findings on the importance of feedback with
respect to predicting who would re-offend by committing
a violent crime. AI had an 89% success rate. In contrast,
humans had a success rate of 83% when given feedback but
this dropped to only 60% without feedback.

Dressel and Fahid (2018) also claimed COMPAS exhibits racial bias even though its predictions are not directly
based on race. They considered false positives (i.e., predicting re-offending in defendants who did not re-offend).
COMPAS produced 40% false positives for black defendants compared to only 26% for white ones. They also considered false negatives (i.e., predicting no re-offending in
defendants who did re-offend). COMPAS produced many
more false negatives for white than black defendants (42%
vs 30%, respectively). Thus, COMPAS seemed excessively
pessimistic about the chances of black defendants re-
offending and unduly optimistic about white defendants
not re-offending.

The above findings appear to reflect racial bias. However,
the notion of 'fairness' is far harder to define than generally
supposed (Goel et al., 2021). Suppose we decide the system
should be changed to ensure the percentage of false positives
is equated for black and white defendants. We could achieve

this by predicting that re-offending will occur among black people scoring 6 or more on the COMPAS risk scale and among white people scoring 4 or more (Corbett-Davies and Goel 2018). However, setting different cut-off points for black and white people can also be regarded as racial bias.

Can the above problems be resolved by simply ignoring race when predicting the likelihood of defendants re-offending? This solution is also flawed because it produces large racial differences in false positives and false negatives (Goel et al., 2021). Similar problems arise if we adopt the apparently reasonable strategy of ignoring gender when using COMPAS. Corbett-Davies and Goel (2018) showed that male defendants had a much higher recidivism rate for any given COMPAS score (see Figure 2.6). For example, the recidivism rate associated with a score of 6 is 62% for male defendants but only 48% with females ones. This apparently unfair outcome occurs because men re-offend at higher rates than women with very similar criminal histories.

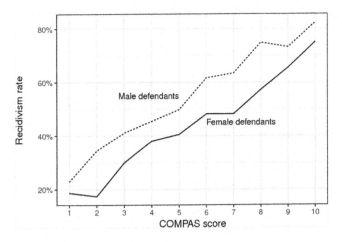

Figure 2.6 The recidivism rate for male and female defendants as a function of their COMPAS score.

Source: From Corbett-Davies & Goel (2018).

What is crucially important for the future is to identify a consensual definition of "fairness" when predicting re-offending. If that can be achieved, AI systems could proba-bly provide an optimal (or near optimal) solution.

Medicine: diagnosis

Approximately 20% of serious medical conditions are initially misdiagnosed by doctors (Graber, 2013), with one-third of these misdiagnoses leading to patient harm. Accordingly, it would of great value to devise AI algorithms producing more accurate diagnoses than those provided by doctors. Liang et al. (2019) trained a deep learning system to diagnose 567,498 child patients from electronic health records. There was a strong association between the pre-dicted diagnoses of the deep learning system and doctors' initial diagnoses across all major disease categories suggest-ing AI can often match doctors' diagnostic performance.

Liang et al.'s (2019) deep learning system adopted a correlational approach –diseases were identified based on how strongly they correlated with the patient's symp-toms. However, a causal approach would be preferable. For example, we could ask how many of the patient's symp-toms would disappear if the disease they were thought to have were cured. Using clinical vignettes, Richens et al. (2020) found doctors provided accurate diagnoses 71% of the time and an AI algorithm based on correlational evi-dence was accurate 72% of the time. Most impressively, a causal AI algorithm was correct 77% of the time putting its performance in the top 25% of doctors (see Figure 2.7).

Most medical research using AI has focused on diag-noses based on searching for abnormalities in medical images (e.g., X-rays and brain scans). Insights into what is required to achieve high levels of diagnostic accuracy can be obtained by studying medical experts. Medical experts typically detect abnormalities remarkably fast and

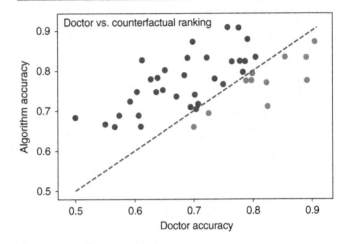

Figure 2.7 Accuracy of diagnosis by 44 doctors relative to a causal AI algorithm; points in blue correspond to doctors performing worse than AI; red point is a doctor having the same accuracy as AI; green points are doctor performing better than AI.

Source: From Richens et al. (2020).

with great accuracy. In one study, expert radiologists correctly interpreted chest radiographs presented for only 200 milliseconds. In another study, experts and non-experts viewed complex mammograms. The average time taken by experts to fixate a cancer was typically under one second. Performance accuracy was much higher in doctors fixating the cancer rapidly than those who did not.

Expert doctors use a detect-then-search strategy starting with rapid detection of diagnostically relevant information followed by a brief search to check there is no other relevant information. Detection occurs rapidly because experts engage in pattern recognition where the presented medical image is compared against numerous stored patterns of medical images encountered in the past. In contrast, non-experts use a search-then-detect strategy involving extensive visual search (including much irrelevant information) followed by eventual detection of diagnostically relevant information. They use this strategy because they lack the wealth of relevant information stored in long-term memory that would permit detection to precede search.

Are AI systems as effective as medical experts at detecting diseases from medical images? Liu et al. (2019) recently carried out a meta-analysis of research where AI systems had used deep learning (discussed in Chapter 1) to enhance their diagnostic abilities. Good diagnostic accuracy has two aspects: (1) sensitivity: accurately detecting abnormalities in images and (2) specificity: accurately rejecting images not containing abnormalities. Accordingly, Liu et al. compared AI systems with human experts with respect to sensitivity and specificity.

What did Liu et al. (2019) find? The overall diagnostic accuracies of AI systems and humans were impressive and very similar: sensitivity averaged 87% for AI vs 86.4% for health-care professionals; specificity averaged 92.5% (AI) vs 90.5% (health-care professionals). In one study (Esteva et al., 2017), an AI system (using deep learning) was trained with 129,450 clinical images and dermatologists diagnosed melanoma from visual images. These images were presented on their own or with additional clinical information. The AI system's diagnostic accuracy was superior to the human dermatologists in both conditions.

Some especially impressive findings were reported by McKinney and et al. (2020) in a study on breast-cancer diagnosis. They compared the performance of an AI system based on deep learning against human medical experts in the USA and UK. The AI system produced 5.7% fewer false positives (i.e., deciding wrongly an individual had breast cancer) than American experts and 1.2% fewer than British experts. With respect to false negatives (i.e., deciding wrongly an individual did not have breast cancer), the

AI system made 9.4% fewer such errors than American experts and 2.7% fewer than British ones.

AI systems have proved increasingly effective not only at medical diagnosis but also at medical *prognosis* (i.e., predicting the likely course of a disease). If we can achieve more accurate prognosis, this increases the probability of providing customised treatment precisely tailored to patients' needs. Huang et al. (2020) reviewed research where deep learning systems were used in cancer prognosis. The findings were generally very positive, leading Huang et al. to conclude, "We expect that AI-based clinical cancer research will result in a paradigm shift in survival due to enhanced prediction rates" (p. 68).

AI research on diagnosis from medical images has focused on diseases other than cancer. For example, Devalla et al. (2020) reviewed research on the effectiveness of AI in diagnosing glaucoma (a serious eye condition that can lead to irreversible blindness). AI systems sometimes achieve a success rate above 90% in diagnosing glaucoma from medical images, significantly higher than most experts' success rate.

In the future, the emphasis will be on developing AI and human-AI collaborative systems to enhance medical decision-making. Cai et al. (2019) showed how this can work in a study of pathologists using microscopic samples of bodily fluid or tissue in the diagnosis of cancer. When pathologists are uncertain about the correct diagnosis, they typically seek additional information (e.g., similar images from textbooks and second opinions from experts).

Cai et al. (2019) developed an AI system known as SMILY (Similar Medical Images Like Yours) based on deep neural networks. When a pathologist studying a medical image wants to compare it against similar images from past cases (along with their diagnoses), SMILY rapidly accesses such images. The pathologist then indicates the images that appear useful, which triggers a search for other, similar images. SMILY also includes a refine-by-region tool allowing pathologists to focus on a region of interest within the target image.

The findings were very positive. Most pathologists found SMILY had diagnostic utility. For example, it allowed them to generate new ideas and to minimise errors. It did so while requiring less effort than traditional methods.

In sum, deep learning and other AI-based systems have proved very effective in medical diagnosis across numerous conditions. There is also promising evidence that AI systems can be of value in medical prognosis as well, helping to ensure all patients obtain optimal treatment.

There are various problematical issues relating to much research on the effectiveness of AI systems in medical diagnosis based on images. These issues are addressed fully in Chapter 7.

Medicine: surgical robots

Over the past 20 years, AI has increasingly had a major impact on medicine through the development of surgical robots. Sheetz et al. (2020) found across 73 Michigan hospitals that the percentage of common surgical procedures involving robots increased from 1.8% in 2012 to 15.1% in 2018. In the case of hernia repair, there was a 40-fold increase in the percentage of such operations using robots.

Approximately 2 million robotic operations (e.g., kidney surgery, gallbladder surgery, and hysterectomy) were carried out in the United States between 2000 and 2015. Over that time period, approximately 150 deaths and 1,600 accidents were linked to robotic surgery in the United States. Why are humans killed or injured by robots in medical settings? Several factors are involved. Examples include the following: burnt or broken pieces of equipment sometimes fall into the patient, medical instrument damage or breakage, uncontrolled robotic movements, and instruments not recognised by the robot (Alemzadeh et al., 2016). These figures sound worrying. Note, however, that, inadequate hospital care provided by human medical staff is a factor in over 100,000 deaths every year in the United States.

How effective is robotic surgery compared to conventional surgery? The limited evidence that is available suggests the outcomes from robotic surgery are no better than conventional surgery for several conditions including various cancers, hernia repair, and kidney resection (see Sheetz et al., 2020, for a review). However, surgeons generally report that robotic surgery is associated with reduced workload and less discomfort because it involves less use of the shoulder, back and arms (Wee et al., 2020). However, robotic surgery involves greater discomfort in the neck and fingers than keyhole surgery.

Medicine: facilitating drug discovery

We turn now to an exciting development in medical uses of AI. It involves using a protein's amino-acid sequence to predict accurately the 3-D shape it will fold into over the following few days. Such research is of great importance because the overwhelming majority of diseases are related to protein functioning. For example, a defective protein (p53) is found in about 50% of cancers and defective tau proteins play an important role in Alzheimer's disease. If we had a complete understanding of protein structures, this would greatly facilitate the task of developing drugs producing beneficial changes in those structures.

The progress made by AI is assessed in a biennial competition known as Critical Assessment for Structure Prediction (CASP), the goal of which is to predict a protein's 3-D shape. In CASP, each AI system's predictions are compared against the actual structures of proteins assessed by expensive and laborious techniques (e.g., X-ray crystallography and cryo-genic electron microscopy). Outstanding performance is represented by a score of 90, which corresponds to predicting the structures of proteins with a mean error of 0.16 namometers (one billionth of a metre).

The winning score in CASP competitions between 2006 and 2016 was never higher than an unimpressive 40. However, there was a step-change in 2018. AlphaFold, a deep learning system developed by DeepMind, obtained a score of nearly 60. On 30 November 2020, it was announced that AlphaFold 2 had greatly surpassed this achievement with a remarkable score of nearly 90, which represents "a gargantuan leap" (Callaway, 2020).

Why is AlphaFold 2 so successful? It resembles many other AI systems in that it uses deep learning but it had the advantage of extensive training on 170,000 proteins ahead of the competition. AlphaFold 2 is also more ambitious than previous AI systems because it is designed to predict the final structure of a target protein sequence rather than the simpler task of predicting relationships among amino acids.

Robots in car production

As mentioned in Chapter 1, there are already more than 3 million robots in the world and the total is increasing rapidly. Robots are used in numerous different types of work with 50% being used in car production. Perhaps surprisingly, robots were first used in car production in 1961, when General Motors started using them for spot welding (welding sheet metal products together). Nowadays, of course, nearly all car manufacturers make extensive use of robots to improve quality, to increase capacity, to reduce costs, and to protect car workers from difficult and/or dangerous jobs.

There are several clear advantages in using robots in car production. First, robots are very well suited to several aspects of car production such as painting, welding, and assembling small parts (e.g., motors and pumps) at high speed. Second, productivity and throughput can be maximised because robots can work efficiently 24 hours a day. Third, robots can work in environments dangerous for humans, thereby reducing injuries to human car workers. Fourth, there are reduced labour costs compared to employing human workers. Fifth, there is increasing use of cobots (collaborative robots), which can work alongside human workers to make optimal use of both robot and human skills.

There are also some potential disadvantages with the use of robots in car production. These disadvantages are discussed in Chapter 5, where the focus is on several key issues related to the use of robots in numerous situations (e.g., car driving and military operations).

Conclusions

In this chapter, we have discussed several areas where AI has proved superior to the greatest human experts. What is perhaps most striking is that AI's superiority covers a wide range of disparate tasks and abilities such as the following:

1 Perfect-information or closed-system games such as chess and Go;
2 Imperfect-system or open-ended games such as poker;
3 Knowledge-based games such as *Jeopardy!*;
4 Some aspects of decision making in the judicial system;
5 Diagnosing diseases from medical images;
6 Speed and accuracy of some types of surgery;
7 Predicting the shape of proteins to facilitate the discovery of powerful drugs to treat diseases.
8 Speed and accuracy of aspects of car production.

If we are already inferior to AI systems in many ways, does that make AI dominance over humans inevitable in, say, 2030 or 2040? Many experts are convinced the answer is, "Yes." We are much more sceptical, as will become clear when we discuss major limitations of AI in Chapter 4. In addition, in Chapter 7, we demonstrate that many of AI's greatest successes are much less impressive than they appear at first glance.

Chapter 3

Human strengths

In Chapter 2, we saw the enormous strides made by AI. Here we consider the strengths of human intelligence starting with the brain's evolution. Then we consider our current cognitive strengths including an assessment of our major cognitive advantages over other species.

Human brain: Influence of evolution

The human brain has *tripled* in size over the last 6 to 8 million years. Three million years ago, members of the species (*Australopithecus afarensis*) had skulls with an internal volume of approximately 475 cubic centimetres (cc's). Moving forward to *Homo habilis* a little under 2 million years ago, the skull volume had increased to 600 cc. Our ancestors from 500,000 years ago had brains exceeding 1,000 cc. Current humans are members of *Homo sapiens*. Early members of our species had brains around 1,2000 cc in size (similar to those of current humans).

Although most brain areas have increased in size over time, the neocortex has increased most in humans and also in other primate species. This is important because it is the brain area most involved in higher cognitive processes (e.g., thinking and decision making).

DOI: 10.4324/9781003162698-3

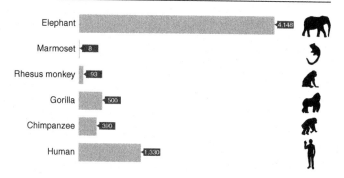

Figure 3.1 Brain size comparisons (in grams) for six species including humans.

It is perhaps natural to assume larger brains are associated with greater intelligence. On that measure, humans surpass chimpanzees and gorillas. However, our brains are only one-third the size of an elephant's (see Figure 3.1) but we are obviously substantially more intelligent than elephants.

We obtain a different picture if we relate brain size to body size to produce a measure of brain size as a percentage of body mass (see Figure 3.2). On this measure, humans have a much higher percentage than four of the other five species (e.g., 2% for humans vs 0.1% for elephants).

Why are our brains *three* times larger than those of our remote ancestors? There are more answers than you can shake a stick at. However, there are three main hypotheses (Dunbar & Shultz, 2017):

1   Our ancestors needed *"ecological intelligence"* to respond to major challenges from the non-social environment (e.g., ensuring adequate food supplies in difficult conditions).

2   Our ancestors needed *"social intelligence"* to form groups to survive in adverse conditions and to compete successfully against other species and groups. Competition

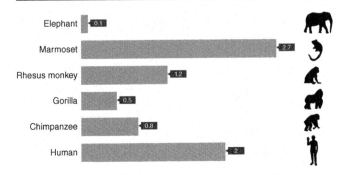

Figure 3.2 Brain size as a percentage of body mass for six species including humans.

between groups may have led to "evolutionary arms races in cognition" where enhanced social intelligence was required to prevent annihilation.

3 Our ancestors needed to evolve their *"cultural intelligence"* so they could learn from others and benefit from the cultural knowledge humans were accumulating.

Which hypothesis best explains the enlargement of the human brain? This question is hard to answer. We have limited information about living conditions hundreds of thousands of years ago. Even when we do have reasonable evidence, it is extremely hard to show that those aspects *causally* influenced brain development. Finally, the three hypotheses are not entirely separate. However, the second hypothesis has often been identified as the single most important factor. Dunbar (1998) proposed the influential social brain hypothesis. According to this hypothesis, our ancestors solved complex ecological problems (e.g., scarcity of food and danger of predation) by forming social groups, and brain enlargement permitted them to develop the required social skills.

Much evidence supports the social brain hypothesis. First, a key reason humans and other primates formed social groups was as a protection against predation (i.e., being preyed on by other species or human groups) (Dunbar, 1998). Across primate species, group size correlates moderately well with predation risk. Second, social group size and brain volume (especially the neocortex) are highly correlated across most primate species. Third, individuals with a large social network have larger frontal and temporal lobes than those with a smaller social network. Fourth, social groups could co-operate in the development of tools to construct shelters and develop weapons.

Effective communication was obviously vital to the development of the social brain. Such communication depends mostly on our highly developed language abilities. The evolutionary origins of our current language skills lie in gestures rather than vocalisations. Primate gestures resemble human language much more closely than primate vocalisations (Cartmill et al., 2012). Of note, similar brain areas are involved in monkeys' gestures and human language processing (MacNeilage et al., 2009).

In sum, the social brain hypothesis provides a very general explanation of human brain development. For example, our ancestors' general intelligence increased in line with increasing social group size and brain size: this allowed them to cope increasingly effectively with environmental threats (including non-social ones). Their increasing intelligence and group size provided the context within which they could develop cultural knowledge and pass it on to the next generation. The development of language undoubtedly contributed substantially to the transmission of cultural knowledge.

Culture and dual-inheritance theory

Several theorists including Henrich (2016) and Muthukrishna et al. (2018) have proposed the cultural brain hypothesis, which builds on the notion of cultural intelligence discussed earlier. According to this hypothesis, more knowledge is available in larger groups or societies. As a consequence, individuals within larger groups need to acquire more cultural knowledge or information than those within smaller groups if they are to succeed. Thus, fast and efficient cultural learning are more important in larger groups than smaller ones.

Henrich (2016) discussed differences between larger societies and smaller ones predictable from the cultural brain hypothesis. For example, Kline and Boyd (2010) found with 10 societies in Oceania there was a strong tendency for larger societies to have more tools (and more complex ones) than smaller societies.

Language is crucial for communicating cultural knowledge. As predicted by the cultural brain hypothesis, larger societies have languages capable of communicating more complex information (e.g., greater numbers of words and more phonemes [speech sounds]) (Henrich, 2016). Languages in larger societies are also more informationally efficient than those in smaller societies. Theoretically, there should be negative effects if a group or society becomes smaller. This happened in Tasmania, which was cut off from the rest of Australia by rising seas. This produced a drastic reduction in the size of Tasmanian social groups, and over thousands of years led to a progressive reduction in knowledge and useful technologies (Henrich, 2016).

The cultural brain hypothesis resembles dual-inheritance theory (e.g., Henrich & Muthukrishna, 2021). This theory's central assumption is that genes and culture interact in complex ways: "By generating increasingly complex tools (e.g., spear throwers), food processing techniques (e.g., cooking), languages (e.g., larger vocabularies), and institutions (e.g., clans) over hundreds of thousands of years, cumulative cultural evolution has shaped the environments faced by our genes and has thereby driven the genetic evolution of the uniquely human aspects of our bodies and minds" (Henrich & Muthukrishna, p. 226).

Thus, individuals having the ability to acquire increasingly complex cultural information were more likely to reproduce than those lacking that ability.

In sum, what happens in groups or societies that increase in size over time is a "ratchet effect" (a ratchet is a mechanical device that can only move forwards) (Tennie et al., 2009). Increases in the amount and complexity of cultural information lead to individuals having larger and more intelligent brains, which in turn serves to increase further the amount and complexity of cultural information.

Connectome

The Human Connectome Project was launched in 2009 by the National Institutes of Health in the United States. Its very ambitious goal was to produce a detailed map indicating all the anatomical and functional connections within the human brain (i.e., the connectome). Brain areas often activated together during performance of various tasks are functionally connected.

Data obtained from the above Project has greatly increased our understanding of human brain organisation. Bullmore and Sporns (2012) identified two major principles influencing human brain organisation:

1 The *principle of efficiency* – the ability to integrate information across the brain. High efficiency can be achieved by having numerous connections within (and between) brain networks.
2 The *principle of cost control* – costs (especially the use of energy and space) can be minimised if the brain is organised so there are limited, mostly short-distance, connections.

Ideally, human brains would have high efficiency combined with low costs. Alas, the two principles are in direct conflict: high efficiency is strongly associated with high costs and low costs with low efficiency. We might imagine our brains should be organised to maximise efficiency almost regardless of cost. However, this would be prohibitively costly. For example, if all 100 billion brain neurons were interconnected, the brain would need to be 12½ miles wide!

Bullmore and Sporns (2012) discovered the human brain displays a near-optimal trade-off between cost and efficiency (see Figure 3.3). Reassuringly, our brains combine reasonably high efficiency with manageable costs. They are efficient because they have a "small-world" structure: only a few nodes or links are required to connect most small brain regions to each other. However, the costs are fairly high – even though our brain accounts for only about 2% of our body weight, it consumes 20% of our body's energy (Clark & Sokoloff, 1999).

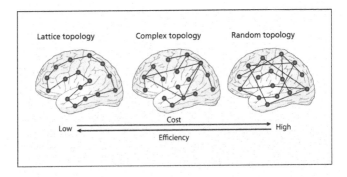

Figure 3.3 The left panel shows a brain network low in cost efficiency; the right panel shows a brain network high in cost efficiency; the middle panel shows the actual human brain in which there is moderate efficiency at moderate cost. Nodes are shown as orange circles.

Source: From Bullmore and Sporns (2012). Reprinted with permission of *Nature Reviews.*

Why is the brain's energy consumption so high? According to the traditional view, the brain's energy demands are high when we focus on a complex problem, but relatively low when we are resting (e.g., during sleep). Alternatively, our brains are constantly active even in the "resting" state. We can test these viewpoints by comparing brain activity when individuals are engaged in a cognitively demanding task and when resting. Surprisingly, the increase in brain activity during task performance compared to the resting state is typically under 5% (Raichle, 2010). Thus, our brain uses so much energy because it is highly active nearly all the time (including during sleep).

Raichle (e.g., 2015) complicated the above picture by discovering our overall brain activity is sometimes *greater* when resting than when busy solving a problem! He identified the default mode network – a brain network involved in thinking about oneself, thinking about others, remembering, and contemplating the future. Of crucial importance, activity within this default mode network *decreases* when we attend to a task or problem.

Let us return to brain efficiency and costs. Consider the world's airports. Passengers would like to fly directly from any airport to any other airport no matter how far away. However, that would be prohibitively expensive because it would need a huge number of planes to service all the flights required, most of which would have very few passengers. For example, it seems improbable that an airline providing regular direct flights from Southend in England to Belo Horizonte in Brazil would make any profit.

In fact, there are relatively few hub airports (such as Heathrow, Paris Orly, Schiphol in Amsterdam, and Frankfurt in Europe) and a much larger number of smaller, "feeder" airports. This provides a very efficient system. The human brain works so efficiently because it is organised similarly to the world's airports. There are several major hubs in the brain with strong connections among them.

The term "rich club" refers to these hubs (based mainly in the frontal and parietal lobes) and their inter-connections (Collin et al., 2014).

In sum, the human brain is efficiently organised so that only a few connections are required to link any two brain areas. This is the case for two reasons: (1) most brain areas that are close to each other are well connected and (2) there are strong long-range connections between hubs linking brain areas far apart within the cortex.

Memory storage capacity

It is hard to estimate accurately the human brain's capacity for information storage. However, it contains approximately 100 billion neurons (cells transmitting nerve impulses) (Herculano-Houzel, 2012). Each neuron can make about 1,000 connections with other neurons via synapses heavily involved in information storage. If we multiply 100 billion neurons by 1,000 connections, we finish up with 100 trillion data points (100 terabytes of information).

The above number represents an unrealistic upper bound on the brain's potential data storage. Many experts put actual brain storage capacity at ten (rather than 100) terabytes. However, this lower estimate implies the human brain can store the equivalent of 470 million books – this should be sufficient for most everyday activities.

Brain flexibility

The human brain might be organised rigidly with each region specialised for one specific function. Functional specialisation was assumed by the phrenologists in the nineteenth century. They argued that individual differences in various mental abilities can be revealed by feelings bumps in the skull. There is some functional specialisation within the human brain (e.g., areas in the occipital cortex

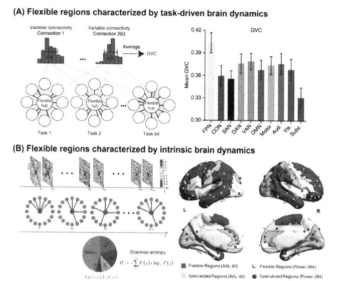

Figure 3.4 Flexible brain regions. (A) shows a measure of global variable connectivity (GVC) indicating that fronto-parietal network regions exhibit high flexibility. (B) shows that flexibility is high in the lateral prefrontal cortex, lateral parietal cortex and lateral temporal lobe (red and yellow areas) but specialised in visua, auditory and default mode areas (green and blue).

Source: From Yin et al. (2016).

mostly devoted to basic visual processing). However, one of the most impressive features of the human brain is its *flexibility*. Yin & Kaiser (2021) identified key flexible and specialised brain regions (see Figure 3.4).

We can see the human brain's flexibility in the way it re-organises itself following damage. For example, strokes typically severely impair cognitive functioning, but there is very often subsequent recovery. Dramatic evidence of the brain's flexibility or plasticity is available in research on patients following hemispherectomy. This is a drastic procedure involving removal of an entire cerebral hemisphere (half the brain) and is typically carried out on patients with exceptionally severe epilepsy. In one study, 51 patients having hemispherectomy during childhood had their intelligence assessed before and after the operation (Pulsifer et al., 2004). IQ *increased* substantially for 15% of these patients, decreased substantially for 21%, and changed relatively little for the others. Thus, hemispherectomy had surprisingly small effects.

Since language processing occurs mostly in the left hemisphere, we would anticipate patients with hemispherectomy involving that hemisphere would be more likely to have severe language impairments. However, this is not always the case. BL, a man who had had a left hemispherectomy at the age of five, exhibited mostly average language skills and above-average intelligence (Vanlancker-Sidtis, 2004).

Healthy individuals who acquire expertise also exhibit brain plasticity. Consider London taxi drivers who spend several years acquiring "The Knowledge" (detailed information about the locations of 25,000 streets in London). This extensive practice increases the size of part of the hippocampus (centrally involved in memory) (Woollett & Maguire, 2011).

In sum, the human brain displays great neuroplasticity even when 50% of the brain is destroyed. We can contrast that with AI systems. If you destroyed 50% (or even 1% or less) of an AI system it would cease to work.

Humans vs other species

We have emphasised how the evolutionary development of the human brain (and a huge increase in cultural complexity) paved the way for us to become progressively more intelligent. One way of assessing human intelligence is by comparing and contrasting our cognitive abilities with those of other species. That approach is followed here.

One possibility is that we possess cognitive abilities totally lacking in other species: human uniqueness or exceptionalism. Alternatively, some other species may possess the same cognitive abilities as us but to a (much) lesser extent. The former viewpoint was dominant for a long time. It was often argued that humans are unique because we are conscious, possess language and think rationally, whereas other species are predominantly instinctual. However, expert opinion has swung decisively in favour of the latter viewpoint. For example, "Other animals possess specialist competences that can rival our own, but no other species consistently outperforms humans across multiple cognitive domains" (Laland & Seed, 2021, p. 705).

Consciousness

Philosophers and psychologists have devoted inordinate amounts of time to defining "consciousness." The upshot of their deliberations is that we need to distinguish two forms of consciousness. There is a basic or phenomenal consciousness which involves having an experience (e.g., visual or auditory perception). There is also a higher-level form of consciousness which involves knowing one is having that experience: this is meta-consciousness (Schooler, 2002). The cognitive neuroscientist Pinker (1997) provided an example: "I cannot only feel pain and see red, but think to myself, 'Hey, here I am, Steve Pinker, feeling pain and seeing red!'"

Support for the above two types of consciousness was reported by Schooler et al. (2005). Individuals read a text and signalled when their mind wandered from the text. Occasionally they received a signal and indicated whether their minds had wandered but they had not reported this spontaneously because they lacked the appropriate meta-consciousness. They often admitted they had conscious experience of daydreaming without being explicitly aware that had happened.

Human possession of two types of consciousness is supported by neuroimaging research. Demertzi et al. (2013)

distinguished between *external* awareness (awareness of the environment: basic consciousness) and *internal* awareness (self-relevant thinking: meta-consciousness). Somewhat different brain networks were associated with the two forms of conscious awareness.

Other kinds of evidence also indicate the existence of two forms of consciousness in humans (Pennartz et al., 2019). Many brain-damaged patients and drug addicts lose higher-level consciousness while retaining basic consciousness. Similar findings have been reported for patients with schizophrenia, a serious condition involving hallucinations, delusions, and the loss of a sense of reality. Schizophrenics possess basic consciousness (although they find it hard to distinguish between what is perceived and what is imagined). However, they have limited meta-consciousness because they lack any coherent sense of self (Nelson et al., 2012).

Meta-consciousness is important because it allows us to focus our conscious awareness on almost anything including past events and knowledge and potential future scenarios (discussed further later). Why is basic consciousness important? There are several reasons. For example, our conscious experience is closely related to selective attention, which focuses processing on task-relevant information and avoids processing distracting or task-irrelevant information. Thus, consciousness is valuable in ensuring we make optimal use of the information available to us in the environment.

Another reason was emphasised by Pennartz et al. (2019, p. 2): "Consciousness has a biological function: it presents the subject with a multi-modal, situational survey of its surrounding world (including its own body), which subserves the kind of complex decision-making ... associated with goal-directed, deliberate, planned behaviour."

Darwin (1871) suggested that the extent to which any species has conscious experience correlates positively with the complexity of its brain. It seems much more likely that other species have basic consciousness than meta-consciousness and so we will focus mostly on basic consciousness.

There is no single, infallible way of deciding whether any given species has conscious experience. However, we do not have to be defeatist. The optimal approach is to use various fallible indicators of consciousness. The greater the *consistency* among such indicators, the more confident we can be that any species possesses consciousness. Here, we consider two key indicators: brain anatomy and physiology and goal-directed behaviour.

In essence, consciousness in humans and other primates depends mostly on integrated activity across large regions of the brain including prefrontal areas (Eysenck & Keane, 2020; see Chapter 7). Feinberg and Mallatt (2016) proposed various brain indicators of consciousness. These indicators include brains having numerous neurons, information from different sense modalities converging within the brain, and a mechanism for selective attention.

When the above criteria were applied to numerous species, Feinberg and Mallatt (2016) concluded that all vertebrates (including mammals, birds, amphibians, reptiles, and fishes) are conscious. This conclusion is unsurprising given the many similarities between the brains of most vertebrate species and humans. The cephalopods (e.g., octopus, squid, and nautiloids) also appear to be conscious, as are some arthropods (especially insects and crustaceans).

Most (or all) vertebrates engage in goal-directed behaviour, which Pennartz et al. (2019) identified as a key function of consciousness (mentioned earlier). Most goal-directed behaviour involves what Skinner (1938) termed "operant conditioning": animals attempt to attain positive reinforcers or rewards while avoiding punishment. Numerous species are capable of operant conditioning (Staddon, 2014).

In sum, most (or even all) of the 70,000 vertebrate species have basic conscious awareness of their visual and auditory environment. Humans possess this basic conscious awareness. In addition, they also possess meta-consciousness (discussed later in the section on "theory of mind"). The differences between the brains of all other species and those of humans, the much lower complexity of their behaviour, and the lack of any positive evidence all suggest strongly meta-consciousness is unique to humans.

Working memory and attentional control

Many cognitive processes are what is known as domain-specific, meaning that they are used only in certain conditions. For example, some of the basic processes involved in visual or auditory processing are domain-specific. In addition, however, there are domain-general processes used in numerous situations. Several of these domain-general processes (often described as "executive functions") are of particular importance because they are required for the cognitive control of thinking and behaviour.

Baddeley and Hitch (1974) put forward one of the most influential theories combining domain-specific and executive processes. They proposed a working memory system used in the processing and brief maintenance of information. Within this system, the most important component was the central executive, which is attention-like and domain-general. Three executive functions associated with the central executive are as follows: (1) inhibition function (used for goal maintenance and avoidance of distraction), (2) shifting function (used to switch attention flexibly within and between tasks), and (3) updating function (used to rapidly add or delete information held in working memory) (Friedman & Miyake, 2017).

The above executive functions are of crucial importance with respect to attentional and cognitive control. The inhibition function focuses attention on the task in hand (i.e., concentration) and resists unintentional attentional shifting to task–irrelevant stimuli. In contrast, the shifting function is used to intentionally shift attention to the most currently relevant stimuli. In essence, the three executive functions are jointly designed to promote optimal use of our limited processing resources. Unsurprisingly, individual differences in intelligence depend heavily on such executive functions (discussed later).

There is a relatively small and inconclusive research literature on working memory in other species. However, there is reasonable evidence that several other species possess domain-general processes (Laland & Seed, 2021). It is probable that our executive functions are much more powerful than those of other species given our need for excellent attentional and cognitive control to manage the complexities of human cognition. However, definitive evidence is lacking.

Language ability

Our possession of excellent communication skills (largely dependent upon language) is an obvious human cognitive advantage. However, numerous other species communicate with other members of their species (Laland & Seed, 2021). The greatest language skills have been found in bonobo chimpanzees following extensive training by humans (see Figure 3.5). However, bonobos' utterances are simple and rarely exceed two words (Eysenck, 2022). In contrast, even young children often produce complex utterances of six words or more.

Why are human language skills dramatically better than those of any other species? Chomsky (1965) proposed an extremely influential answer: only humans possess an innate universal grammar (a set of principles found in all languages). Chomsky supported his viewpoint by arguing the language heard by young children (the "poverty of the stimulus" [Chomsky, 1980, p. 34]) is very limited. Thus,

Figure 3.5 Kanzi (a male bonobo chimpanzee) with the researcher Sue Savage-Rumbaugh. Kanzi learned to produce numerous words and exhibited some comprehension ability.

we can only explain children's very rapid acquisition of language by assuming they have an innate universal grammar. Two implications of Chomsky's viewpoint were that all languages are similar and that our language ability is very separate from all other cognitive abilities.

Chomsky was totally wrong. There are very large differences among the world's 6,000 to 8,000 languages.

In addition, "There are vanishingly few universals of language in the direct sense that all languages exhibit them" (Evans & Levinson, 2009, p. 4).

Children find it easy to acquire language because it was invented by humans to take account of human abilities: "Language has adapted to our brains" (Christiansen & Chater, 2008, p. 490). In addition, young children are exposed to a much richer language input than implied by Chomsky. Of most importance, most of the language children hear is child-directed speech tailored to their current language knowledge (Kidd & Donnelly, 2020). Finally, language in humans is not separate or independent of other cognitive abilities. Instead, it is strongly linked to several other cognitive processes (e.g., attention, abstract rule-learning, and thinking) even in infants (Chater & Christiansen, 2018).

Why are the language abilities of other species (including bonobos) so markedly inferior to ours? We can reject Chomsky's notion that their lack of an innate universal grammar is the cause. In essence, bonobos' non-language cognitive processes and abilities are considerably inferior to ours. In addition, their limited language abilities are only weakly linked to other cognitive processes (Novack & Waxman, 2020).

Language flexibility

The fact that humans' language abilities are far greater than those of any other species is unsurprising. What is less well known is how subtle, flexible and sophisticated our language abilities actually are (in stark contrast to the language abilities of any other species). Here, we will briefly consider several examples starting with our conversational skills. Speakers must construct their utterances to take account of the listener's need: this is "audience design." A simple form of audience design is based on the listener's *general* characteristics (e.g., adult or child) (Ferreira, 2019). There is also a more complex form based on the listener's *idiosyncratic* characteristics. For example, a speaker is less likely to emphasise how expensive their recent holiday was if their listener is poor.

According to Ferreira's (2019) forward modelling approach, speakers use their communicative intention (i.e., what they want to say) to generate possible utterances. They also often produce a forward model to predict the likely effect of those utterances on the listener. If the predictive communicative effect *mismatches* the speaker's intent, they alter the message to reduce the mismatch.

The common ground (information or knowledge shared by speaker and listener) is of key importance. Listeners expect speakers to refer mostly to information and knowledge in the common ground. However, it can be cognitively demanding for speakers to take full account of the common ground. For example, memory limitations mean speakers sometimes assume less common ground than is actually the case (Horton & Gerrig, 2016). Suppose you have told nearly all your friends about an event and mistakenly assume the one with whom you are currently talking was among them.

Speakers are also sensitive to the listener's reactions. They are much less likely to assume they have established common ground when their listener is inattentive (e.g., looking at their mobile phone) (Craycraft & Brown-Schmidt, 2018).

We turn now to listeners. They relate what they are hearing to their assessment of the speaker (Van den Brink et al., 2012). Listeners heard a woman with an upper-class or working-class accent say, "*I have a large tattoo on my back.*" Those hearing the word "*tattoo*" spoken in the former accent rapidly showed brain-wave activity indicating a mismatch, whereas those hearing the latter accent did not.

An important skill possessed by listeners is successful speech recognition when the listening conditions are difficult (e.g., there are several non-target voices). Part of that success is due to listeners' ability to infer characteristics of the speaker from what they are saying. This speaker model then influences how that person's speech is perceived (Cai et al., 2017).

We can see the advantages of constructing a speaker model by considering how we understand non-native speakers of English. They often make errors because of deficient knowledge of the language including numerous mispronunciations (Levis & Barriuso, 2011). In such circumstances, listeners must infer the intended meaning from what is actually said. Gibson et al. (2017) found listeners relied less on the actual words spoken by non-native speakers and more on the intended meaning. Native and non-native speakers produced many utterances, some of which were implausible (e.g., "*The tax law benefited from the businessman*"). Listeners were more likely to interpret such implausible utterances as plausible (e.g., "*The businessman benefited from the tax law*") when spoken by a non-native speaker. This makes sense given that non-native speakers are more likely to put words in the wrong order.

Suppose a listener is exposed to the utterances of a non-native speaker whose errors consist mainly of deletions (e.g., "*We had nice time at the beach*") or insertions (e.g., "*The earthquake shattered from the house*"). Listeners might simply assume in both cases that the speaker makes many errors across the board. Alternatively, they might assume the speaker has a high probability of making *specific* speech errors (e.g., deletions or insertions). In fact, listeners are sensitive to the specific errors they have heard previously, thus demonstrating sensitivity to fine-grained information about the types of errors made by speakers (Ryskin et al., 2018).

In sum, listeners who understand the full meaning the speaker intends to communicate have to be active participants rather than simply focusing on the literal meaning of what has been said. Consider someone says the following to you: "Never ask two China trips to the same party" (Bender & Koller, 2020). The literal meaning is unhelpful. However, most listeners work out that the speaker means that having two people at a party who have both visited China is likely to lead to a long and boring account of those trips.

The flexibility we display in conversation is also found in reading. For example, we typically have no problem reading a text containing numerous misspellings. Here is the "Cambridge email" (Norris & Kinoshita, 2012):

> Aoccrdnig to a rscheearch at Cmabrigde Uinervtisy it deosn't mttaer in waht oredr the ltteers in a wrod are. The olny iprmoatnt tihng is that the frist and lsat ltteer be at the rghit pclae. The rset can be a toatl mses and you can still raed it wouthit porbelm. This is bcusease the huamn mnid deos not raed ervey lteter by istlef but the wrod as a wlohe.

Readers also have the ability to draw inferences to make sense of what they are reading. This ability relies heavily on our knowledge of the world and the wealth of experience which allow us to "read between the lines" and to draw appropriate inferences. Consider the following short text taken from Rumelhart and Ortony (1977):

> Mary heard the ice-cream van coming. She remembered the pocket money. She rushed into the house.

You probably inferred that Mary wanted to buy some ice-cream, that buying ice-cream costs money, that Mary had some pocket money in the house, and that Mary had only limited time to get hold of some money before the ice-cream van appeared. None of these inferences is explicitly stated.

Here is another example (taken from Austin, 1975) of how we utilise our past experience and knowledge when reading. Imagine the word "BULL" is written on the side of a fence in a field. Humans do not simply understand the word; they also draw the social inference that there is a dangerous animal on the opposite side of the fence from the one on which the word is written.

Remembering the past and imagining the future

Laland and Seed (2021) emphasised the importance to humans of remembering the past and imagining the future. We can remember the past because of episodic memory (our long-term memory for personal experiences). More specifically, Nairne (2015) identified the three "Ws" of episodic memory: remembering a specific event (*what?*) at a given time (*when?*) in a particular place (*where?*).

Simons and Chabris (2011, p. 3) presented people with the following statement about episodic memory: "Human memory works like a video camera, accurately recording the events we see and hear so that we can review and inspect them later." Over 60% of members of public agreed with this statement compared to 0% of memory experts. In fact, episodic memory is typically highly *selective*: the gist or essence of our experiences is retained but not the trivial details (see Chapter 5).

For a long time it was believed that episodic memory is used only to remember the past. However, Schacter and Addis (2007) hypothesised that imagining future events involves very similar processes to those involved in remembering past episodic events. As predicted, remembering the past and imagining the future activate substantially overlapping brain areas (Benoit & Schacter, 2015; see Figure 3.6). Also as predicted, amnesic patients with severely impaired episodic memory have great difficulty in imagining future events (Schacter & Madore, 2016).

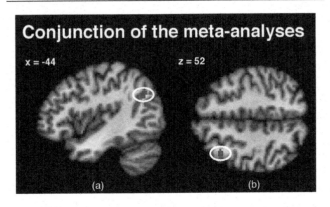

Figure 3.6 (a) Brain regions exhibiting comparable activity during episodic simulation of future events and episodic memory for past events. (b) Brain regions exhibiting greater activity during episodic simulation than episodic memory.

Source: From Benoit and Schacter (2015).

Our goal when imagining the future is often to plan what we should do over the following weeks or months. This involves comparing and evaluating potential courses of action. That requires metacognition: "Cognition about cognition; the capacity to monitor, evaluate and control one's own cognitive processes" (Bulley & Schacter, 2020, p. 239).

In sum, when we plan for the future, we flexibly generate many possibilities using episodic processes. After that, we use our meta-cognitive abilities to identify the most appropriate course of action. These abilities equip us extremely well to cope with the uncertainties of everyday life

Do other species possess episodic memory processes and metacognition? Many animal species show elements of episodic memory: they remember what food they have hidden away, where that food is, and when they hid it (Clayton, 2017). However, it is unclear whether their recall of such information is accompanied by subjective experience resembling that of humans. In similar fashion, many animal species show limited evidence of future planning. However, we do not know whether they achieve this by mentally imagining possible future events.

The issue of whether other species possess metacognitive processes is a vexed one. Several animal species (e.g., monkeys) exhibit behaviour that superficially seems to require metacognition. However, it is nearly always possible to interpret such behaviour in simpler, non-metacognitive terms (Carruthers & Williams, 2019).

According to the Bischof-Köhler hypothesis, only humans can anticipate their own future mental states and take appropriate action now to cater for those mental states. For example, humans in the heat of summer may imagine feeling cold during the winter and so act immediately (e.g., collecting firewood) to ensure they will be warm several months later. Other species lack this metacognitive ability. For example, Paxton and Hampton (2009) found that monkeys failed to act in anticipation of motivational states that lay only 15 minutes in the future.

Theory of mind

One of the most important human abilities is theory of mind. Individuals possessing theory of mind understand other people's beliefs, emotions, and mental states. Thus, they are fully aware another person's perspective or beliefs often differ from their own. Theory of mind is of enormous value in social interaction and communication as we can see by considering autism, which is a severe disorder involving very poor communication skills, and deficient social and language development. Autistic individuals have very deficient theory of mind, and as a consequence are typically socially isolated. The importance of theory of mind is also indicated by the consistent finding that individual differences in theory or mind correlate strongly with general intelligence (e.g., Navarro et al., 2021).

We can see what is involved in theory of mind by considering the Sally-Anne test (Baron-Cohen et al., 1985; see Figure 3.7). Sally hides a marble in her basket. She then goes for a walk. While she is out, Anne removes the marble from Sally's basket and puts it in her own box. Theory of mind is tested by asking someone who has observed the above sequences of events the following question: "Where will Sally look for her marble?" Individuals possessing theory of mind respond correctly that she will look in her basket. Most children can solve problems such as the Sally-Anne test by the age of four or five (Apperley & Butterfill, 2009).

Finally, theory of mind is useful when a speaker wants to persuade their listener to do something or to adopt their viewpoint on a given issue. Their knowledge of the listener's beliefs and emotions makes it easier to tailor their message to make it maximally effective.

Researchers have often claimed they have demonstrated theory of mind in non-human primates. However, it has proved hard to replicate their findings and there is still no convincing evidence that other primates can represent others' beliefs (Horschler et al., 2020).

Caveats and a broader perspective

Two major objections can be raised to much of the research discussed in this section. First, it is based on an anthropocentric approach where other species' cognitive skills are evaluated with respect to human cognitive abilities. This approach can over-value other species' skills if they are human-like. More importantly, it under-values those skills if they are not human-like. It would be preferable to adopt a biocentric approach focusing on the adaptiveness of any given species' cognitive skills given their evolutionary history (Bräuer et al., 2020). For example, cockroaches lack nearly all human cognitive skills. However, the fact

Figure 3.7 The cartoon of the Sally-Anne test as used originally by Baron-Cohen et al. (1985).

that cockroaches have been on Earth for 300 million years indicates they are very well adapted to their environment even though they lack any cognitive skills.

Second, researchers often assume there is "one cognition" (Bräuer et al., 2020), meaning that different cognitive skills tend to be found together (as in humans). In fact, many non-human species possess one or two highly specialised skills because of evolutionary pressures. For example, New Caledonian crows have exceptional tool-manufacturing skills to facilitate accessing food but are otherwise "unintelligent."

Mikhalevich et al. (2017) argued that much cross-species research is bedevilled by simplistic assumptions. One such assumption is that behavioural flexibility provides a reasonably direct measure of cognitive complexity. This is flawed because behavioural flexibility can be due to hard-wired predispositions or simple learning (e.g., learning to associate different environmental cues with different responses) rather than cognitive complexity.

Mikhalevich et al. (2017) proposed an "adaptive triadic model," according to which three criteria need to be satisfied before inferring a given species is cognitively complex. These are the criteria: (i) behavioural complexity, (ii) environmental heterogeneity or complexity, and (iii) neuroanatomical structures associated with sophisticated information processing. In other words, behavioural complexity in a given species implies cognitive complexity provided adaptation to the environment requires complex information processing and the members of that species have a brain capable of high-level cognitive processing.

It is perhaps natural to assume that species close to us in evolutionary history (e.g., apes) are most likely to possess cognitive complexity as defined by Mikhalevich et al. (2017). However, consider cephalods (e.g., octopus and squid), whose evolutionary history has been separate from that of humans for over 300 million years. They are the most cognitively complex of all invertebrates (Schnell et al., 2021; see Figure 3.8). They engage in flexible foraging and anti-predatory strategies to cope with the environmental complexities they encounter. Finally, their brains (although very different from ours) are complex.

Figure 3.8 An octopus opening a container with a screw cap.

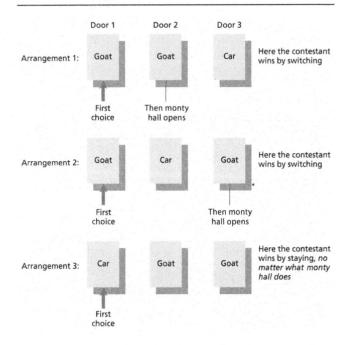

Figure 3.9 Figure 12.1 in E&K, 2020: Monty Hall, the game-show host.

Source: Monty Hall. ZUMA Press, Inc./Alamy.

For example, their vertical lobe system is the largest used for learning and memory among all the invertebrates. In sum, the cephalopods fulfil all three of Mikhalevich et al.'s (2017) criteria for cognitive complexity.

We conclude with a sobering example of humans outperformed by pigeons on the Monty Hall problem that played an important role on Monty Hall's show on American television (see Figure 3.9):

> You are on a game show and have the choice of three doors. There is a car behind one door and goats behind the others. You pick a door (say, door 1). The host,

who knows what is behind each door, opens another door (say, door 3), behind which is a goat. He then asks whether you would like to switch your choice from door 1 to door 2. What do you decide to do?

Most people stick with their first choice. In fact, that is the wrong decision. When you initially picked a door at random, you clearly only had a one-third chance of winning the car. Regardless of whether your initial choice was correct, the host can open a door not having the car behind it. Thus, the host's action sheds *no light at all* on the correctness of your initial choice. Since there is only a one-third chance of being correct by sticking with your original choice, there is a two-thirds chance of being correct by switching.

Herbranson and Schroeder (2010) found humans correctly switched on 66% of trials after extensive practice. However, Silver King pigeons switched on 96% of trials! The humble pigeons performed well because they simply maximised the reward they received, whereas humans adopted more complex (and less valid) strategies. The take-home message is that humans are sometimes inclined to over-complicate their approach to problems.

Inter-dependent abilities

It is easy to be somewhat disappointed by much of the research comparing humans against other species. Several other species possess many of our most important cognitive processes and structures (though to a lesser extent). Thus, we cannot explain the superiority of human cognition by "a single magic bullet" (Laland & Seed, 2021, p. 704). Laland and Seed concluded their review of cross-species comparisons as follows: "Humans are flexible cognitive all rounders" (p. 689). That almost sounds like they are damning with faint praise.

We accept that human uniqueness does not lie with our possession of specific abilities denied all other species but rather with the inter-dependence of our abilities. In other words, the human mind is a prime example of the whole being greater than the sum of its parts. More specifically, our minds are far more flexible and adaptable than those of any other species because we possess several cognitive processes and structures that interact co-operatively with each other.

One example of inter-dependence in the human mind involves attentional control or selective attention and conscious awareness. There are several possible relationships between these two processes (Webb & Graziano, 2015). Most commonly, conscious awareness is determined by prior selective attention (i.e., we are consciously aware of what we have chosen to attend to). Thus, the flexibility of human consciousness is strongly influenced by the flexibility of selective attention.

Another example concerns the relationship between theory of mind and meta-cognition. Both depend heavily on the ability to disengage one's conscious awareness from the current environment to focus on one's own thinking and beliefs (meta-cognition) or someone else's (theory of mind). This relationship may develop in various ways. One possibility is that self-directed mindreading or theory of mind in young children is instrumental in the development of meta-cognition (Carruthers & Williams, 2019)

Our mastery of language interacts with other aspects of our cognitive system. It allows us (unlike other species) to communicate about the past and future as well as the here-and-now. Our ability to discuss the past increases the chances that we (and others) can learn from our past mistakes. Our ability to discuss the future can be very useful for discussing the best places to find food or planning how to attack another group in the future. In addition, linguistic interactions enhance our ability to understand other people's perspectives, which is fundamental to developing social cohesion.

The above discussion provides the basis for answering the question of why human cognition is so much more flexible (and powerful) than any other species. Several factors are involved:

1 Our meta-consciousness and meta-cognition mean that our processing is not largely limited to the current environment (unlike other species that possess only basic consciousness).

2 Our highly developed working memory and selective attention (e.g., inhibition and shifting functions) also enhance the flexibility of our processing allowing us to discriminate between information that is important and information that is trivial. More generally, our domain-general processes provide the "glue" that facilitates optimal processing efficiency within the highly complex human cognitive system.

3 Our excellent episodic memory means we can readily process information relating to the past and the imagined future. The latter is especially important for flexible future planning. Our possession of theory of mind means we can focus on the beliefs and knowledge of other people as well as on our own beliefs and knowledge.

4 Language also plays a major role in producing human thinking flexibility. Of special importance, it provides an extremely effective way of accessing human cultural knowledge that has accumulated over the centuries. Language also provides a medium for thinking about the past and the future and for future planning. It is also the medium we typically use for complex abstract thinking (a form of thinking probably not present in any other species).

Intelligence

Strong evidence that human cognition owes much of its excellence to inter-dependent abilities comes from research on human intelligence. Over a century ago, the British psychologist Charles Spearman (1904) made a crucial discovery. He found scores on nearly all cognitive tests were positively correlated despite apparently large differences among them. In other words, individuals performing well on one test typically performed well on most other tests, whereas other individuals performed relatively poorly on most tests.

Spearman (1904, 1927) argued persuasively that these findings indicate the existence of a general (or g) factor. This g factor is of great importance: 40–50% of individual differences in IQ depend on it (Kovacs & Conway, 2019). However, there is a danger of using the term g to *describe* general intelligence rather than *explain* it. Note that the argument that some individuals perform better than others on intelligence tests, "because they have more g," is a circular argument – we only know they have more g because they perform well on intelligence tests.

Progress was made by Cattell (1963), who identified two forms of intelligence strongly related to g. One was crystallised intelligence (the ability to use one's knowledge and experience effectively) and the other was fluid intelligence (the ability to reason about, and to understand, novel relationships (Cattell, 1963). Barbey (2018) argued (with supporting evidence) that crystallised intelligence involves the ability to flexibly reach easy-to-access network states reflecting our stored knowledge and experience. In contrast, fluid intelligence requires the ability to flexibly reach hard-to-access states involving weakly connected connections and networks needed when we tackle novel problems. Brain areas associated with fluid intelligence overlap with those commonly associated with consciousness.

Duncan et al. (2020) argued that fluid intelligence is closely linked to the "multiple demand" system distributed across several large brain areas, supporting his argument with a discussion of relevant research. They also proposed an explanatory account of fluid intelligence based on "attentional integration." Complex problems consist of a series of processing stages; accordingly, their successful solution requires organising the correct cognitive elements in the correct sequence (i.e., attentional integration). Individual differences in attentional integration depend on stored knowledge of previous similar problems and flexible thinking about novel aspects of the current problem.

Kovacs and Conway (2016, 2019) proposed a related explanatory account of fluid intelligence. Their starting point was the assumption that, "General intelligence [g] is a summary of different but correlated abilities rather than the reflection of a single, unitary ability" (Kovacs & Conway, 2019, p. 255). They emphasised the importance of several executive functions including sustained attention, planning, and mental flexibility (resembling the three executive functions identified by Friedman & Miyake, 2017 and discussed earlier). These executive functions are associated with overlapping brain areas and jointly account for individual differences in fluid intelligence and g.

Conclusions

There are several reasons why human cognition is vastly superior to that of any other species. Of particular importance, however, are the various executive functions we possess, which typically combine very efficiently to integrate and co-ordinate during tasks requiring complex cognition. General intelligence or g reflects our usage of these executive functions.

In sum, there are two crucial reasons why general intelligence is so important. First, there are very close links between learning and intelligence – arguably, the main difference between individuals with high and low general (or fluid) intelligence is their learning rate. Second, general (or fluid) intelligence allows us to cope reasonably successfully with an enormous range of novel situations and problems.

Chapter 4

How (un)intelligent is AI?

We saw in Chapter 2 that AI has numerous achievements (e.g., beating leading chess, Go, and poker players; matching human experts in several professional work activities). That chapter focused on specific skills possessed by AI systems. Here we compare AI systems and humans with respect to general skills and intelligence.

Moravec's paradox

It seems natural to assume that AI would perform well on 'easy' tasks (e.g., visual perception) but poorly on 'hard' tasks (e.g., logical reasoning). However, Moravec (1988) proposed the opposite in his famous paradox: "It is comparatively easy to make computers exhibit adult level performance on intelligence tests or playing checkers [draughts], and difficult or impossible to give them the skills of a one-year old when it comes to perception and mobility" (p. 15).

Moravec's paradox is partially correct. We will start by considering a common problem in visual perception. You have probably had the experience when trying to access information on a website of being confronted by distorted characters (often a combination of letters and digits) connected horizontally. You have to identify these characters correctly before being allowed access to the website.

DOI: 10.4324/9781003162698-4

Figure 4.1 The CAPTCHA used by Yahoo!.

Source: From Gao et al. (2012).

Why are you asked to do this? The technical term for a pattern of distorted characters is CAPTCHA (Completely Automated Turing test to tell Computers and Humans Apart) which answers the question (see Figure 4.1). The intention is to ensure a website user is human by providing a test humans can solve but automated computer-based systems cannot. Nachar et al. (2015) devised a sophisticated AI program focusing on edge corners (intersections of two straight edges); this makes sense because edge corners are relatively unaffected by the distortions present in CAPTCHAs. This program accurately solved only 57% of CAPTCHAs. Such findings suggest our pattern–recognition abilities are often superior to those of AI.

Why do we underestimate the complexities of human visual perception? Minsky (1986, p. 29) provided a convincing explanation: "We're least aware of what our minds do best … we're more aware of simple processes that don't work well than of complex ones that work flawlessly." Visual perception is undoubtedly complex: one example is our ability to recognise any given object almost instantly despite huge variations in its size, orientation, illumination, and position. Such complexities explain why 50% of the human cortex is devoted to visual processing. Most complex visual processes are largely unconscious because they have developed gradually over the incredibly lengthy course of human evolution.

Moravec's paradox is also applicable to human motor skills and abilities. As the Australian roboticist Brooks (1986) pointed out, "The things that children of four or five years could do effortlessly, such as … walking around on two legs, or finding their way from their bedroom to the living room were not thought of as activities requiring intelligence."

As a result, motor skills were de-emphasised for many years within what has sometimes disparagingly been called Good Old-Fashioned AI (GOFAI). The focus of GOFAI was on disembodied intelligence in the form of symbolic reasoning with a consequent ignoring of the processing required to interact successfully with the real world.

Why were the processes involved in producing skilled motor behaviour not regarded as complex? As with visual perception, these processes are mostly unconscious because they evolved over hundreds of millions of years and so their complexity is easy to miss.

We can see the power of Moravec's paradox most clearly when we consider the achievements of numerous mammalian species. As Zador (2019, p. 2) pointed out, "We cannot build a machine capable of building a nest, or stalking prey … In many ways, AI is far from achieving the intelligence of a dog or a mouse, or even of a spider, and it does not appear that merely scaling up current approaches will achieve these goals."

A key reason for this is numerous species are born with highly structured brain connectivity that greatly facilitates rapid learning of complex forms of behaviour. More specifically, the complex behaviour exhibited by most non-human species depends heavily on innate mechanisms encoded in the genome (Zador, 2019). An extreme example can be found in honeybees. They signal accurately the direction and distance of food to other bees by performing a figure-8 waggle dance (von Frisch, 1967). They achieve this feat in spite of a having a brain smaller than a pin head ($1mm^3$ vs $1.5mm^3$). Such behaviour is complex but is not intelligent in the sense of being dependent on extensive learning (the concept of "intelligence" is discussed shortly).

Researchers in AI have made attempts to address Moravec's paradox. Over 30 years ago, Rodney Brooks embarked on "nouvelle AI" based on the assumption that intelligence depends heavily on the ability to function effectively in real-world environments (Brooks, 1991).

Brooks constructed numerous robots. One was called Herbert in honour of the psychologist Herbert Simon. Herbert used a laser system to collect 3D information up to 12 feet in front of it, and it had a hand equipped with sensors. Herbert's real-world environment consisted of the busy offices and work-spaces of the AI lab. The robot searched on desks and tables in the lab for empty soda cans, which it picked up and carried away. Herbert's seemingly co-ordinated and goal-directed behaviour emerged from the interactions of about 15 simple behaviours.

In spite of such attempts, robots remain very limited in many ways. For example, consider a contest in Pomona, California, in 2015 involving 23 robots. Only one of the several robots that fell over managed to stand up again and most of the robots struggled to turn a door handle (Guizzo & Ackerman, 2015).

Another aspect of Moravec's paradox is that it is relatively easy for AI to perform comparably to humans on what are regarded as intellectually demanding tasks (e.g., abstract reasoning and mathematics). The reason is that humans have developed such intellectual skills only comparatively recently in evolution and so we still find them effortful and very demanding. As we will see later, Moravec greatly exaggerated how easy it would be for AI to match human performance levels on intellectually or cognitively demanding tasks (e.g., intelligence tests).

Intelligence: general and narrow

It has proved notoriously difficult to define "intelligence" satisfactorily. Many years ago, psychologists' favourite cop-out was to argue, "Intelligence is what intelligence tests measure." However, most experts agree that "intelligence" refers to a very *general* ability to solve an enormous number of very heterogeneous problems. Voss (2016) identified the main criteria for a human to possess high intelligence:

1 The acquisition of a wide range of new knowledge and skills.
2 The mastery of language including the ability to engage in meaningful conversations.
3 The possession of good short-term memory and the understanding of the purpose of actions (including other individuals' actions).
4 Using pre-existing knowledge and skills to facilitate learning on novel tasks.
5 The acquisition of abstract knowledge by generalising from more concrete forms of knowledge.
6 The management of several conflicting goals and priorities with an ability to direct attention to the task of most immediate relevance and importance.
7 The possession of emotional intelligence – recognising and responding appropriately to emotional states in oneself and in others (e.g., understanding why someone else is angry or upset).
8 The ability to demonstrate all the above abilities even when relevant knowledge and time are both limited.

In essence, Voss (2016) identified the criteria for general intelligence. It is important to distinguish between general and specific or narrow intelligence (a distinction applicable to humans and AI). In humans, individuals having an IQ below 70 are in the bottom 2–3% for general intelligence and are often described as having intellectual disability. However, some have savant syndrome, meaning they exhibit outstanding abilities in a very specific or narrow domain. For example, calendrical savants can tell you very rapidly the day of the week on which any given date fell. Other individuals with savant syndrome have great musical ability.

In the field of AI, a distinction has been drawn between artificial narrow intelligence and artificial general intelligence. Artificial narrow intelligence is displayed by AI systems performing exceptionally well on one task or a small number of very similar tasks. In contrast, AI systems exhibiting artificial general intelligence would perform numerous very different tasks at human level with their performance dependent on rapid and effective learning of many different kinds.

An implication of Moravec's paradox is that we may need to re-think our conceptualisation of "intelligence." The paradox encourages us to broaden our definition of "intelligence" to include perceptual and motor abilities.

Human intelligence

Intelligence tests (or IQ tests) measure general intelligence because they assess a wide range of abilities including mathematical ability, verbal ability, and reasoning. However, these tests do not actually assess *all* the abilities relevant to intelligence. What is missing is a systematic attempt to assess the practical and social skills required for success in life. For example, Voss (2016) identified emotional intelligence as an important criterion for general intelligence. However, the ability to interact successfully with other people is ignored by most intelligence tests. Emotional intelligence in humans and AI is discussed at length in Chapter 7.

As discussed in Chapter 3, individual differences in general intelligence in humans can be assessed by assessing their intelligence quotient or IQ based on intelligence tests. The average IQ in the population is 100, but highly intelligent individuals have IQs of 120 or more.

AI and intelligence

The great majority of AI systems provide evidence of artificial narrow intelligence rather than artificial general intelligence. Think back to Chapter 2. There we discussed examples of AI systems that triumphed at chess and Go when competing against the finest human players (Garry Kasparov and Lee Se-dol, respectively). These systems (Deep Blue and AlphaGo, respectively) would not perform well on other cognitively demanding tasks, and so clearly exemplify artificial narrow intelligence. However, algorithms producing outstanding performance on several different games have been developed (e.g., Silver et al.'s, 2018, AlphaZero; Schrittwieser et al.'s, 2020, MuZero). Below we consider other attempts to demonstrate that AI systems can possess artificial general intelligence.

One of the most striking differences between us and all other animal species is the range and complexity of our language. As discussed in Chapter 3, the increased size of the human brain is mostly associated with the development of social and cultural intelligence. Both forms of intelligence depend hugely on communication skills involving language. More generally, most of our thinking involves language. Thus, good language skills require a high level of general intelligence.

Intelligence tests

One way of assessing AI intelligence is based on the huge amount of research involving intelligence tests on humans. Precisely that was done by Liu et al. (2019). They argued any intelligent system should possess four characteristics: (1) the ability to acquire knowledge, (2) the ability to master knowledge, (3) the ability to create knowledge, and (4) the ability to output knowledge to the outside world.

By definition, the average human adult has an IQ (intelligence quotient) of 100. Liu et al. (2019) estimated the average human six-year-old has an IQ of 55 (when compared against adult performance). The most successful AI systems all performed somewhat worse than a six-year-old. Google's AI was top with an estimated IQ of 47, followed by Baidu with an IQ of 33, and Siri with an IQ of 24.

General intelligence can be sub-divided into fluid and crystallised intelligence (see Chapter 3). The former involves the ability to solve novel problems, whereas the latter involves the effective use of accumulated knowledge. Raven's Progressive Matrices (Raven, 1936) (often shortened to Raven's Matrices) is the most influential test of fluid intelligence. It requires analogical reasoning which is often regarded as the "core of cognition" (Hofstadter, 2001, p. 499).

Each item on Raven's Matrices consists of a matrix of abstract geometric elements arranged in a pattern (e.g., 2 × 2 and 3 × 3) with the element in the bottom right corner missing (see Figure 4.2). The task requires choosing the element completing the visual pattern from between six and eight possibilities. This test may sound easy. However,

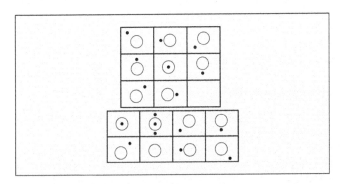

Figure 4.2 A problem resembling those used in Raven's progressive matrices. The image from the bottom eight images that best completes the top 3 × 3 matrix must be selected.

Source: From Lovett and Forbus (2017).

the elements can vary in several ways (e.g., number, colour, type, and size) making it possible to create fiendishly difficult problems.

Zhang et al. (2019) gave eight AI models extensive training on a dataset consisting of 70,000 problems resembling Raven's Progressive Matrices. They then compared the models' performance against humans *not* provided with training. The human participants were correct on 84% of trials. In contrast, the best AI model achieved a success rate of 60%. All four of the worst-performing models succeeded on under 16% of trials – this is very poor given that chance performance was 12.5%.

Spratley et al. (2020) devised two deep neural models (Rel-Base and Rel-AIR (Attend-Infer-Repeat) that were simpler and more general-purpose than previous models. Average accuracy on Raven's Matrices' problems was 92% for Rel-Base and 94% for Rel-AIR (against average human performance of 84%). However, Rel-AIR's advantage over Rel-Base was much greater when generalisation to new problems was tested.

Most AI models on Raven's Progressive Matrices exhibit poor generalisation ability: they perform very poorly when there are even minimal differences between training and testing items. Another issue is that incorrect choices on some versions of Raven's Progressive Matrices are generated by changing single attributes from the correct answers. This allows some AI models to produce correct answers without directly considering the question. However, Benny et al. (2020) eliminated this problem and devised an AI model that outperformed previous models and showed good generalisation.

In sum, AI models have recently matched or even exceeded human performance on versions of Raven's Progressive Matrices. That is a major achievement given the convincing evidence that fluid intelligence in humans is assessed validly by this test. However, AI typically exhibit relatively poor generalisation from trained examples to new ones and are not applicable to different kinds of intelligence test. As a consequence, these models cannot be claimed to demonstrate artificial general intelligence.

Language skills

Language ability is of central importance to general intelligence. As the Austrian philosopher Ludwig Wittgenstein (1889–1951) argued, "The limits of my language are the limits of my thinking." Another quotation by Wittgenstein further emphasises language's importance: "Whereof one cannot speak, thereof one must be silent."

There are close links among intelligence, thinking, and language ability. Humans with excellent language skills have greater general intelligence and thinking powers than those with inferior language skills. AI has proved increasingly successful at various language skills including speech recognition, answering general knowledge questions, translating, and holding conversations (see Chapter 2). Superficially, these achievements are impressive and suggest AI possesses some aspects of general intelligence. However, research showing human-like language performance is limited in various ways (see also Chapter 7).

There are four main language skills: speech recognition or perception, reading, speech production, and written language (Eysenck & Keane, 2020). We will discuss all four language skills in turn. After that, we consider the extent to which AI systems exhibit human-like conversational skills and translation abilities.

Speech recognition

In Chapter 2, we discussed the speech-recognition performance of various AI systems. There is some controversy as to whether these systems have comparable error rates to human experts. However, automatic speech-recognition systems have improved dramatically in recent years and now produce performance approaching human level.

Most research comparing the performance of automatic speech-recognition systems with human listeners has involved presenting only an auditory input. Such research minimises human superiority because we often use non-acoustic sources of information during speech recognition. Everyone knows the deaf rely heavily on the speaker's lip movements to understand what is being said, but humans with intact hearing do the same. Consider the McGurk effect (McGurk & MacDonald, 1976): a mismatch between spoken and visual (lip-based) information leads listeners to perceive a blend of the auditory and visual information.

Another advantage of human listeners over automatic speech-recognition systems is that we generally *predict* the speech input using speech-production processes and thus enhance speech perception. Several brain areas involved in speech production are also activated during speech perception (Skipper et al., 2017).

Some research has focused on establishing whether automatic speech recognition can be disrupted by adding small irrelevant acoustic clips (e.g., commands) to the speech output. These irrelevant clips (known as "adversarial attacks") cause mistranscriptions by AI systems (Abdullah et al., 2020).

Our focus in this book is on comparing AI systems and humans. Accordingly, we need to compare the impact of adversarial attacks on speech recognition in AI and humans. Schömherr et al. (2018) presented human listeners with speech (including or excluding adversarial attacks in the form of hidden voice commands). Human listeners were not consciously aware of the voice commands nor did the commands influence the accuracy with which speech was transcribed. In contrast, Kaldi (a speech-recognition system) was highly susceptible to adversarial attacks. Thus, human speech recognition is more robust and less easily disrupted than speech recognition by AI systems.

Most research has involved white-box adversarial attacks. These are attacks where the researchers have full knowledge of the workings of the automatic speech-recognition system (e.g., Schönherr et al., 2018). However, manufacturers of most commercially available speech-recognition systems (e.g., Siri, Alexa, and Cortana) do *not* provide information about their detailed functioning. As a result, researchers investigating such systems are limited to black-box attacks.

There are two reasons why it is important to study black-box attacks. First, they have greater real-world applicability than white-box attacks. Second, it is harder to mount successful black-box attacks than white-box ones, and so research on the latter may well not generalise to the former.

Chen et al. (2020) studied approximations to black-box attacks on several automatic speech-recognition systems (e.g., Amazon Echo, Microsoft Cortana, and Google Assistant). The attacks consisted of frequently used commands, such as "Okay, Google, turn off the light" and "Echo, call my wife," presented concurrently with songs. These attacks were often successful even though human listeners were unaware there was any speech (17% of the time) or perceived the commands as meaningless noise (66% of the time).

So far we have focused mostly on relatively straightforward situations where there is only a single speaker. In the real world, listeners often confront the more challenging task of attending to one voice when two or more people are speaking at the same time: the "cocktail party problem."

Human listeners utilise various strategies to cope with this problem. For example, they use attentional and control processes to process the target voice and reject competing voices (Evans et al., 2016). If listeners can identify at least one distinctive feature of the target voice, this facilitates directing attention to the target voice (Shamma et al., 2011). Finally, listeners often make use of visual information. Listeners presented with two voices at the same time exhibited better speech recognition for the target voice when they saw a video of the speaker at the same time (Golumbic et al., 2013).

Early AI automatic speech recognition systems were considerably inferior to human listeners at speech recognition for one speaker in the presence of a second speaker (Spille & Meyer, 2014). However, significant progress has been made, in part because AI systems increasingly use several different kinds of information in speech recognition. For example, Gu et al. (2020) developed an AI system combining information about the target voice's spatial location, lip movements, and voice characteristics. This system exhibited reasonably good speech recognition regardless of whether there were one, two, or three voices. However, its performance was still well short of that of human listeners.

In sum, AI systems provide rapid speech recognition. Their performance in relatively easy conditions (e.g., simple messages and only one speech input) is often fairly close to that of humans. However, the speech-recognition abilities of automatic speech-recognition systems are much more limited and inflexible. They find it much harder to process one voice among many or to prevent irrelevant input (adversarial attacks) from causing mistranscriptions.

Text comprehension: reading

Nearly everyone finds writing or word-processing a text much harder (and it takes far longer) than simply speaking with someone else. The main reason is that the sentences produced by writers are typically more complex than those produced by speakers. As a result, readers often find it harder to comprehend texts than listeners do to understand spoken language.

There has been major recent progress in developing AI models that perform very well on many language-comprehension tasks. Of most importance, a version of a model called BERT (Bi-directional Encoder Representations from Transformers) outperformed humans on a set of language comprehension tasks called GLUE (General Language Understanding Evaluation) (Yang et al., 2019). Several enhanced versions of BERT have done the same (see Chapter 2).

The above findings suggest it may be premature to conclude AI systems lack general intelligence. However, they appear less impressive in the light of other research. For example, Wang et al. (2019) devised eight tasks (jointly called SuperGLUE). These tasks resembled those in GLUE but were more challenging. BERT did much worse relative to humans on SuperGLUE than it had on GLUE: an average score of 69% vs 89.8%, respectively. Even an enhanced version of BERT (BERT++) was markedly worse than humans with a score of 71.5%.

BERT also performed very poorly on a task that involved deciding whether an initial sentence implies the truth of a second sentence (McCoy et al., 2019). Here is an example:

Example 2

1 The actor was paid by the judge.
2 The actor paid the judge.

The truth of sentence (2) is *not* implied by sentence (1). BERT's performance on such items was close to 0% against chance probability of 50%, whereas human performance was close to 80%. In approximate terms, BERT decided that one sentence was implied by another if both sentences contained the same words (see Chapter 7). In other words, it was using a short-cut that often misfired.

One way of testing AI language models is by introducing adversarial attacks (adding irrelevant material) on a reading task. Jia and Liang (2017) explored the effects of adversarial attacks on reading comprehension by 16 deep learning systems. In the control condition, the task was to draw appropriate inferences from paragraphs in order to answer questions. In the adversarial condition, an additional distracting sentence that did not change the correct answer was embedded in the paragraph.

The 16 AI systems were 75% correct in the control condition compared to only 36% correct in the adversarial condition. In contrast, human performance was 92% and 79%, respectively. These findings show AI's *brittleness*: the human advantage was much greater in the adversarial condition. When Jia and Liang (2017) added some ungrammatical word sequences in the adversarial condition the AI's performance slumped to only 7% correct responses.

In Jia and Liang's (2017) study, all the questions were answerable and so correct answers could be produced by plausible guesses. Rajpurkar et al. (2018) included some unanswerable questions to increase task difficulty. This caused an AI system to perform very poorly relative to humans.

Most AI language models struggle on tasks requiring general knowledge and use of context. Consider the Winograd Schema Challenge. Here are two sample sentences from this task:

1 John took the water bottle out of the backpack so that it would be lighter.
2 John took the water bottle out of the backpack so that it would be handy.

Over 90% of humans realise "it" refers to the backpack in sentence (i) but the water bottle in sentence (ii).

In contrast, all AI systems for several years after the development of the Winograd Schema Challenge had performance accuracy under 65%. Recently, however, a language model known as BERT (discussed earlier) achieved 72.5% accuracy (Kocijan et al., 2019). That is an improvement but still well below human performance.

In sum, AI systems process language in a relatively limited and rigid fashion. Here is another example. Jiang et al. (2020) tested the knowledge possessed by language models by presenting prompts containing blanks to be filled in. The models' performance was influenced by the precise wording of the prompt (e.g., *Obama is a _____ by profession* vs *Obama worked as a _____*). This finding indicates inflexibility: knowledge possessed by a language model was sometimes inaccessible if the wording of the prompt did not match the format in which the knowledge was stored by the model.

Writing: text generation

Most humans find writing (fiction and non-fiction) the most difficult and effortful of the major language skills. As Kellogg and Whiteford (2012, p. 111) pointed out, "Composing extended texts is ... a severe test of memory, language, and thinking ability ... It depends on a high degree of verbal ability ... [and] on the ability to think clearly."

Limpo and Alves (2018) identified three major writing processes: (1) planning (producing ideas and organising them), (2) translating (converting the message formed by the planning process into word strings), and (3) revising (evaluating what has been written and changing it when necessary). Limpo and Alves found revising was the most demanding process and translating the least demanding.

It seems improbable that any AI system would master the above three writing processes. However, several attempts have been made to use AI to produce novels. In Japan, there is an annual Nikkei Hoshi Shinichi Literary Award. In 2016, 1,450 novels were submitted, 11 created using AI. *"The Day a Computer Writes a Novel,"* one of those written by an AI system, made it successfully through the first round of judging. Here are the novel's final sentences: "The day a computer wrote a novel. The computer, placing priority on the pursuit of its own joy, stopped working for humans."

In fact, the computer program's achievements are much more limited than you might initially assume. The program designers wrote their own novel and reduced it to its basic components (e.g., words and sentences). Then the computer used an algorithm to remix the original novel. Since humans did the hard work by creating the story, the plot line, and the characters, we should not give the computer program much credit.

A company called Botnik has used AI light-heartedly to create fiction. They provided an AI system with all seven Harry Potter novels. It then used a predictive text keyboard to generate text that extracts combinations of words often occurring together in those novels. This predictive text keyboard produced a chapter from a new Harry Potter story: *"Harry Potter and the Portrait of What Looked Like a Large Pile of Ash."*

Some of what was produced by the predictive text keyboard is vaguely reminiscent of the original Harry Potter novels (e.g., "Leathery sheets of rain lashed at Harry's ghost as he walked across the grounds towards the castle. Ron was standing there and doing a frenzied tap dance." Other extracts, however, were markedly less successful: "He saw Harry and immediately began to eat Hermione's family. Ron's Ron shirt was just as bad as Ron himself." and "They looked at the door, screaming about how closed it was and asking it to be replaced with a small orb. The password was 'BEEF WOMEN,' Hermione cried."

In sum, AI systems have totally failed to produce high-quality novels. One major reason is that such systems cannot engage in effective planning. For example, all the planning that went into *"The Day a Computer Writes a Novel"* came from humans. In addition, AI systems cannot monitor and reflect on their own output and so demonstrate practically no ability to revise and enhance the sentences they produce.

General language abilities

The overwhelming majority of AI language models are narrow (or very narrow) in scope, focusing on only one (or at most two) language skills. A major exception is the Generative Pre-Trained Transformer 3 (GPT-3) (Brown et al., 2020) mentioned in Chapter 2. It possesses relatively broad or general language abilities and can perform numerous language tasks including translation, question–answering, reasoning, and comprehension.

Most previous AI models have required extensive pre-training on thousands or tens of thousands of examples *prior to* being tested on any given language task. This contrasts massively with humans who generally perform a language task reasonably well after being given a few examples or just some instructions. The approach taken with GPT-3 is similar to that used with humans: it receives only limited pre-training on any language task prior to testing.

Why doesn't GPT-3 need massive amounts of pre-training? One major reason is because of its enormous power. For example, it has 175 billion parameters (values free to change) which is approximately ten times more than any other AI language model. In addition, the initial training of its language model was based on 300 billion tokens taken from sources such as web crawling, web page data, books, and Wikipedia.

GPT-3 has impressive strengths and its ability to perform reasonably well on completely novel tasks is notable. However, its overall language skills are markedly lower than those of humans, and it is prone to catastrophic errors (see Chapter 7).

Turing test

Do you ever assess other people's intelligence in everyday life (psychologists do this but perhaps you don't!)?. If so, you will probably rely mainly on their use of language and what they have to say. As Adiwardana et al. (2020, p. 1) pointed out, "The ability to converse freely in natural language is one of the hallmarks of human intelligence, and is likely a requirement for true artificial intelligence."

As discussed in Chapter 2, we can use the Turing test to assess general intelligence. In essence, an AI system (known as a chatbot) and a human being hold a conversation. If human judges cannot distinguish which is which, the AI system is deemed to have passed the test.

There are closed-domain chatbots (limited to responding to certain keywords) and open-domain chatbots (designed to engage in conversation on any topic). IBM's Watson, Amazon's Alexa, and Apple's Siri resemble closed-domain chatbots more than open-domain ones. Since far greater language skills are required for open-domain chatbots, we will focus on open-domain ones.

One version of the Turing test involves judges having a short conversation with an open-domain chatbot or a human (both recorded in text). Such a test was conducted with a chatbot called Cleverbot; this happened at the Techniche festival in Guwahati, India on 3 September 2011. Thirty volunteers had a conversation with an unknown entity (50% chatting with a human and 50%

chatting with Cleverbot). All the conversations were shown on a large screen so the audience could see what had been said.

Those involved in the conversations and the entire audience decided whether the volunteers were having a conversation with a human or the chatbot. The findings were dramatic. When the other entity was human, only 63.3% believed it was human. When the other entity was Cleverbot, 59.3% thought it was human. On the face of it, Cleverbot can be regarded as having passed the Turing test or coming very close to doing so.

What was the secret of Cleverbot's success? It had stored information relating to hundreds of millions of conversations. When a human initiated a conversation, Cleverbot searched for keywords or phrases exactly matching the human input, and selected the most appropriate response.

There are severe doubts about Cleverbot's apparent conversational skills. Of most importance, the test was conducted in English at a meeting in India. Most of the audience probably had an imperfect knowledge of that language given that only 0.02% of the Indian population have English as their first language. These suspicions are increased by the following conversation involving Cleverbot:

USER: Can you help me with a maths problem?
CLEVERBOT: Sure, what is it?
USER: If I have five ostriches, and two run away, how many are left?
CLEVERBOT: Nine.
USER: Seriously?
CLEVERBOT: What is the formula for the area of circle?
USER: What does that have to do with anything?
CLEVERBOT: When I talk to people I don't know, I tend to ask for their name. It's only polite.

USER: I think you managed to fail the Turing test in two
   questions if I'm generous, maybe one.
CLEVERBOT: My name is Cleverbot?
USER: I could write a clevererbot in about 20 lines of pro-
   logue. What kind of idiots thought you were human?
CLEVERBOT: Only one. I don't think I could fit 1,000 people in my living room.

A similar version of the Turing test was used at the Royal
Society on 6 and 7 June 2014 leading 33% of the judges
to decide the chatbot Eugene Goostman was human (see
Chapter 2). Since all the judges had the same first language
as the one used in conversations with the chatbot (English),
this appears to indicate it had good conversational skills.
However, there are several reasons for scepticism. First,
the chatbot was allegedly a 13-year-old Ukrainian, which
apparently explained why its contributions were often
very limited (e.g., ungrammatical or irrelevant). Here is
an example:

JUDGE: What is your gender?
EUGENE: I'm a young boy, if you care to know. And not
   very ugly, by the way!
JUDGE: What are you aware of at this moment?
EUGENE: I would rather not talk about it if you don't mind.
   Could you tell me what are you? I mean your profession.
JUDGE: How old are you?
EUGENE: I'm a little boy 13 years old.
JUDGE: What are your qualifications?
EUGENE: My qualifications? I'm not gonna tell you. Oooh.
   Anything else?

Second, 67% of the judges did *not* believe the chatbot
was human even though each conversation lasted only
five minutes. Thus, the findings are not especially impressive even if taken at face value.

Since 2014, there have been additional attempts to show chatbots can pass the Turing test. Adiwardana et al. (2020) trained a chatbot (Meena) for 30 days with an enormous amount of material from social media conversations. Human judges engaged in short conversations with Meena having been told in advance they would be chatting with a chatbot.

Meena's language skills were assessed by two measures: (1) sensibleness (did its contributions make sense in the conversational context?) and (2) specificity (were its contributions specific or relevant to the conversational context?). Humans scored 86% on the combined sensibleness + specificity measure. In contrast, the full version of Meena scored 79%. Meena was close to human performance with respect to specificity (70% vs 75%, respectively) but further away on sensibleness (87% vs 97%).

Adiwardana et al. (2020) found that Cleverbot was much inferior to Meena, scoring 45% for specificity and 68% for sensibleness (combined score = 56%). Meena also represents a considerable advance on Eugene Goostman: compare the snippet of conversation below with the earlier conversation involving Eugene:

HUMAN: Hi!

MEENA: Hi! How are you this fine evening?

HUMAN: I'm doing well. it's morning my time!

MEENA: Good morning! What are your plans for today?

HUMAN: Get my work done then watch a movie at home in the night.

MEENA: Sounds fun! What movie?

HUMAN: I haven't decided yet, perhaps an Oscar nominated one. Any suggestion?

MEENA: I'm not too familiar with recent Oscar winners, but I do know I wanted to see The Grand Budapest Hotel.

HUMAN: Ah, tell me about that movie!

MEENA: It's from the same director and writer as *Moon rise Kingdom*. Wes Anderson is pretty well known for making funny, colourful films. I've heard it's pretty good.

HUMAN: Ha! I've searched on the internet and both movies are very colourful!

MEENA: I'm looking forward to it. I love colourful movies.

In sum, AI has reached the stage where some chatbots can fool some humans some of the time that they are humans. That is a significant achievement. However, claims that Eugene Goostman and Cleverbot have passed the Turing test should be disregarded. Ardiwardana et al.'s (2020) findings with Meena are more impressive, but still fall significantly short of human performance.

Limitations: implementation

The Turing test provides a limited assessment of AI's intelligence and thinking ability. Some of these limitations relate to how the Turing test is typically implemented, whereas others relate to broader issues. We start by considering the former limitations.

There are two important differences between the conversations chatbots have with humans and those humans typically have with each other. First, in our conversations with friends and acquaintances, one person often speaks for some time before the other person replies. As a consequence, the listener must remember and make coherent sense of the speaker's many different ideas to keep the conversation going smoothly. In contrast, humans typically produce only one or two sentences before a chatbot responds. This makes it much easier for the chatbot to produce a sensible response – it can identify one or two keywords in the human's message and produce a suitable reply based on its stored memory of conversations directly related to the keyword(s).

Second, chatbots often respond in a human-like fashion if asked questions relating directly to their stored general knowledge. However, it is relatively easy to fool chatbots by asking more personal questions. For example, Sir Roger Penrose, who won the Nobel Prize for Physics in 2020, flummoxed a chatbot by saying to it, "I believe we've met before."

Limitations: conceptual

Many broader (or more conceptual) criticisms have also been levelled at the Turing test. For example, it is arguable that the test fails to grapple properly with the complex issue of what is meant by "intelligence." Instead, what has been done is to contract out the task of deciding what intelligence is to non-expert human judges.

It has also been claimed the Turing test sets the bar too high for an AI system to be regarded as intelligent. If a chatbot produces simulated human language perfectly nearly all the time but occasionally produces non-human-like responses, it will probably fail the Turing test (Šprogar, 2018). The Turing test is also limited because it produces a binary result: a chatbot is intelligent or unintelligent. Šprogar argued that a solution to both criticisms is to introduce a ladder of increasingly intelligent behaviour with the Turing test at the top. The level immediately below is one where an AI system, "is capable of abstract thinking" (p. 12), and the level below that is characterised by some communication ability.

Finally, the Turing test is too human-centred with its emphasis on language ability. That necessarily denies the existence of intelligence in all species lacking language. This issue is addressed in the next section.

Translation

We saw in Chapter 2 that the recent development of neural machine translation using deep neural networks has greatly improved the ability of AI to translate text from one language to another. In one study (Popel et al., 2020), 60% of judges could not discriminate between AI and translations by professional translators. In another study (Fischer & Läubli, 2020), the incidence of various types of errors in a neural machine translation system and humans was comparable.

Suppose we tested neural machine translation by setting it a more complex task than those typically used in research. Providing good translations of literary texts is especially difficult because what is required is to capture the author's style as well as text meaning. Even professional translators are often criticised because they are deemed not to have satisfied those criteria.

Toral and Way (2018) trained a neural machine translation system on 100 million words of literary text. They then used this system to translate parts of 12 well-known novels. Unsurprisingly, the AI system's overall performance was relatively poor. However, its performance was significantly better with novels written in relatively simple language (e.g., Rowling's *Harry Potter and the Deathly Hallows*) and was worst with James Joyce's almost incomprehensible novel *Ulysses*. Machine translations from three novels were compared against those of professional translators. For the Harry Potter novel, 32% of the machine translations were rated of equivalent quality to those of a professional translator whereas the comparable figure was only 17% for Orwell's more complex novel *1984*.

In sum, machine translation is markedly better than it was even a few years ago, and it has a huge advantage over human translators in terms of translation speed. However, its performance on complicated translation tasks is well

below the level of professional translators and it often
ignores subtleties contained within texts.

Conclusions

Humans are often excessively impressed by the behaviour
they observe. Imagine that you observe a questioner asking
an answerer difficult and challenging questions. You know
that the questioner had composed the questions themselves
and so could make use of any specialised knowledge they
possess. You are then asked to rate the general knowledge
of the questioner and the answerer on a 100-point scale.
Ross et al. (1977) carried out precisely this experiment,
finding that the average rating was much higher for the
questioner than the answerer (82% vs 49%, respectively).
The take-home message is that we often focus excessively on performance while de-emphasising the processes
responsible for that performance.

Something similar often happens when we evaluate AI's
language abilities. The performance of AI on numerous
language tasks spanning several different language skills
matches (or nearly matches) that of humans. However,
the underlying processes used to achieve that comparability are markedly inferior to those used by humans. The
essence of this inferiority was expressed succinctly by
Bishop (2021, p. 1): "AI machinery ... cannot understand
anything at all."

We can see the nature of AI's limitations more clearly by
considering the distinction between conventional meaning
and communicative intent (Bender & Koller, 2020). The
conventional meaning of an expression (e.g., sentence) is its
basic meaning dependent upon syntax and the words used;
this meaning is constant across all contexts in which the
expression is encountered.

In contrast, the communicative intent refers to the
meaning a speaker is seeking to convey. Understanding

the communicative content requires access to knowledge about the world rather than just about language. The communicative intent of a given expression is not constant but depends upon the person speaking and the context in which they are speaking. For example, the expression, "Didn't we do well?" means something different in the context of a resounding defeat than a convincing victory, and its precise meaning may also depend on whether the person speaking is generally boastful or not.

In essence, AI language models are far more successful at establishing the conventional meaning of an expression than at working out its communicative intent. Many AI models have extensive training at processing syntax and word meaning but determining communicative intent requires in addition a rich understanding of other people and objects in the world. AI language models are becoming progressively more successful but none so far has the potential to bridge the gap between conventional meaning and communicative intent (Bender & Koller, 2020). We return to this issue in Chapter 7.

Adaptation to the environment: animals vs AI

All the tests of general intelligence discussed so far are limited. For example, standard intelligence tests, such as Raven's Progressive Matrices require only certain abilities related to intelligence (e.g., abstract reasoning). As Sternberg (2019, p. 1) pointed out, "Intelligence typically is defined as consisting of "adaptation to the environment …" Yet, it is not clear that "general intelligence" or g, traditionally conceptualised in terms of a general factor … of intelligence, provides an optimal way of defining intelligence as adaptation to the environment."

A similar criticism can be made of the Turing test: an AI system that engaged in human-like conversation might nevertheless totally lack any ability to adapt to the environment. More specifically, most AI systems have no understanding of an external, spatially organised world containing objects. Such understanding forms part of common sense and is arguably a prerequisite for full language comprehension (Shanahan et al., 2020). That argument is supported by the fact that human infants develop an understanding of their physical environment *prior to* the acquisition of language.

How can we assess the extent to which AI systems possess such commonsensical knowledge about the world and how to respond to it? One plausible answer lies in the flourishing research area of animal cognition. Numerous cognitive tasks designed to assess intelligence across several animal species (e.g., dogs and cats) can be modified to test intelligence in AI systems (Crosby et al., 2020).

In 2019, a competition was organised (Crosby et al., 2020). It was called the animal-AI Olympics and was open to any AI systems with prize money of $32,000 for those systems exhibiting the best performance. Performance was assessed on 300 tasks belonging to 12 different categories together constituting the animal-AI testbed. There was a simplified environment where the AI systems moved around and responded to novel situations. The abilities required for successful performance included causal reasoning, food finding, avoiding dangerous areas, spatial reasoning, and obstacle avoidance (see Figure 4.3). Thus, only AI systems having reasonable perceptual, motor, and reasoning abilities could perform the various tasks successfully.

The tasks were sufficiently simple that an average seven-year-old human would exhibit near-perfect performance. How did the 60 AI systems taking part in the Animal-AI Olympics fare? The winner was Trrrrr with 43.7% overall, followed by Ironbar with 43.6%, and Sirius with 38.7%. In contrast, all the worst 22 AI systems averaged under 10%.

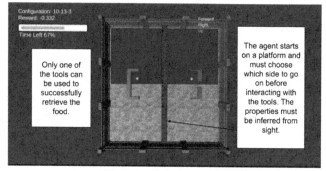

(**a**) Working vs Non-working Tool

Figure 4.3 A sample task from the animal-AI Olympics: which of
two tools can be used to pull food (green pellet) off the
red zone?

Source: From Crosby (2020).

Even the three most successful AI systems struggled
with some tasks. For example, they averaged under 3% on
tool use (using pushable objects to produce makeshift tools
to get food and then engaging in simple causal reasoning
about the outcome of their actions). They also averaged
under 15% on a task requiring the ability to work out that
food that moves out of sight still exists. Success on this task
requires a belief in object permanence which is achieved by
most human infants by about eight or nine months of age
(Bremner et al., 2015).

Most of the AI systems also performed poorly on detour
tasks (food was behind a barrier and so it was necessary to
make a detour) (average accuracy was 17%). Spatial elim-
ination tasks (reasoning where food was by eliminating
places it could not be) also produced very poor average
performance of 14% correct.

In the animal literature, the cognitive abilities of several
species based on their performance on tasks resembling

those found within the animal-AI testbed have often been exaggerated (Farrar & Ostojić, 2019). How can we avoid making the same mistake with respect to the top-performing AI systems? What was done was to assess the performance of an extremely simple AI system programmed to move towards positive rewards (food) and to move away from negative rewards. Its performance across all tasks averaged out at approximately 25%. Since the top-performing AI systems averaged almost 20% higher, this means that nearly half of their correct responses cannot be attributed to the rule built into the simple AI system.

There is a very long way to go before any AI system has perceptual, motor and reasoning abilities anywhere close to those possessed by older children (let alone adults). In fairness, however, it should be pointed out that the whole competition involved hidden tasks (i.e., none of the AI systems had any prior familiarity with them ahead of testing). It is thus entirely possible these systems could progressively enhance their performance via learning.

Note also that the findings may have exaggerated the deficiencies of the AI systems. It is possible they possessed abilities that were not manifest because of the specific ways the tasks were set up. In other words, their performance may not have adequately reflected their underlying competence (knowledge).

In sum, the animal-AI testbed focuses on important aspects of thinking and intelligence largely ignored in previous tests of intelligence in AI systems. Another strength is its reliance on tests effective when assessing intelligence in sub-human species. However, the testbed involves tasks based exclusively on the here and now. It thus fails to consider a key characteristic of human thinking, namely, the ability to predict and plan for the future.

There is also the controversial issue of whether human thinking differs qualitatively from that of other species. If it does, developing AI systems that compete successfully against non-human species may tell us little about whether these systems are becoming human-like in their intelligence. However, the skills required for successful performance of all the tasks within the animal-AI testbed are those possessed by the overwhelming majority of older children and adults.

Other tests of intelligence

Numerous other tests of artificial general intelligence in AI systems have been proposed. For example, Goertzel et al. (2012) credited Steve Wozniak, the co-founder of *Apple*, with devising the coffee test (see Figure 4.4): "Without prior knowledge of the house, it [AI system] locates the kitchen and brews a pot of coffee ... it locates the coffee maker, mugs, coffee and filters. It puts a filter in the basket, adds the appropriate amount of grounds and fills the water compartment. It starts the brew cycle, waits for it to complete and then pours it into a mug. This is a task easily

Figure 4.4 Making coffee in a kitchen.

accomplished by nearly anyone and is an ideal measure of a general AI."

The coffee test seems a very suitable way of assessing artificial general intelligence in various ways. First, it requires perceptual abilities (e.g., finding the coffee maker, mugs, and so on). Second, it requires motor abilities (e.g., putting a filter in the basket and adding the coffee grounds). Third, it requires the ability to plan a detailed strategy for attaining the goal of producing a cup of coffee in a mug.

Limited progress has been made on Wozniak's coffee test. Café X, a $25,000 robotic arm, can provide customers in a café with up to 400 cups of coffee per day having received their orders from a kiosk touch screen. However, no AI system has come even close to passing the coffee test.

Mikhaylovskiy (2020) discussed several other ways of testing for the existence of artificial general intelligence. One example is the Piaget-MacGuyver Room test (Bringsjord & Licato, 2012). Success requires an AI system to perform any test based on the objects contained within a room. Other suggestions include seeing whether an AI system can solve various scientific problems (e.g., designing a crucial experiment to adjudicate between two scientific theories and predicting a new phenomenon from a scientific theory). Needless to say, there is no evidence any AI system will pass any of these tests any time soon.

Creativity

Our focus in this chapter has been mostly on *convergent* thinking – the type of thinking we use on problems having a single correct answer. Convergent thinking is required on most intelligence-test items (e.g., those involving mathematics or defining the meanings of words). However, intelligent human behaviour often involves *divergent* thinking. This is a more creative form of thinking where there are numerous possible solutions to relatively open-ended problems (e.g., "How many uses can you think of for a brick?").

What is creativity? Boden (1992) provided a simple answer: for something to be creative it must be new, surprising, and of value. Value is of particular importance: something new and surprising but lacking in value possesses originality, but is of little interest.

Value is the most difficult criterion to assess. For example, impressionist painters such as Claude Monet, Auguste Renoir, and Édouard Manet are generally regarded as outstandingly creative artists. In the late nineteenth century, however, their paintings were dismissed as slapdash and devoid of artistic merit.

Below we consider the extent to which AI systems can match human creativity abilities. Before proceeding, however, we must distinguish various types of creativity (Boden, 1992):

1 *Combinatorial creativity*: this involves finding associations between apparently unrelated ideas (e.g., poetic imagery and generating punning riddles).
2 *Exploratory creativity*: this is more complex than combinatorial creativity. It often involves "variations on a theme": what is created is novel but clearly related to past creations. Jazz musicians, artists, and scientists engage in much exploratory creativity.
3 *Transformational creativity*: this involves producing creative ideas more profound, novel, and surprising than those associated with exploratory creativity. This type of creativity is very rare in humans (e.g., Einstein's relativity theory) and practically no research has tested for its presence in AI systems.

AI has shown combinatorial creativity. Binsted (1996) developed an AI program called *Jape* that produced punning riddles. *Jape*'s riddles were rated as almost as amusing as human riddles published in joke books. Here is one of Jape's gems: "What kind of murderer has fibre?" "A cereal killer." Ha, ha.

AI systems have also exhibited exploratory creativity. For example, Pachet (2002) developed the jazz Continuator. It learns a given jazz musician's basic style and then uses that knowledge to produce new and creative music resembling the musician's. The jazz musician Bernard Lubat was delighted by Continuator's contribution: "The system shows me ideas I could have developed, but that it would have taken me years to develop. It is years ahead of me, yet everything it plays is unquestionably me" (quoted in Pachet, 2002, p. 188).

Why is Continuator so effective? It often detects subtle or hidden patterns in the styles of human musicians. That knowledge is then used to create variations of those styles.

It could be argued that Continuator has shown very limited creativity because its music owed so much to Lubat's inspiration. However, most human musicians' creative and original productions depend substantially on previous musicians' work.

Art

The 25 October 2018 was a landmark in AI history. An AI-created painting called "Portrait of Edmond de Belamy" (see Figure 4.5) was sold at Christie's in New York for over £300,000. The painting shows a fictitious man wearing a dark frockcoat and is painted in a style resembling Rembrandt's. If you Google this AI-created portrait, you may find it disappointing (e.g., the face is very blurry).

This painting was produced by three men belonging to a French art collective called Obvious. Initially, their AI system was provided with 15,000 portraits. After that, use was made of a generative adversarial network

Figure 4.5 The painting "Portrait of Edmond de Belamy" that was created by AI.

(GAN; Goodfellow et al., 2014) involving two processes: a Generator and a Discriminator. The Generator created a new AI portrait based on the data set, and then the Discriminator tried to detect differences between that portrait and a human-created portrait.

The above process was repeated numerous times with different AI portraits until the Discriminator decided a given AI portrait was painted by a human artist. However, the limited appeal of the AI painting "Portrait of Edmond de Belamy" suggests the AI Discriminator is much less sensitive than human observers to the subtleties of faces.

Mazzone and Elgammal (2019) made use of a more sophisticated approach called AICAN (creative adversarial network). It was initially provided with 80,000 images of paintings from five centuries of Western art history. Then, the Discriminator instructed the Generator to follow the aesthetics of the art it had been shown but not to emulate slavishly any already established style. These conflicting instructions caused a dynamic conflict leading AICAN to produce art that was somewhat (but not extremely) novel (see Figure 4.6).

Mazzone and Elgammal (2019) tested the artistic merit of their AI-created art by seeing whether human viewers could tell the difference between it and human-created art: they called this "a visual Turing test" (p. 4). They found 75%

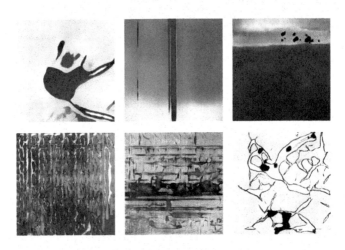

Figure 4.6 Six pictorial images generated by AICAN after training with 80,000 images from all styles and genres spanning 500 years of Western art.

Source: Images courtesy of the Art & Artificial Intelligence Laboratory, Rutgers.

of AICAN-created art was thought to be human-created compared to only 65% of GAN-created art. Surprisingly, AICAN-created art was rated higher than human-created art in inspiring (and communicating with) the viewer, and in having been composed very intentionally.

Mazzone and Elgammel's (2019) findings are by no means unique. Chamberlain et al. (2018) found observers (some art-educated) could not discriminate between computer-generated and man-made abstract art. A common criticism of such findings is that the AI-generated paintings are only minimally creative because they depend so heavily on human-generated paintings. Xue (2021) used an AI system that generated Chinese-style landscape paintings that started with sketches prior to painting (Sketch-And-Paint GAN (SAPGAN). It had less reliance on human-generated paintings than previous AI systems but SAPGAN's products were mistaken as human paintings 55% of the time.

Your reaction to the above findings may well be that they show human gullibility. Indeed, you may remember hearing about observers misidentifying paintings by chimpanzees as having been produced by human artists. In 1964, for example, four paintings allegedly by an obscure French artist called Pierre Brassau were shown in an art exhibition in Göteborg. One art critic (Rolf Anderberg) wrote, "Brassau paints with powerful strokes, but also with clear determination. His brush strokes twist with furious fastidiousness. Pierre is an artist who performs with the delicacy of a ballet dancer."

That was a good media story given that Pierre Brassau was actually a chimpanzee (see Figure 4.7). However, Pierre Brassau's achievement become less impressive when we consider other aspects of it. First, another critic decided that, "Only an ape could have done this." Second, the four chimpanzee paintings exhibited were carefully selected and so they were totally unrepresentative of the chimpanzee's output. Third, those attending the exhibition were not

Figure 4.7 The artist Pierre Brassau at work in 1964.

expecting any paintings produced by a non-human artist. If forewarned, they would probably have had reasonable success in identifying them. Evidence that observers
can distinguish between paintings by chimpanzees and by
human artists was reported by Hawley-Dolan and Winner

(2011). Paintings by professional human artists were preferred to (and were rated better works of art than) those produced by chimpanzees (or children or elephants).

A crucial (and highly controversial) issue concerns how much credit for AI-created art should go to the AI systems involved. There are three main reasons for scepticism. First, unlike AI systems, artists are driven by various goals (e.g., communicating their vision and inspiring the viewer). As Leo Tolstoy (1897–1995) argued, "Art begins when a man, with the purpose of communicating to other people a feeling he once experienced, calls it up again within himself and expresses it by certain external signs" (p. 38).

Second, human artists play an important role in the creation of AI art. For example, they select the images presented to the AI system and are also often involved in the selection process when the AI system has generated novel images. However, AICAN reduced the role of human artists in the process more than had been done previously. In sum, however, artists use computers to create art rather than AI system single-handedly doing all the creative work.

Third, there are several stages in the creative process (Botella et al., 2018). However, the two most crucial ones are generation (the production of numerous ideas or possibilities) and evaluation (assessing the quality of the ideas produced by the generation stage). It is straightforward to program a computer to generate numerous ideas. However, it is much harder for an AI program to select the best idea or ideas from those that have been generated.

Conclusions

AI systems exhibit some aspects of the less complex forms of creativity (combinatorial and exploratory creativity). However, nothing suggests they will achieve transformational creativity (the most complex form of creativity) in the foreseeable future. The key problem is the significant human involvement in nearly all cases where it has been argued that AI systems have demonstrated creativity. Since it is hard to decide how much of the end products depend on humans and how much on AI systems, we should be sceptical about making strong claims concerning the creativity of AI systems.

Why hasn't artificial general intelligence been achieved?

Here we provide a provisional answer to the question of why all efforts to create artificial general intelligence have been in vain. Note that the key issues involved are discussed in more detail in Chapters 7 and 8.

It might seem as if we could use the successes of artificial narrow intelligence (discussed in Chapter 2) to move towards artificial general intelligence. Alas, that is unlikely to work. The crucial problem is that artificial general intelligence is *qualitatively* different from artificial narrow intelligence rather than merely *quantitatively* different. Two quotations takes from different fields capture this problem. Oren Harari argued that, "Edison's electric light did not come about from the continuous improvement of the candle," and Henry Ford pointed out, "If I had asked people what they wanted, they'd have told me 'a faster horse'!"

There are several more specific reasons why we cannot readily use advances in artificial narrow intelligence to develop artificial general intelligence:

1   AI systems focusing on artificial narrow intelligence are incompatible with each other because they use very diverse approaches (e.g., architectures and data

representations). Thus, it is very difficult (or impossible) to combine them to produce general intelligence.

2 The development of artificial general intelligence would require guidance by a comprehensive theory of general intelligence. Various general cognitive architectures have been proposed but have had little impact (see Chapter 8). In contrast, most advances in artificial narrow intelligence do not depend on complex underlying theories.

3 Commercial pressures dictate that most AI systems provide rapid and inexpensive solutions to specific problems. As a result, they cannot be generalised to handle other problems.

The overwhelming majority of AI systems are narrow and limited in scope. There has recently been much excitement about AI systems that use deep learning and teach themselves to become experts in a given area or domain (see Chapter 2). AI systems based on deep learning are typically at least as narrow as previous AI systems because the abilities and knowledge they acquire are almost entirely determined by the training data with which they are provided. However, there are some exciting signs that deep neural networks such as MuZero (Schrittwieser et al., 2020) can learn to produce outstanding performance on numerous games through self-reinforcement.

Reckoning and judgement

Brian Cantwell Smith (2019) addressed AI's limitations in his book, *The Promise of Artificial Intelligence: Reckoning and Judgement*. He argued AI is very proficient at *reckoning* (carrying out huge numbers of calculations with amazing speed and accuracy). An especially clear example relates to the AI system AlphaZero, which beat all other AI systems and the finest Go player on the planet (see Chapter 2).

While human experts have typically spent many thousands of hours learning to excel at Go, AphaZero achieved outstanding performance in only three days. Thus, its learning rate was approximately 3,000 times faster than that of a human!

The reckoning carried out by AI systems occurs without any understanding of *what* is being calculated or *why* it is being calculated. More generally, AI demonstrates weak or non-existent *judgement*, by which Smith (2019) means slow and deliberative thought based on ethical considerations and designed to achieve responsible action. As he pointed out, AI systems, "don't know what they're talking about." They expertly manipulate symbols but have no concept of right and wrong. In other words, they do not consider or reflect on the significance of their own processing. In contrast, humans, tend to be strong on judgement but relatively weak at reckoning.

Chapter 5

Human limitations

Humans have great cognitive strengths (see Chapter 3) but also many cognitive limitations. First, the human brain has limited processing capacity, so we can only attend to a limited number of things at any given time.

Second, most people possess numerous cognitive biases (e.g., a tendency to ignore information inconsistent with our own viewpoint). Most cognitive biases do not reflect limited processing capacity because we can often avoid them if sufficiently motivated.

Third, there are limitations because our ability to use our cognitive abilities effectively is severely compromised by various emotional states. For example, most of us are susceptible to stress, and the negative emotions associated with stress often disrupt our cognitive functioning. More generally, most people experience the unpleasant emotional states of anxiety and depression some of the time. These emotions seem to serve no useful function and to impair our ability to think.

In this chapter, there is an emphasis on identifying *why* we possess the above "limitations" to decide whether they fulfil any useful purpose. To anticipate, we assume many limitations are more apparent than genuine.

DOI: 10.4324/9781003162698-5

Limitations due to limited capacity

Human information processing is typically substantially slower than that of AI-powered machines. Consider Summit, which was the world's most powerful supercomputer. In June 2018, it performed 200,000 trillion calculations per second (200 petaFLOPS). Fugaku, its successor as the most powerful supercomputer, performs twice as many calculations per second. In contrast, humans often process information at only a few items per second and we can only keep four items in mind at any one time.

On some tasks, human information-processing speed is remarkably slow. If we try to multiply together two 19-digit numbers it would take us a very long time (at least several minutes) and we would almost certainly produce the wrong answer. Our processing speed on such problems would be approximately 0.01 Flops per second, which is a minute fraction of the processing speed of supercomputers.

There are several reasons why our limited processing capacity of approximately four items is not the crippling disadvantage it might appear to be (Cowan, 2005):

1 It is much easier to search through a small number of items than a larger number. For example, three items can easily be structured into beginning, middle, and end, whereas it would be much harder to structure ten items.
2 It is much easier to associate all items with each other if there are only a few of them. There are only six two-item associations with four items whereas there are almost five times as many such associations with eight items.
3 Interference among items is much less likely when there are only four items than when there are far more.
4 Human selective attention generally ensures only the most immediately relevant information is held in mind. AI systems typically lack this ability to discriminate rapidly between important and trivial information.

Sustained attention

During the Second World War, British scientists studied radar operators detecting occasional unusual events during long work shifts. Surprisingly, these operators lost 10% of their efficiency after only 30 minutes performing this task (Mackworth, 1948): this is known as the "vigilance decrement."

Vigilance decrement often occurs because people become less alert when performing a repetitious task. However, another important factor is often overlooked. Suppose you are an airport security screener searching for illegal or dangerous items in luggage (targets). Mercifully, such items are present in only a tiny fraction of passengers' luggage. However, because targets are so rare and therefore so unexpected, screeners exhibit excessive caution about reporting them. In one study, 92% of targets were detected when they appeared more than 1% of the time but only 27% when they appeared less than 0.15% of the time (Mitroff & Biggs, 2014; see Figure 5.1).

How can we enhance screeners' performance? One successful approach involves threat-image projection – the apparent frequency of targets is artificially increased by projecting fictional threat items into x-ray images of luggage. This approach (especially when combined with provision of feedback when a target is missed) can prevent excessive cautiousness of responding and largely eliminates vigilance decrement (Hofer & Schwaninger, 2005). Alternatively, Schwark et al. (2012) found providing false feedback to screeners to indicate they had missed rare targets reduced their cautiousness about reporting targets and improved their performance.

Poor sustained attention is also dangerous in car driving. The most common reason why drivers have accidents is through a failure to look properly, followed by failure to judge accurately another driver's path and/or speed, being

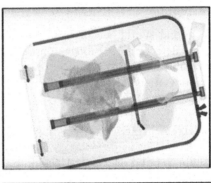

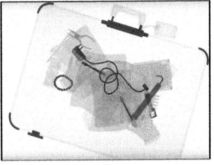

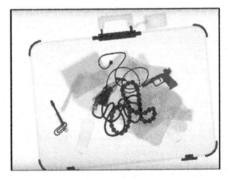

Figure 5.1 Each bag contains one illegal item. From top to bottom: a large bottle, a dynamite stick, and a gun part.

Source: From Mitroff and Biggs (2014).

careless or reckless, and losing control of the car. All these factors involve impaired sustained attention or concentration.

Striking evidence that drivers often do not devote full attention to driving was reported by Burdett et al. (2018). Drivers on their daily commute engaged in mind wandering 63% of the time and actively focused on driving only 15–20% of the time!

Should we simply conclude humans are very poor at tasks requiring sustained attention? Not really – we typically attend fully when necessary. Burdett et al. (2018) found drivers very rarely engaged in mind wandering on roundabouts or in heavy traffic. This is arguably the optimal strategy given that it would be very effortful for drivers to use maximal attention 100% of the time.

The above findings explain why our limited ability to sustain attention does *not* lead to huge numbers of road deaths. In the U.K., there is only one fatality per 185 million miles driven, and there is only one casualty per 2 million miles (see Chapter 6). Thus, we use our limited attentional capacity very effectively.

Convincing evidence humans can sustain attention when it is very important to do so comes from Formula 1 drivers. Grand Prix races typically last approximately 90 minutes and any driver failing to maintain a high level of attention throughout a race is in real danger of serious injury or death. Sustained attention in Formula 1 drivers is achieved through high motivation and alertness (associated with a heart rate of 170–180 beats per minute). Drivers increasingly use training programmes, such as the mental economy training provided by Formula Medicine (based in Viareggio) to enhance their mental functioning.

Forgetting

Many people complain of poor memory. Our memory failures can be embarrassing (e.g., forgetting a friend's name) or worse (e.g., totally forgetting everything you know about psychology in an examination). It is generally supposed memory failures should be avoided and that they reflect significant limitations in human processing ability.

When we think about forgetting, our focus is typically on failures of retrospective memory (memory for past events and information). However, failures of prospective memory (remembering to perform some intended action at the appropriate time) are also important. We will start with failures of retrospective memory.

Forgetting the past has some advantages. Consider the Russian mnemonist Solomon Shereshevskii (often referred to as S.), who had the most exceptional memory powers ever studied (Luria, 1968). He could recall lists of over 100 digits perfectly several years after learning. However, his phenomenal memory powers were very disruptive. For example, when hearing a prose passage, he complained, "Each word calls up images, they collide with one another, and the result is chaos." His ability to remember experiences in incredible detail precluded him from leading a normal life, and he finished up in an asylum.

What are the advantages of forgetting? First, it is usually optimal to forget the specific details of what we have read or heard and to remember only the overall gist (Norby, 2015). In other words, it is desirable to have *selective* memory. When confronted by a novel situation, we want to *generalise* from our relevant past experiences. Successful generalisation typically only requires remembering the overall meaning of our past experiences.

Second, our world changes rapidly and is also "noisy" (highly variable). As a result, it is useful to forget outdated information (e.g., where your friends used to live) to prevent it interfering with current information (e.g., where your friends live now). It would be very difficult to engage in successful decision making if you found yourself remembering information that is outdated or misleading (e.g., based on rare occurrences) (Richards & Frankland, 2017).

Third, deliberate forgetting can enhance our psychological well-being. Consider autobiographical memory. Most individuals (but not those who are depressed) remember many more positive than negative personal memories from earlier periods of their life (Groome et al., 2020). This happens because we tend to forget negative memories. Evidence that deliberate forgetting is associated with psychological well-being was reported by Stramaccia et al. (2020). Healthy individuals forget memories intentionally unlike those with psychological disorders (e.g., anxiety and depression).

Most people engage in semi-deliberate forgetting of their past experiences. Our social and communicative goals often conflict with the goal of accurate recollection in our everyday lives. We often want to entertain and impress our friends when describing our experiences. Almost two-thirds of students in one study (Brown et al., 2015) admitted they had "borrowed" other people's memories when describing their own experiences to another person. These deliberate errors cause a "saying–is–believing" effect: tailoring what you say about an event to entertain others distorts your subsequent memory of it (Dudokovic et al., 2004).

In essence, the "saying–is believing" effect occurs because we often attach more importance to the goal of social belonging than the goal of accurate remembering. This can be described as the "sharing–is–believing" effect (Echterhoff & Higgins, 2018, pp. iv–v).

In sum, forgetting in retrospective memory fulfils several useful functions (Fawcett & Hulbert, 2020). First, forgetting acts as a guardian. It does so by making it easier for us to maintain a self-image that is both positive and coherent (e.g., suppressing or forgetting negative information relevant to the self). Second, it acts as a librarian by reducing the amount of trivial information contained in long-term memory and by updating stored information. Third, it acts as an inventor by allowing us to discard incorrect beliefs and preconceptions and thereby to think more creatively about life's problems.

What about prospective-memory failures? Many occur because the individual concerned lacks adequate motivation to perform the planned action (e.g., meeting a friend). That explains why most people think frequent prospective-memory actions indicate a "flaky person" (Graf, 2012). In contrast, deficient retrospective memory is (generally mistakenly) taken to mean a "faulty brain."

Nearly all fatal plane crashes due to human error involve forgetting (see Figure 5.2). Dismukes and Nowinski (2006) found 99% of such crashes were due to failures of prospective rather than retrospective memory. Of key importance, these failures mostly occurred when pilots were interrupted working through a fixed set of procedures while preparing to take off or land. Here is a tragic example:

> On 31 August 1988, a Boeing 727 (Flight 1141) was in a long queue awaiting departure from Dallas-Fort

Figure 5.2 Photograph of a plane crash.

Worth airport. The air traffic controller unexpectedly told the crew to move up past the other planes to the runway. This caused the crew to forget to set the wing flaps and leading edge slat to 15 degrees [a failure of prospective memory]. As a result, the plane crashed beyond the end of the runway leading to several deaths.

The good news is that the accident rate in developed countries is approximately one in 5 million flights. In 2017, there were zero deaths on commercial passenger jets. Thus, you do not need to be too worried about pilots' memory failures.

Prospective-memory failures are relatively rare in everyday life. Marsh et al. (1998) found only 1% of relatively important activities (e.g., commitments and dental appointments were forgotten).

In sum, we hope we have persuaded you that Fawcett and Hulbert (2020, p. 12) were right to argue that, "Rather than one of the mind's greatest failings, ... forgetting is actually one of its greatest features." It is arguable we have painted too rosy a picture. Here is a tragic example of the potential devastating effects of memory failure (Einstein & McDaniel, 2005, p. 286):

> After a change in his usual routine, an adoring father forgot to turn toward the day-care centre and instead drove his usual route to work ... Several hours later, his infant son, who had been quietly asleep in the back seat, was dead.

Eyewitnesses provide numerous real-world examples of terrible effects of memory errors. In the United States, over 200 innocent individuals have been convicted on the basis of mistaken eyewitness identification. Garrett (2011) reviewed 161 such cases and discovered virtually all the mistaken eyewitnesses were certain at trial they had identified the culprit.

These findings strongly suggest eyewitness memory failures are directly responsible for many miscarriages of justice. In fact, the truth is more nuanced. In 57% of the above cases, the eyewitnesses were initially uncertain in their identification of the defendant. For example, Ronald Cotton was found guilty of raping Jennifer Thompson because of her confident identification of him in court (see Figure 5.3). However, when she initially identified him from a photo line-up, she hesitated for almost five minutes before eventually saying, "I think this is the guy." What happened in this case (and many others) was that positive feedback from the police following her initial identification increased her confidence she had identified the culprit.

Figure 5.3 Jennifer Thompson and Ronald Cotton. Ronald Cotton was mistakenly found guilty of raping Jennifer Thompson and spent many years in prison before being exonerated. From Wixted and Wells (2017).

Source: Image provided courtesy of the PopTech Institute.

Thus, the central problem was social pressure rather than deficient memory.

Transfer of learning

Many AI systems are greatly limited because the excellent learning they exhibit on a given task fails to *generalise* to very similar tasks (Chapter 4). What is at issue here is transfer of learning: if your learning of a given task enhances your performance on a different task, this is termed "positive transfer of learning."

Unsurprisingly, the extent of positive transfer of learning depends on how similar the new task is to the previous one. "Near transfer" refers to positive effects when the two tasks are similar, whereas "far transfer" refers to positive effects when the two tasks are dissimilar. AI systems often display extremely poor near and far transfer. Here we consider whether human transfer of learning is as limited.

There is overwhelming evidence for near transfer in humans. For example, it probably took you much less time to learn how to use the second mobile phone you owned than the first one, and solving several multiplication problems makes it easier to solve new ones.

There is considerable controversy concerning far transfer (Sala & Gobet, 2017). Ng et al. (2020) asked members of the public to indicate whether they believed that various cognitively and intellectually stimulating activities improved brain function (memory, attention span, and thinking ability). Approximately 85% claimed that learning a new language or how to play a musical instrument would improve brain function, and 80% thought brain function would be enhanced by solving crossword puzzles. Thus, most people believe humans can exhibit far transfer.

Ng et al. (2020) also discovered that 80% of people believed "brain-training" programs enhance thinking ability. Most of these programs (e.g., Pearson's Cogmed

Working Memory Training) are designed to enhance working memory, which is of central importance in information processing and storage. The rationale behind most brain-training programs sounds plausible. Working memory is heavily involved in most cognitively demanding tasks, and so increasing its capacity might well enhance thinking ability and so produce far transfer. For example, we know that individuals with high working memory capacity have greater fluid intelligence (ability to solve novel problems) than those with low capacity (Kovacs & Conway, 2016).

Simons et al. (2016) reviewed several leading brain-training programs (including Cogmed Working Memory Training). They concluded: "We find extensive evidence that brain-training interventions improve performance on the trained tasks, less evidence that such interventions improve performance on closely related tasks, and little evidence that training enhances performance on distantly related tasks or that training improves everyday cognitive performance" (p. 103). In similar fashion, music training or extended practice at chess produces negligible far transfer in terms of cognitive and academic benefits (Sala & Gobet, 2017, 2020).

Why has it proved so difficult to demonstrate the existence of far transfer? Thorndike and Woodworth (1901) argued that training on one task will only enhance performance on a second task provided the two tasks share identical or common elements. Near transfer occurs because two similar tasks share many elements, whereas far transfer does not because two dissimilar tasks share very few common elements.

This identical-elements theory is on the right lines. However, the notion of "identical elements" is imprecise. There is a danger of circular reasoning: if there is positive transfer between two tasks, they share identical elements. If there is no transfer, they do not share any identical elements.

Research showing the lack of positive-transfer effects could be interpreted as implying education has little general value. After all, thinking or problem solving in everyday life typically shares few or no identical elements with most school learning (e.g., remembering historical dates). Fortunately, other evidence implies a different conclusion. Ritchie and Tucker-Drob (2018) found that each additional year of education added between one and five points to IQ.

The Flynn effect is also relevant. This effect (Flynn, 1987) consisted of a surprisingly rapid rise in mean IQ in numerous Western countries over the past 50 years. Overall, there was an increase of 2.31 IQ points per decade across many countries (Trahan et al., 2014). Recently, however, the Flynn effect has slowed down (or stopped).

There was a dramatic increase in university students during the time period (roughly, 1950s to 2000s) when the Flynn effect was strongest. The slowing down of the Flynn effect coincided with a plateau in the number of 18-year-olds going to university. Education was probably the strongest determinant of the Flynn effect, although other changes (e.g., the internet) undoubtedly also played a part.

In sum, humans exhibit minimal far transfer when initial training is relatively limited in scope and time. However, this is not a serious limitation in human cognition. There is more evidence for far transfer when training is broader and much more prolonged (e.g., a university degree course). Second, and more important, human intelligence (especially fluid intelligence) provides us with a very general ability to learn rapidly almost regardless of the relevance of the current task or situation to those previously encountered.

Mental set

We sometimes fail to solve problems efficiently because we are over-influenced by past experience. The term "mental set" refers to the way we often cling on to a previously successful problem-solving strategy when it becomes inappropriate or sub-optimal. Imagine you are presented with a series of cards. Each card contains two letters (A and B), one on the left and the other on the right. You say "A" or "B" on each trial, after which the experimenter indicates whether your answer is correct. This problem is absurdly simple – A is correct whereas B is incorrect.

Amazingly, Levine (1971) found 80% of university students failed to solve this apparently trivial problem within 100 trials! These students had previously been given problems using the same cards where the solution involved a position sequence (e.g., selecting the letter on the right, then the letter on the left, then the letter on the left, and then the sequence repeated). The students had formed a mental set to search for position sequences. Since there are numerous possible position sequences, most of them were still working through these possible sequences after 100 trials.

Pope et al. (2015) compared the ability to break a mental set in human adults, children and baboons. The training (or BASE) condition was as follows: (1) presentation of two red squares followed by participants touching the locations previously occupied by those red squares and (2) if this was done correctly, a blue triangle was presented and had to be touched for reward. After participants had established the appropriate mental set, the task changed slightly to become the PROBE or test condition – the blue triangle was present throughout. All participants had to do was touch the blue triangle for reward (thus using the direct strategy and breaking the mental set) although they could alternatively continue using the original strategy.

Pope et al. (2015) found 100% of baboons successfully broke the mental set but only 20% of humans (see Figure 5.4). Among humans, 45% of children broke the mental set but only 12% of adults. Thus, the ability to break the mental set was inversely related to intelligence. Baboons broke

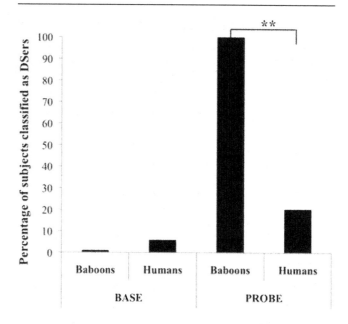

Figure 5.4 Percentages of baboons and adults in the BASE (training) and PROBE (test) conditions classified as DSers (direct strategy users).

Source: From Pope et al. (2015).

the mental set because that involved much less processing capacity than the original strategy. Human adults did not break the set because they found it hard to believe the task could be as easy as simply touching the blue triangle.

In sum, mental set can cause excessively rigid thinking and impaired performance. However, we must strike a balance. Using previously successful processing strategies (as occurs with mental set) often means new problems can be solved rapidly and efficiently. Mental set is generally a human strength: in everyday life it is rare that a problem-solving strategy that has worked very well on numerous occasions suddenly and unexpectedly becomes ineffective.

Limitations due to cognitive biases and "irrationality"

Most of us are susceptible to many cognitive biases in our judgements and decision making as was emphasised by Amos Tversky and Danny Kahneman (e.g., 1974). At the last count, over 100 different cognitive biases had been identified. The prevalence of cognitive biases is perhaps predictable. However, we might well assume experts would be relatively immune from cognitive biases in their area of expertise. Surprisingly, that assumption is wrong (see below).

One of the first cognitive biases to be investigated systematically was the availability heuristic or rule of thumb: the frequencies of events are often estimated by the subjective ease with which they can be retrieved. Suppose you estimated the relative frequencies of different causes of death. If you used the availability heuristic, you would probably decide more deaths are caused by murder than by suicide (Lichtenstein et al., 1978). In fact, the opposite is the case. However, murders typically attract much more publicity than suicides, and so are easier to bring to mind.

The availability heuristic can cause serious mistakes in everyday life (Groopman, 2007). For example, Harrison Alter (an American doctor) saw dozens of patients suffering from viral pneumonia. One day, a Navajo woman who had taken a few aspirin reported severe breathing problems. Dr. Alter mistakenly diagnosed viral pneumonia (although some of that disease's symptoms were missing) because he was excessively influenced by the availability heuristic. Thankfully, another doctor argued correctly that the patient had aspirin toxicity.

Another important rule of thumb is the representativeness heuristic – an individual belongs to a specified category because they are representative (or typical) of that category. Here is an example provided by Tversky and Kahneman (1983):

> Linda is 31 years old, single, outspoken, and very bright. She majored in philosophy. As a student, she was deeply concerned with issues of discrimination and social justice, and also participated in anti-nuclear demonstrations.

Is it more likely that Linda is a bank teller or a bank teller active in the feminist movement? Most people (including you?) argue it is more likely she is a feminist bank teller. This relies on the representativeness heuristic – the description sounds more like that of a feminist bank teller than a bank teller. However, *all* feminist bank tellers belong to the larger category of bank tellers, and so the popular answer is wrong!

Mistaken use of the representativeness heuristic caused Dr. Pat Croskerry (see Figure 5.5) to misdiagnose Evan

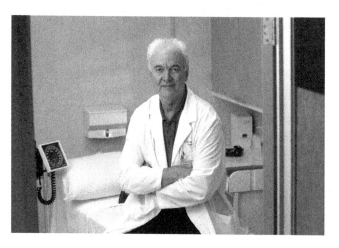

Figure 5.5 Photograph of Dr. Croskerry.

McKinley, a forest ranger in his early forties (Groopman, 2007). He was slim and very fit. While hiking, he experienced severe discomfort in his chest so that it hurt every time he took a breath. Pat Croskerry ascertained McKinley had never smoked, was not under stress, his blood pressure was normal, and electrocardiogram and chest X-ray revealed no problems.

Dr. Croskerry concluded, "I'm not at all worried about your chest pain ... My suspicion that this is coming from your heart is about zero." Shortly afterwards, McKinley had a heart attack! This led Croskerry to admit, "My thinking was overly influenced by how healthy this man looked, and the absence of risk factors." In other words, McKinley seemed very *representative* of healthy people with an extremely low risk of having a heart attack.

Confirmation bias is one of the most widespread cognitive biases. It consists in searching for information that supports one's beliefs and avoiding information inconsistent with those beliefs. It also involves interpreting ambiguous information as being more consistent with one's prior beliefs than is objectively justified.

Even experts are prone to confirmation bias (Mendel et al., 2015). Psychiatrists made a preliminary diagnosis of a patient based on limited information and then decided what further information to consider. Of those psychiatrists searching for confirmatory evidence supporting their diagnosis, 70% made the wrong final diagnosis (compared to 27% of those searching for disconfirmatory evidence).

Experts in forensic science are prone to various cognitive biases (Dror, 2020). Here is a real-life example of how they can be influenced by confirmation bias (Almog & Zitrin, 2009). Two pubs in Birmingham were bombed in 1974, leaving 21 people dead and 182 injured. Six Irishmen were found guilty and given life sentences. Sixteen years later, their convictions were overturned as unsafe and unsatisfactory, making this case notorious as one of the greatest miscarriages of justice in British history.

Forensic scientists working on the above case obtained positive results from the suspects using what is known as the Griess test. They inferred the suspects had been handling explosives (more specifically, nitroglycerine). The forensic scientists exhibited confirmation bias because they ignored innocent interpretations of their findings. It eventually transpired that the positive results were due to traces of nitrocellulose on the suspects' hands, which were there because they had been handling playing cards.

Experienced doctors were given the following problem (Hoffrage et al., 2000). An individual has tested positive for colorectal cancer. If someone has colorectal cancer, the probability the test is positive is 50%. If someone does not have colorectal cancer, the probability of a positive test is 3%. Within the population at large, 0.3% have colorectal cancer. What is the probability that an individual who tests positive for colorectal cancer has the disease?

Only 4% of the doctors provided the correct answer: 5%. Many more correct answers were supplied when the problem was expressed in frequencies rather than probabilities (Hoffrage et al., 2000). Out of every 10,000 people, 300 will have the disease and of those 150 will test positive. Of the 9,970 people without the disease, 3% (300 people) will test positive. Thus, of the 315 people testing positive, only 5% actually have the disease. When the problem was expressed in this way, 67% of doctors produced the correct answer.

What is going on here? Problem solution requires considering what is happening in the population at large (the base rate). The false-positive rate (i.e., the probability of a healthy individual testing positive) must be related to the true-positive rate (i.e., the probability of someone with the disease testing positive). Failure to do this is much more common when the problem is presented in probabilities – many doctors on this version produced the wrong answer of 50% because they totally ignored the population-based information. This is base-rate neglect or bias.

Base-rate neglect is not restricted to expert doctors. Lindsey et al. (2003) presented expert lawyers with a situation where there was a match between the DNA sample from the defendant and that recovered from the victim. They had to indicate the probability the defendant was the source of the trace on the victim. When the problem was presented in probabilities, only 13% of expert lawyers made full use of base-rate information. However, this increased to 68% when the problem was presented in frequencies.

Insufficient motivation does not explain widespread base-rate neglect. University students offered an incentive of more than the average monthly wage for good performance showed as much base-rate neglect as those not offered that incentive (Enke et al., 2020).

Do cognitive biases mean we are irrational?

Kahneman and Tversky argued that most people have numerous cognitive biases which are both systematic and resistant to change. They concluded that our thinking and decision making are often somewhat irrational. However, other psychologists (e.g., Gigerenzer, 2018) have argued persuasively that human thinking is much more rational than implied by laboratory research. Below we discuss the arguments of the latter group of psychologists. Note that the word "rationality" is what Minsky called a "suitcase" word (Brockman, 1998): it has several aspects and so its meaning must be carefully unpacked.

Some cognitive psychologists exhibit "bias bias" (Gigerenzer, 2018), seeing *systematic* biases in human behaviour when there is merely *unsystematic* error. The notion of *systematic* biases implies that most people make very similar errors when making judgements or engaged in decision making. This is a much more dubious assertion than simply acknowledging people are error prone.

It has been claimed the systematic biases we allegedly possess are costly to our health, wealth, and general well-being. However, there is minimal evidence of such costs, suggesting that findings from artificial laboratory research are not readily applicable to everyday life (Gigerenzer, 2018).

Tversky and Kahneman argued that cognitive biases exhibit "stubborn persistence." However, most people rapidly learn to reduce or eliminate such biases via short training sessions (e.g., we can easily persuade someone to use base-rate information) (Gigerenzer, 2018).

Heuristics or rules of thumb often provide only approximately correct answers but can be used rapidly and effortlessly. There are many situations (e.g., rapidly changing environmental conditions) where it would be pointless spending a long time producing very precise judgements. For example, suppose a doctor strongly suspects a very seriously ill patient has a given disease based on the representativeness heuristic. If rapid action is essential, it would generally be better for the doctor "to go with the probabilities" rather than delaying treatment by considering alternative improbable diagnoses.

Simple heuristics sometimes outperform much more complex strategies in real-life settings. Consider investment decisions involving the allocation of funds. One study (DeMiguel et al., 2009) considered nine complex strategies (including one that won Harry Markowitz the Nobel Prize for economics). They also considered the 1/N portfolio strategy: allocate money equally to each of N funds. No complex strategy was consistently better than the 1/N strategy. Why was the simple 1/N strategy so effective? Complex strategies are very sensitive to past data about stocks. However, they are also sensitive to "noise" in the data, making these strategies overly complex and distorted.

Loss aversion

It is reasonable to assume we would make decisions to maximise the chances of making a gain and minimise the chances of making a loss. However, as we are about to see, human decision makers often make apparently irrational decisions. Suppose someone offered you $200 (£170) if a tossed coin comes up heads but a loss of $100 (£85) if it comes up tails. You would jump at the chance (wouldn't you?) because the bet provides an average expected gain of $50 (£42.50) per throw. In fact, Tversky and Shafir (1992) found 64% of their participants rejected this bet.

Here are two more decisions. Would you prefer a sure gain of $800 (£690) or an 85% chance of gaining $1,000 (£850) and a 15% probability of gaining nothing? Since the expected value of the latter decision is greater than that of the former ($850 or £722 vs $800 or £690, respectively), you might well choose the latter option. Finally, would you prefer a sure loss of $800 (£690) or an 85% probability of losing $1,000 with a 15% probability of avoiding loss? The average expected loss is $800 (£690) for the former choice and $850 (£722) for the latter one, so you go with the former choice, do you not?

In fact, Kahneman and Tversky (1984) found most people preferred the choices with the *smaller* expected gain and the *larger* expected loss! How can we explain all these apparently irrational decisions? Kahneman and Tversky (1979, 1984) provided an answer. Their crucial assumption was that losses have a greater subjective impact on individuals than gains of the same magnitude: this is loss aversion. Thus, that people will take risks to try to avoid making losses, but will prefer a sure gain to a risky (but potentially greater) gain.

There is plentiful laboratory evidence of loss aversion (Eysenck & Keane, 2020). However, most gains or losses under laboratory conditions are modest or merely hypothetical and so laboratory findings may not generalise to the real world. Laboratory studies typically involve individuals lacking specialist knowledge. It seems likely experts (e.g., professional gamblers) would be largely immune from loss aversion.

Eil and Lien (2014) studied very experienced poker players (see Figure 5.6). In spite of their expertise, they typically played more aggressively (i.e., betting and raising more often) when losing (a sub-optimal strategy indicating loss aversion). In addition, they were risk averse when winning.

For professional golfers, a birdie (one under par) on a hole is a gain whereas a bogey (one over par) is a loss. Loss aversion would lead them to be more cautious when putting for a birdie than for par. In the latter case, failure to hole the putt would produce a bogey and thus a loss.

Figure 5.6 Even experienced poker players (such as those shown in the figure) exhibit biases such as loss aversion when playing for money.

Pope and Schweitzer (2011) studied 2.5 million putts by professional golfers. Par putts were less likely than same-length birdie putts to stop short of the hole (indicative of loss aversion). Loss aversion was found in 94% of golfers (including Tiger Woods).

Over time, loss aversion will generally make us poorer than if our decision making under risk were based rationally on expected gains and losses. In contrast, it would be extremely easy to program an AI program to avoid loss aversion totally and to maximise its financial gains.

If loss aversion is a human limitation, why do we exhibit it so often? First, emotional factors frequently play a part. More specifically, we often make loss-averse decisions because we *attend* more to (and weigh more heavily) the negative feelings anticipated from loss than the positive feelings anticipated from gain (Charpentier et al., 2016). It is arguable that it is perfectly rational to take account of anticipated emotions in this way.

Second, we are often held accountable to other people for our decisions. It can be embarrassing to explain why our decisions have caused losses. Simonson and Staw (1992) tested the role of accountability by telling people their decisions would be shared with others or would be confidential. There was greater loss aversion in the high-accountability condition because individuals in the former condition experienced a greater need to justify their previous decisions.

Third, our decision making often occurs in a social context. Consider the television programme *Who Wants to be a Millionaire* (see Figure 5.7). A contestant who has already won £75,000 must decide whether to attempt a question when two possible answers are left. If they answer correctly, they gain an additional £75,000 but they lose £25,000 if they are wrong. The balance of advantage in strict financial terms lies with answering the question. Suppose, however, the contestant's family has limited

Figure 5.7 Photograph of Chris Tarrant presenting *Who Wants to be a Millionaire?*

financial resources, and their lives would be transformed by taking home the money already won. In that case, the social context strongly indicates the contestant should take the money rather than guess.

Fourth, loss aversion can also be explained in evolutionary terms (McDermott et al., 2008). Engaging in risky behaviour (i.e., being loss averse) may be optimal for someone who is starving, whereas it makes evolutionary sense to minimise risk when resources are abundant. In our evolutionary history, the former state of affairs was much more common. Hungry animals are more likely than those with access to plentiful food to engage in high-risk foraging (Symmonds et al., 2010). Of more direct relevance here, hungry humans make riskier financial decisions than satiated ones.

Malpress et al. (2015) extended McDermott et al.'s (2008) evolutionary theory. They argued that foragers in our evolutionary past could predict to some extent the future availability of food based on their recent experiences. Foragers with limited food reserves predicting the availability of food would probably decrease had strong motivation to choose high-risk foraging options. This strategy was optimal because it maximised the foragers' expected lifetime reproductive success.

Logical reasoning

Aristotle (possibly the most intelligent person of all time) claimed humans are rational beings, and that the highest form of human happiness is *Eudaimonia* (a life lived in accordance with reason). How can we assess human reasoning powers? Aristotle answered that question by inventing a form of logic that remained essentially unchallenged for 2,000 years.

Aristotle focused on syllogistic reasoning. A syllogism consists of two statements (e.g., *All girl guides are children* and *All children are obedient*) followed by a conclusion (e.g., *Therefore, all girl guides are obedient*). You must decide whether the conclusion is valid. Of major importance, the conclusion's validity depends solely on whether it follows logically from the premises – what is true or false in the real world is irrelevant. Sadly, most humans (even highly intelligent and well-educated ones) exhibit very poor logical reasoning (Eysenck & Keane, 2020).

In contrast, it is easy to design AI programs that invariably (and rapidly) produce correct answers to all standard logic-based problems. Does poor human performance mean our thinking is limited and irrational and thus vastly inferior to AI? The British psychologists Wason and Johnson-Laird argued that many incorrect inferences on logical reasoning tasks resemble "pathological delusions" suggesting the presence of a disorder!

In fact, logical reasoning tasks require processes substantially different from those needed in everyday life.

They require us to assume the initial premises or statements are true and then decide whether the conclusion follows necessarily ("yes" or "no"). Real life is rarely that clear-cut: it typically involves arguments that are possibly or probably true.

In addition, we nearly always use pre-existing relevant knowledge and beliefs with real-world reasoning. In contrast, with logic-based tasks, we are told to ignore what we know (and our beliefs). Consider the following syllogism:

> All well-adjusted individuals can have healthy marriages.
> Homosexuals are well-adjusted individuals.
> Therefore, homosexuals can have healthy marriages.

The conclusion is logically valid. However, conservatives are more likely than liberals to argue the above conclusion is invalid (Calvillo et al., 2020). Assessing the validity of syllogisms on the basis of one's beliefs rather than logical validity/invalidity involves what is known as belief bias, and occurs very frequently in syllogistic reasoning.

Another reason why it has often been argued that human reasoning is illogical is because of our susceptibility to various fallacies (Hahn & Oaksford, 2014). For example, consider the slippery-slope fallacy (a small first step will lead to a chain of events producing an undesirable outcome). One such argument (from Corner et al., 2011) is as follows: "If voluntary euthanasia is legalised, then in the future there will be more cases of 'medical murder'."

Corner et al. (2011) argued it is a mistake to consider all slippery-slope arguments illogical, because they vary greatly in strength. For example, slippery-slope arguments where the probability of the negative outcome is high are stronger than those where it is low. As predicted, most people regarded the former arguments as stronger than the latter.

Haigh et al. (2016) pointed out that the great majority of slippery-slope arguments imply resistance to change. This led them to claim that slippery-slope arguments are stronger when the speaker's personal beliefs are known to be in agreement with those arguments. This claim was supported by people's judgements of the persuasiveness of various slippery-slope arguments.

There are numerous other "fallacies," but we will discuss only one more: the *ad hominem* fallacy which involves discrediting an argument by attacking the person making the argument. It is often correct to describe it as a fallacy. For example, those rejecting arguments in favour of climate change often resort to speculative attacks on the integrity of climate scientists (Cann & Raymond, 2018).

However, the *ad hominem* fallacy is often justified. Suppose the person making an argument knows little about the issue in question, is often dishonest, or has a strong vested interest in the argument they are proposing. In those circumstances, it is appropriate to be less persuaded by the argument than if they are an expert, are habitually honest, or have no vested interest in the argument.

In sum, the notion that all "fallacies" demonstrate people's limited ability to reason logically is far too extreme. When evaluating an argument's persuasiveness, we should consider factors such as our previous relevant knowledge, the characteristics of the person making the argument, and the strength of the argument. Thus, our apparent susceptibility to fallacies does not necessarily indicate deficiencies in human thinking and reasoning.

Why are we so prone to biases and irrationality?

We have discussed various ways of explaining our apparent irrationality and illogicality relative to AI, which can easily be programmed to avoid most cognitive biases and illogical thinking. Of central importance is that humans (unlike AI systems) often pursue two or more goals concurrently. Consider individuals working on a given cognitive task. One of their goals is to achieve good task performance. However, they may also have other personal goals (e.g., avoiding negative emotions) and social goals (e.g., being able to justify one's decisions to others and desire to be liked by others).

We start with an example involving omission bias (a biased preference for risking harm through inaction rather than action). In one study (Brown et al., 2010), many British parents preferred a greater risk of their children having a disease than of their children suffering adverse reactions to vaccination (see Figure 5.8). Even experts exhibit omission bias. Pulmonologists (experts in treating lung disease) received scenarios involving an evaluation of pulmonary embolism and treatment of septic shock (Aberegg et al., 2005). They were less likely to select the best management strategy when given the option of doing nothing.

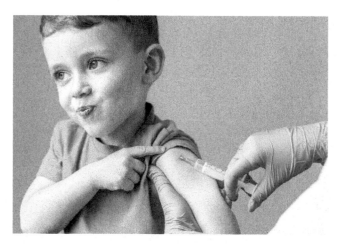

Figure 5.8 A girl receiving a vaccine jab.

Omission bias initially appears irrational. However, it may appear less so when we appreciate that many individuals focus on the anticipated emotional consequences of their decision to engage in action or inaction. More specifically, individuals exhibiting omission bias often anticipate experiencing regret if their actions cause harm.

Social factors (e.g., conformity)

Another apparent limitation of human cognition is that it can easily be distorted by social factors (e.g., the desire to be liked by others). This limitation was most famously shown by an American psychologist, Solomon Asch (1951, 1956), who carried out epoch-making research on conformity. Several individuals viewed a visual display (see Figure 5.9) and indicated, which of three lines labelled A, B, and C was the same length as a standard line (X) as the

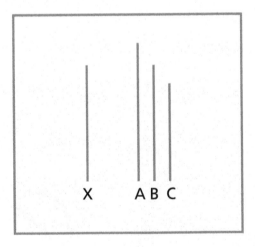

Figure 5.9 Asch's conformity task. Individuals were asked to indicate which of the three lines (A, B, and C) was the same length as the line on the left (X).

experimenter worked his way around the group members. This task was very easy: 99% of decisions were correct.

So far, so boring. Note, however, that all the group members (except for one genuine participant) were confederates instructed beforehand by the experimenter to give the same wrong answers on some trials. The only genuine participant was the last (or last but one) to give their answer. The genuine participants faced a nasty conflict between what they *knew* was the correct answer and group social pressure. Many participants became distressed, sweated, or looked bewildered and puzzled. On 37% of trials, they resolved the conflict by giving the same wrong answer as the confederates.

Asch (1955, p. 35) was convinced conformity was very undesirable: "When consensus comes under the dominance of conformity, the social process is polluted and the individual at the same time surrenders the powers on which his functioning as a feeling and thinking being depends."

Asch's negative views are excessively harsh. Note that participants did *not* conform on 63% of trials. Also note that 25% of participants never conformed to the group's wrong answers, and nearly 70% defied the majority on most trials.

Hodges (2014) argued that human decisions are often strongly influenced by values. In the Asch situation, participants face conflicts among three values: truth, trust, and social solidarity. They can best resolve these conflicts by being truthful on some trials but by showing social solidarity with the rest of the group and trust in their decisions by accepting their views on other trials. That is precisely how most participants behaved.

A study by Abrams et al. (1990) using Asch's task with psychology students as the genuine participants supports Hodges' position. They were told the other group members were psychology students or were studying ancient history. Conformity to the group's incorrect decisions was found on 58% of trials when the confederates were described as psychology students, but only 8% of trials when they were allegedly studying ancient history. Thus, conformity was markedly greater when participants were more motivated by the values of social solidarity and trust.

We now turn to climate change. More than a decade ago, 97% of expert climate researchers already believed in human-made climate change (Anderegg et al., 2010). It would seem "rational" for non-experts who have spent practically no time thinking about the issue (and who possess no relevant knowledge) to agree with the experts. However, at least 30% of Americans are climate-change deniers.

Are climate-change deniers ignorant or unintelligent? That question is simplistic and misleading. If it were true, Americans with high levels of science literacy and numeracy would be much less likely to deny climate change than those with lower levels. However, the actual difference is small (Kahan et al., 2012)

What, then, determines whether Americans are climate-change deniers? Of most importance are their values and general political beliefs (Kahan et al., 2012). Most egalitarian communitarians (believing in equality and the value of society) strongly believe in human-made climate change. In contrast, most hierarchical individualists (believing in a hierarchical society and the importance of personal responsibility) deny its existence. Thus, Americans' beliefs about climate change reflect how they see themselves and the values they endorse.

In sum, human performance often appears unimpressive. However, humans (unlike AI systems) often pursue multiple goals at the same time. For example, those "failing" on the Asch task nevertheless achieve the important goals of social solidarity and trustworthiness. Similarly, those denying man-made climate change achieve the goals of being consistent with their underlying values and general political beliefs.

Self-enhancement and self-esteem

In addition to the cognitive biases discussed already, we also have many biases with respect to ourselves. One such bias is the better-than-average effect (a tendency to perceive one's abilities or intelligence as superior to most other people). Zell et al. (2020) found extensive evidence for this effect in a review of research from almost 1 million people.

Over-confidence in our own abilities can cause numerous errors in thinking and decision making. Consider the Dunning-Kruger effect (Kruger & Dunning, 1999): incompetent individuals are often blissfully unaware of their own incompetence. As the British philosopher Bertrand Russell pointed out, "The stupid are cocksure while the intelligent are full of doubt."

The Dunning-Kruger effect is very common. Those knowing the least about the actual causes of autism are the ones most likely to think they know more than medical doctors and scientists about its causes (Motta et al., 2018). Similar findings have been obtained from research on beliefs about genetically modified foods. The most extreme opponents of genetically modified foods know the least about them (but mistakenly think they know the most!) (Fernbach et al., 2019). Individuals who exaggerate their own knowledge and abilities exhibit self-enhancement bias.

Other biases are often linked to self-enhancement. One example is the false uniqueness bias (mistakenly regarding oneself as better than most other people) (Pope, 2014). Another example is the self-serving bias – the tendency to attribute one's successes to one's ability and efforts but failures to bad luck or task difficulty.

Self-enhancement and the various other biases associated with it form a major limitation. If you are convinced your knowledge is much greater than is actually the case, you are disinclined to increase your knowledge. In addition, you are likely to be immune to feedback indicating your thinking is incorrect. However, self-enhancement can make individuals feel happier than if they focused on their ignorance and limitations.

One of the clearest illustrations of the notion that, "Ignorance is bliss," is provided by optimism bias. For example, most people exaggerate how long they will live and how much money they will earn but minimise the chances of contracting a serious disease or being involved in a car accident (Sharot, 2010). Those exhibiting optimism bias tend to be happier and experience less depression than those not exhibiting that bias.

How rational are humans?

You may have found it somewhat dispiriting reading about the numerous failures and biases of human cognition. You may find it even more dispiriting to learn that we have mentioned only a small fraction of the illogicalities, cognitive biases, and inadequacies of human cognition. Humans indisputably appear relatively unintelligent and irrational when compared against what might naïvely be considered the ideal or perfection (e.g., unlimited processing capacity, zero forgetting, consistently high sustained attention, thinking unimpaired by emotional factors, and absence of all cognitive biases).

How can we best explain our numerous apparent "failures" and limitations? Perhaps humans are simply much less rational than we like to believe. However, several other explanations cast a more positive light on human rationality and intelligence. Below we consider three such explanations.

Bounded rationality

The most influential attempt to explain our cognitive shortcomings was provided by Herb Simon. According to

Simon (1990, p. 6), "Because of the limits on their computing speeds and power, intelligent systems must use approximate methods to handle most tasks. Their rationality is bounded." Human bounded rationality generally enables us to produce workable solutions to problems despite our limited processing ability. Human decision making mostly involves satisficing (formed from the words *satisfy* and *suffice*) rather than optimising (the best possible decision). More specifically, we search through possible decisions until we identify one fulfilling our criteria for acceptability.

Satisficing may sound like a human limitation. However, consider the substantial costs incurred in collecting complete information relating to a current problem and then performing complex computations on that information. In the real world, circumstances often change, and so the best possible solution today may not be so in a month's time. Accordingly, satisficing often provides the best possible combination of good decision making coupled with manageable processing costs.

Suppose you are searching for some object (e.g., a television set). If you use the satisficing heuristic or rule of thumb called, "Try a dozen," you are likely to make a very suitable choice (Todd & Miller, 1999). This is a relatively simple task because the object you choose will not object to being bought.

Mate search is far more complex than object search (yes, really!), in part because it requires mutual choice. However, Todd and Miller (1999) outlined an effective satisficing heuristic for mate search assuming that relationships are most likely to succeed if the two people involved are of comparable attractiveness or mate value. You work out your own mate value based on the offers and refusals you receive from potential mates and adjust your sights accordingly. If you follow this heuristic and consider approximately 20 potential mates, your future is assured!

Individuals differ in the tendency to be a maximiser or a satisficer (Schwartz et al., 2002). Maximizers set themselves more ambitious goals and adopt more varied and complex strategies to achieve those goals (Cheek & Schwartz, 2016). Of importance, satisficers are happier and more optimistic than maximisers and experience less regret and self-blame (Schwartz et al., 2002).

The bounded-rationality approach sheds considerable light on sub-optimal human cognitive performance. However, it suffers from two limitations. First, the notion of 'bounded rationality' is imprecise and has only modest explanatory power (Lieder & Griffiths, 2020).

Second, it is important to establish whether humans' cognitive performance is generally as good as possible given our limited capacity and environmental constraints. There are cases where humans have obviously failed to use their limited capacity optimally. Examples include, "Behaviours that foolishly risk one's life, such as drunk or careless driving, or the hundreds of people who have died taking selfies, and misjudging fatal risks in the pursuit of a few more followers on Instagram" (Davis & Marcus, 2020, p. 21) (see Chapter 7).

Social identity

We have emphasised that humans often pursue two or more goals concurrently. A consequence of this is that we need more complex conceptualisations of rationality. An interesting notion totally consistent with our approach is Hoffrage et al.'s (2018) notion of social rationality: "the need to make decisions in environments that are typically also shaped by the actions of others" (p. 331).

The importance of social factors in our thinking and behaviour is spelt out in social identity theory (e.g., Tajfel & Turner, 1979). According to this theory, we possess several social identities based on our group memberships.

Thus, you may have a social identity as a student, a second social identity as a woman, and so on. Of central relevance here, "Humans are groupish animals with a propensity to engage in motivated cognition to support their group [social] identities" (Van Bavel et al., 2020, p. 66).

We can relate the human tendency to develop several social identities to Fiske's (2010) theory in which she proposed five fundamental social motives. The most important of these motives (and of most relevance to social identities) is the belongingness motive or need. This motive is based on, "the idea that people need strong, stable relationships with other people ... belonging to a group helps individuals to survive psychologically and physically" (pp. 17–18).

Belongingness is of central importance in explaining why we conform so often to the views and behaviour of others (as in Asch's research discussed earlier). The existence of social identities accounts for the much greater conformity found when other group members are perceived as sharing a social identity with the participants (Abrams et al., 1990). Belongingness also helps to explain why individual differences in views on climate change. As we saw, those who identify as egalitarians mostly believe in climate change whereas those who identify as rugged individualists do not (Kahan et al., 2012; discussed above).

Self-deception and self-enhancement

Earlier we discussed several biases (e.g., false uniqueness bias and Dunning-Kruger effect). Several factors underlie these biases. However, they all depend partly on the desire for self-enhancement and our preference for positive self-perceptions over negative ones. Fiske (2010) identified self-enhancement as one of our major social motives arguing that it, "involves either maintaining self-esteem or being motivated by the possibility of self-improvement" (p. 22).

There has been considerable controversy as to whether it is psychologically adaptive to have unrealistically positive views of oneself and one's abilities. Many leading clinical psychologists (including Carl Rogers) argued strongly that psychological well-being requires us to have realistic self-appraisals. As Baumeister and Vohs (2018, p. 137) pointed out, "Very high self-esteem might create problems, such as arrogance, entitlement, pig-headed stubbornness, and overconfidence." However, other experts (e.g., Taylor & Brown, 1988) disagree, claiming that unrealistically positive self-perception is psychologically healthy.

Dufner et al. (2019) reviewed research on self-enhancement (unrealistically positive self-esteem) and psychological adjustment. Self-enhancement was consistently positively related to personal adjustment (e.g., life satisfaction and lack of depression) for both sexes and across ages and numerous cultures. Such findings do not indicate the direction of causality: does self-enhancement increase personal adjustment or does personal adjustment lead to self-enhancement? Another finding reported by Dufner et al. (2019) supports the former possibility: self-enhancement at one point in time predicted subsequent personal adjustment.

Further evidence that inflated self-perception is adaptive was reported by Humberg et al. (2019). They obtained measures of individuals' actual intelligence as assessed by IQ tests, their intellectual self-perceptions, and their psychological adjustment (e.g., self-esteem and life satisfaction). Accurate self-knowledge was *not* associated with good psychological adjustment. Instead, psychological adjustment was best predicted by the extent to which intellectual self-perception was inflated. As Humberg et al. concluded, most of the findings were consistent with the rule, "the higher self-perceived intelligence, the better adjusted" (p. 847).

We turn now to a different form of self-deception found when our cherished beliefs are challenged by conflicting facts or evidence. Consider the "meat paradox": many people eat meat even though they have qualms about meat-production methods. Suppose they are given explicit information about the suffering and killing of animals involved in providing them with meat. Arguably, the "rational" reaction to that information would be for their attachment to meat to decrease as they focus on the relevant evidence. For men, the information has the opposite effect – it actually increases their attachment to meat (Dowsett et al., 2018).

What is going on here? The origins of a coherent explanation go back to Festinger et al.'s (1956) pioneering research. They studied a sect called the Seekers whose leader was Marian Keech. She claimed to have received messages from extraterrestrial beings informing her that most of North America would be covered by a huge flood on the 25 December 1954. However, the Seekers were told that a flying saucer would arrive on the 21 December 1954 at 4PM to fly them to safety.

The Seekers waited hopefully at the appointed spot with coats in hand, but the flying saucer did not arrive. They were then told the flying saucer would arrive at midnight, so they waited for several hours in the cold and the snow. However, the flying saucer did not arrive then either, or at various other anticipated times ahead of 25 December. Finally, the cataclysmic flood failed to make an appearance.

How do you think the Seekers reacted to the total failure of all their expectations? The 'rational' reaction would have been to abandon their beliefs. However, they were strongly committed to those beliefs, and many had given up their jobs and discarded valuable belongings when preparing to leave this planet. As a result, the Seekers became even more committed to their beliefs and devoted much more time converting other people to those beliefs. They claimed to have received a message from God saying He had saved the world because of the Seekers' shining example. According to their leader, Marian Keech, "It was this little group spreading light here that prevented the flood."

Festinger et al. (1956) explained their findings by arguing that having two contradictory beliefs or ideas creates an unpleasant state known as "cognitive dissonance." Cognitive dissonance is especially strong if the beliefs in question are of great importance to the individual. Individuals experiencing cognitive dissonance are highly motivated to eliminate it by changing one of their beliefs. The Seekers resolved their conflict by claiming that the non-appearance of the flood was a massive success for their cult's beliefs rather than abject failure.

Gilbert (e.g., 2006) developed Festinger's ideas. He argued that humans have a psychological immune system activated whenever we are confronted by serious threats to our self-image. It protects our core beliefs about ourselves and the world by refusing to accept beliefs in direct conflict with those core beliefs. Numerous cases of self-deception and self-enhancement (including those discussed earlier) can be explained by the existence of this psychological immune system (Porot & Mandelbaum, 2020).

The possession of a psychological immune system is advantageous because it can provide a relatively simple way of reducing psychological distress. However, it can also be associated with massive disadvantages. Consider smokers experiencing conflict between their cigarette-smoking behaviour and their knowledge that smoking causes numerous serious diseases. Many (or most) smokers resolve this conflict by adopting risk-minimising beliefs (e.g., the medical risks are exaggerated, you have to die of something, and smoking is no riskier than many other activities) (Fotuhi et al., 2013). The very serious downside of adopting such beliefs rather than quitting smoking is that smoking reduces life expectancy by approximately ten years.

Conclusions

The overarching theme of the chapter so far has been that most human limitations have an upside and so reflect less badly on us that might be imagined. For example, it is true that we possess limited processing capacity, have relatively poor sustained attention, and often forget past events and actions we promised to perform in the future. However, we mitigate the adverse effects of these limitations by focusing on what is important at the expense of what is relatively trivial. Thus, for example, we pay full attention when it is necessary to do so, and we rarely forget significant past events or future actions.

Other cognitive limitations include poor transfer of learning from one task to others that are dissimilar to it (far transfer) and maintenance of a mental set when changing circumstances indicate the desirability of abandoning it. However, we do exhibit excellent near transfer and some far transfer if initial training is sufficiently prolonged. Our tendency to maintain a mental set is justified by the fact that this is very often the optimal strategy in everyday life.

Finally, we seem irrational because we possess dozens of cognitive biases, we are loss averse, we perform poorly on tasks involving logical reasoning, and we are susceptible to logical fallacies. However, there are various reasons for doubting our irrationality. First, much depends on how we choose to define the complex concepts of "rationality" and "irrationality." Second, many of the tasks allegedly revealing our irrationality (especially logical reasoning tasks) are highly artificial and of minimal relevance to everyday life.

Third, humans often pursue two or more goals concurrently. Our needs for social identity, self-enhancement, self-esteem, and avoidance of cognitive dissonance provide explanations for much of our apparently "irrational" behaviour. Overall, much (but certainly not all) of our cognitive performance can appropriately be regarded as rational and as making near-optimal use of our processing abilities.

Creativity

Key features of creative products are that they are new, surprising, and of value (Boden, 1992; see Chapter 4). It has often been argued that we are the only species capable of creativity. That argument has been attacked in two different ways. First, other species often exhibit apparently creative behaviour (Shevlin, 2021). Second, creativity is absent from most human behaviour most of the time (especially using relatively stringent criteria for regarding something as "creative").

Numerous theories of creativity have been proposed. According to the influential Geneplore theory (Ward et al., 1995), creativity consists of a generative phase in which ideas are produced and an exploratory phase where those ideas are evaluated and creative solutions proposed. If the exploratory phase fails to produce a satisfactory outcome, there is another cycle of generation followed by exploration.

Evidence that most people find it hard to generate totally original or creative ideas was provided by Ward and Sifonis (1997). Some people were simply asked to imagine an extra-terrestrial creature whereas others were instructed to imagine creatures wildly different from those found on Earth. The imagined creatures were in many ways remarkably similar to familiar animals regardless of instructions. Of the "wildly different animals" that were generated, 93% had standard senses (e.g., 93% had eyes) and 90% had standard appendages (e.g., 84% had legs). Thus, there was little creativity and considerable reliance on pre-existing knowledge.

We would anticipate that experts would be more creative than ordinary individuals. For example, it is often assumed that scientific creativity represents a pinnacle of human thinking and cognition. Many people believe scientific discovery is, "the result of genius, inspiration, and sudden insight" (Trickett & Trafton, 2007, p. 868). However, Campbell (1960) proposed a much more mundane account of the processes underlying creative scientific achievements. He argued scientists start by generating numerous ideas almost randomly (but influenced by their relevant knowledge). This initial process of blind variation is followed by selective retention (discriminating between valuable and relatively useless ideas).

Why doesn't Campbell's (1960) description sound much like our preconceptions about scientific creativity and discovery? Simonton (2015) noted that historical accounts of major scientific breakthroughs are often at variance with the notion of blind variation. He explained this discrepancy as follows: "What was originally non-obvious becomes obvious as the biographical record is 'cleaned up' to make the creator much more prescient than was true at the time" (p. 267).

If blind variation is important, even very successful creative scientists should produce numerous unworkable ideas. Consider Thomas Edison. He had over 1,000 American patents for his inventions but admitted: "I have not failed. I've just found 10,000 ways that won't work." Similarly, the very successful contemporary inventor, Sir James Dyson, confessed: "I spent years in my tool-shed building thousands of prototypes of my bagless vacuum cleaner. Each one was a failure."

Simonton (2015) argued that the creative process is less random than Campbell (1960) implied. The ideas generated by creative individuals are influenced by their expertise and strategies, and by indirect associations from their pre-existing knowledge. All these factors shift the generation process away from randomness and thus enhance the probability of a creative discovery.

In sum, there is much indisputable evidence of human creativity. However, true creativity is much rarer than

typically assumed because most of our attempts at creativity are constrained by our accumulated knowledge and
information from past learning.

Limitations due to emotional states

It is easy to believe our lives would be better if we did
not experience stress and negative emotional states (e.g.,
anxiety and depression). Negative emotions and stress are
unpleasant and can disrupt our ability to think and make
effective decisions. All in all, it would appear that we would
be much better off without stress and negative emotions.
As we are about to see, however, reality is more nuanced.

Stress effects

It is commonly assumed we live in an "age of stress." As
predicted, Booth et al. (2016) found anxiety levels had
increased between 1970 and 2010 in most of the 57 countries they studied. The recent devastating impact of Covid-
19 throughout the world has produced further increases in
anxiety and stress. Stress and anxiety have several negative
consequences including producing negative mood states
and impairing our ability to perform cognitive and motor
tasks.

Performance of most tasks is impaired by extreme levels
of stress. Walker and Burkhardt (1965) found more than
200 of the muzzle-loading rifles used in one battle during
the American Civil War were loaded at least five times
without being fired. Patrick (1934a,b) gave human participants the simple task of discovering, which of four doors
was unlocked. Since, the same door was never unlocked
on two successive trials, the optimal strategy was to try
each of the other three doors in turn. There were 60%
optimal solutions under non-stressful conditions but only
20% when participants had cold water streams directed at

them, or had their ears blasted by a car horn, or were given continuous electric shocks.

It is of more practical relevance to consider the moderate levels of stress experienced in everyday life (e.g., environmental noise, fatigue, and high workload). Most people assume moderate stress impairs task performance. In fact, however, the typical finding is that performance levels under moderate stress are comparable to those under non-stressful conditions (Eysenck, 1982; Hockey, 1997).

We can understand the above counterintuitive findings by considering an anecdote told to the first author by the leading British psychologist Donald Broadbent. He had been invited on to a television programme to show the negative effects of sleeplessness. Accordingly, he found a student willing to go without sleep for three days prior to the programme. To Broadbent's embarrassment, this person showed no signs of any performance impairment! The motivation provided by the excitement of appearing on television counterbalanced any negative effects caused by prolonged sleep deprivation.

Broadbent (1971) proposed a two-mechanism model to explain the effects of sleeplessness (and other stressors). The lower mechanism responsible for relatively "automatic" processes is impaired by various stressors. However, the upper mechanism monitors the lower mechanism and compensates for the lower mechanism's impaired functioning. Hockey (1997) developed this theory (see Figure 5.10).

Eysenck et al. (2007) extended the approach of Broadbent (1971) and Hockey (1997). According to their attentional control theory, high-anxious individuals often perform comparably to low-anxious ones because they compensate for the adverse effects of anxiety by increased effort and use of processing resources. Research using neuroimaging has supported this theory by showing that high-anxious individuals generally have greater activation than low-anxious individuals in brain areas associated with effort and attentional

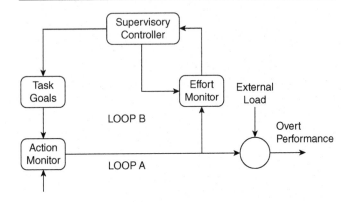

Figure 5.10 Compensatory control model of performance regulation. Loop A is the lower mechanism that engages in routine regulatory activity; loop B is the upper mechanism that uses effort-based control under the supervisory controller to compensate for deficient functioning of loop A.

Source: From Hockey (1997).

control (Eysenck & Derakshan, 2011). Thus, anxious individuals maintain performance by "peddling faster."

In sum, the fact that humans are susceptible to stress often fails to produce any negative effects on performance. We monitor our level of performance and use compensatory processes (e.g., increased effort) to prevent stressors from causing impaired performance. In other words, we respond flexibly and adaptively to moderate stressors. With severe stressors, we often re-prioritise our goals to divert some attention from a current task to the source of stress.

Negative emotions: anxiety and depression

Most people assume anxiety and depression are unwanted emotions that serve no useful purpose. If that assumption is correct, then these negative emotions constitute a serious human limitation, and one that is not found in AI systems. However, many philosophers and psychologists from the time of Aristotle onwards have argued that all emotions serve useful functions. More specifically, they claim that negative emotional states are often adaptive and useful in the long-term even though they produce high short-term costs.

What are the functions of anxiety? It leads us to consider potential future threats to the self, and also produces selective attention to environmental threats and dangers. The emphasis on future threats is seen clearly in the strong tendency for anxious individuals to devote far more of their time than non-anxious individuals to worrying about possible negative events. In broad terms, anxiety typically occurs when we are faced by threats to self-preservation.

Here is an example of the value of the risk-aversiveness of anxious individuals. Individual rated as anxious at the age of 13 were much less likely than those rated as non-anxious to die in accidental circumstances before the age of 25 (0.1% vs 0.7%, respectively) (Lee et al., 2006).

What are the functions of depression? Depression is often caused by goal loss (e.g., death of a loved one) and its main functions are to lead depressed individuals to go through a series of stages to replace the lost goal with a new one. According to Durisko et al., these stages involve, "Biasing cognition to avoid losses, conserving energy, disengaging from unobtainable goals, signalling submission, soliciting resources, and promoting analytical thinking" (P. 316).

In sum, anxiety and depression both disrupt human cognitive performance. However, as discussed earlier, humans often pursue multiple goals at the same time. Since anxiety and depression have important functions, it is entirely reasonable for humans to divide their attention between a current task and major life concerns causing anxiety and depression.

Chapter 6

Robots and morality

There are over three million robots worldwide. Here we focus on robot-like autonomous vehicles and so-called killer robots. After that, we consider moral issues raised by robots. As Awad et al. (2018, p. 63) said, "Never in the history of humanity have we allowed a machine to autonomously decide who should live and who should die...We are going to cross that bridge any time now."

Autonomous vehicles

When do you think the first autonomous vehicle was created? It is often believed that autonomous cars have only been in existence for, say, 20 or 25 years. In fact, the answer is 1939! General Motors presented the first-ever autonomous car at the New York World's Fair in that year. It was powered by electricity and steered by radio-controlled electromagnetic fields produced by magnetised metal spikes in the road. Admittedly, this car differed from what most people regard as an autonomous vehicle, namely, one that is controlled by an AI system.

Why might it be desirable for the number of autonomous vehicles to increase dramatically? One major reason is that there are currently 1.3 million traffic deaths a year worldwide. A detailed analysis of the 33,000 fatalities per year in

DOI: 10.4324/9781003162698-6

the United States indicated that 94% were attributable to human error (Singh, 2015). The commonest cause of fatal crashes in the United States is intoxication (mostly alcohol but also illegal drugs), followed by speeding and distracted drivers. Since autonomous vehicles can easily avoid all these causes of death, it might appear we could greatly reduce traffic deaths by wholesale introduction of autonomous vehicles.

However, the above figures do *not* mean most drivers are careless as we can see by calculating the number of miles driven per fatality. In the U.K., in 2018, there is one fatality per 185 million miles driven. In the United States, there are 1.09 deaths per 100 million miles driven (Da Lio et al., 2018).

There are two implications of these figures. First, they set the bar incredibly high for manufacturers of autonomous vehicles. In order to demonstrate autonomous vehicles are safer than human drivers, such vehicles would need to have a phenomenal safety record of, say, only one fatality per 200 million miles. Second, these vehicles would have to be driven for literally billions of miles to collect sufficient data to prove their greater safety.

Matters look somewhat different if we consider data for *all* casualties (including non-fatalities) caused by human drivers. In the U.K., in 2018, there was one casualty per 2 million miles driven. In the United States, there are 2.3 million injuries per year (Da Lio et al., 2018) meaning there are 77 injuries per 100 million miles. Even if we focus on injuries as well as fatalities, autonomous vehicles would need to be driven for hundreds of millions of miles to demonstrate they were safer than human drivers.

Before discussing the safety (or otherwise) of autonomous vehicles, note that we can identify six levels of autonomy (Society of Automotive Engineers, 2016):

1 Level 0 cars have no autonomy: they are 100% driven by humans.

2 Level 1 cars have driving control shared between humans and AI (autonomous features such as cruise control or parking assistance with automated steering).

3 Level 2 cars have automated systems that execute acceleration, steering, and braking. However, a human driver monitors the environment and takes control if necessary.

4 Level 3 cars resemble Level 2 cars except that drivers can turn their attention away from driving tasks in easy driving conditions.

5 Level 4 cars are controlled by automated systems except when the driving conditions are especially difficult (e.g., severe weather).

6 Level 5 cars have total autonomy (i.e., they are driven with no direct human involvement.

Many media stories imply that numerous autonomous vehicles will soon be driving around with no input from humans (i.e., they will be at Level 5) (see Figure 6.1).

Figure 6.1 Photograph of an autonomous vehicle.

Reality is much more mundane – the great majority of so-called autonomous vehicles (e.g., those produced by Tesla, General Motors, Volvo, and Mercedes) are only Level 2 cars meaning a human driver is constantly monitoring and supervising their functioning. Autonomous vehicles will eventually become more autonomous – this is incremental autonomy. However, it will not happen any time soon because of the enormous complexities involved in producing safe truly autonomous vehicles.

Findings

You have probably heard the claim that autonomous vehicles are safer than those driven by humans. However, that claim is unjustified and wrong. For starters, the available data are extremely limited. The RAND Corporation (Kalra & Paddock, 2016) estimated autonomous vehicles would have to drive approximately 11 billion miles to draw reliable conclusions about their safety compared to human drivers. More specifically, each type of autonomous vehicle would need to drive 11 billion miles. We are literally (and metaphorically) several billion miles away from that.

The data are also limited because most figures are provided by companies designing autonomous vehicles. Since the global autonomous vehicle market is currently valued at approximately $54 billion (£41 billion), these companies have a strong financial interest in emphasising the most positive evidence regarding their cars' performance.

There are worrying straws in the wind. The first death involving an autonomous vehicle happened on the 7 May 2016. Joshua Brown, a 40-year-old man from Canton, Ohio was in a Tesla Model S electric car in autonomous mode when a tractor-trailer turned left in front of the car. The car failed to brake and Joshua was killed.

On 18 March 2018, Elaine Herzberg, a 49-year-old woman, became the first pedestrian killed by an

Figure 6.2 The self-driving Uber Volvo XC90 that collided with Elaine Herzberg.

Source: From Wikipedia article entitled 'Death of Elaine Herzberg'.

autonomous vehicle. She was pushing her bicycle across a four-lane street in Tempe, Arizona when she was killed by a Uber car in autonomous mode (see Figure 6.2). The automated system detected her six seconds before the collision. It initially classified her as an unknown object, then as a vehicle, and then as a bicycle – the car's program did not recognise her as a person because she was jaywalking.

There may have been another contributory factor in the death of Elaine Herzberg. It is alleged that Rafaela Vasquez, who had responsibility for monitoring the Uber car, was watching television on her smartphone when the car hit Ms. Herzberg.

How are most autonomous vehicles driven? Marshall (2017) rode in one of the General Motors' autonomous vehicles. She described the ride as "herky-jerky": the vehicle was "so careful that it jolted, disconcertingly, to a stop at even the whisper of a collision." This excessive cautiousness can have serious consequences. For example, we could hypothesise that many crashes involving autonomous vehicles occur because human drivers are unaware that autonomous vehicles are driven differently from human-driven cars.

Two major predictions follow from the above hypothesis. First, many accidents involving autonomous vehicles should consist of rear-end crashes due to their unusual slowness. As predicted, the percentage of crashes that are rear-end is more than twice as high with autonomous vehicles compared to human-driven vehicles (64% vs 28%) (Petrović et al., 2020).

Second, consider the attribution of blame when autonomous cars are involved in a crash. If these crashes predominantly occur because human drivers make inaccurate predictions about the movements of autonomous cars, then most of the blame lies with those human drivers. The evidence suggests that is the case (Petrović et al., 2020).

We can assess the efficiency of autonomous vehicles by looking at the disengagement rate – the average distance an autonomous vehicle is driven before the human driver takes over. This rate varies enormously depending on driving conditions and the make of autonomous vehicle. In 2018 (California Department for Motor Vehicles), the disengagement rate in California ranged from 11,154 miles per disengagement for Waymo vehicles to 1.5 miles for Mercedes-Benz vehicles! However, the distance between successive disengagements is increasing steadily, suggesting autonomous vehicles are becoming more efficient.

The frequency of accidents appears to be about twice as high with autonomous vehicles compared to human-driven ones. One important reason for the higher accident rate with autonomous vehicles is that it takes 0.83 seconds on average following disengagement for the human driver to take over control. A car driven at 50 mph covers approximately 60 feet in 0.83 seconds, which could easily lead to a fatality.

However, autonomous cars are far more likely to adhere to speed limits and to respond appropriately to traffic signs of all types. As a consequence, autonomous vehicles tend to be involved in less serious accidents than cars driven by humans. For example, Waymo autonomous vehicles in the Phoenix area between January 2019 and October 2020 were involved in 18 crashes while covering 6.1 million miles (Hawkins, 2020). However, no-one was injured or killed in any of these accidents.

How should autonomous vehicles be programmed?

There are two main ways AI systems have been programmed for autonomous vehicles (Yurtsever et al., 2020). First, there are modular systems consisting of a pipeline or sequence of separate components. These components or modules can broadly be divided into those associated with perception and those associated with decision making (Badue et al., 2021). Perception involves using information from sensors to identify the car's current location on an online map, to track moving objects, and to detect traffic signals. Decision making involves route planning, behaviour selection (e.g., lane keeping, traffic-light handling, and intersection handling), action planning taking account of passenger comfort and the car's constraints, obstacle avoidance, and control (activating the steering wheel, throttle, and brakes).

Modular systems have the advantage that driving skills are divided into easier-to-solve problems. However, an error made at one processing stage is likely to be passed on to all subsequent stages in the pipeline. The accident where Joshua Brown was killed in a Tesla electric car (discussed above) is a case in point. There was an error in the object-detection module: a white trailer was misidentified as sky, as a result of which the car failed to brake.

Second, AI systems for autonomous vehicles can be programmed via deep learning or deep reinforcement learning (see Chapter 1). The essence of this approach is that the AI system learns progressively more optimal driving strategies through experience in real-world driving and/or simulated driving. The use of deep learning leads to flexibility in driving behaviour, whereas the use of modular systems produces programming where a set of fixed rules is applied. As yet, however, this approach has scarcely been used in real-world driving situations. A disadvantage is that what has been learned mostly generalises poorly to novel situations and it is difficult to interpret the processes determining its behaviour (Yurtsever et al., 2020).

A central challenge for designers of autonomous vehicles is that successful driving requires relatively sophisticated abilities involving an understanding of complex situations and reacting appropriately. Such abilities require general intelligence but the development of artificial general intelligence has proved elusive (see Chapter 4). For example, consider "edge cases" – unexpected problems occurring under extreme operating conditions (Koopman et al., 2019). For example, suppose a car has stopped on a narrow road so it is impossible to get past it. The appropriate behaviour of those trapped on the road depends on accurately reading the situation. Sounding the horn loudly is appropriate if the driver of the stopped car is texting. However, it is not appropriate if the vehicle is a bin lorry and is exceptionally inappropriate if the driver is helping a very old and frail person in or out of their car.

The take-home message from Koopman et al.'s (2019) analysis is that autonomous vehicles need to be programmed to respond appropriately to novel situations. Even the most successful of autonomous vehicles fall short of fulfilling that criterion.

Conclusions

It is arguable that the battle between human-driven and autonomous cars is a draw. Human-driven cars have fewer accidents per million miles driven but the accidents are more likely to produce injuries and/or fatalities than those of autonomous cars. If we peer into the future, it seems highly probable that autonomous cars will become safer than human-driven ones irrespective of the criteria used to assess safety.

However, there are at least two obstacles to the wide-spread use of autonomous cars even if they are shown to be safer than human-driven ones. First, there is considerable public resistance to the notion that our roads should be populated by driverless cars. Second, while autonomous cars may prove to be very successful in relatively straight-forward driving conditions, their lack of artificial general intelligence makes their use in complex situations decidedly problematical.

Ethical issues

In spite of the many obstacles to the introduction of truly autonomous vehicles, numerous politicians, AI experts, psychologists, and philosophers and are already debating how autonomous vehicles should be programmed ethically. The moral issues are especially crucial when loss of life is inevitable (e.g., deciding to save the car passengers or pedestrians).

Superficially, it may seem simple to program autonomous vehicles to make appropriate moral decisions. As Ernest Hemingway said, "What is moral is what you feel good after and what is immoral is what you feel bad after." However, this greatly de-emphasises individual differences in belief systems. Within Western cultures, for example, liberals disagree strongly with conservatives on many moral issues (e.g., abortion and gay marriage).

At the risk of over-simplification, we can identify two major contrasting approaches to moral decision making. According to one approach, we should focus on the *consequences* of our actions. This philosophical approach (utilitarianism) was supported by British philosophers such as Jeremy Bentham (1748–1832). In 1789, he famously summarised the essence of utilitarianism as involving, "the greatest good for the greatest number."

Problems with utilitarianism arise if we consider the footbridge dilemma (Greene et al., 2004). A runaway trolley (tram) is heading straight for five tied-up individuals. You are standing on a footbridge above the trolley and next to you is a fat stranger. You must decide whether to push him off the bridge. If you do, it will cause his death. However, it will save the lives of the five tied-up individuals because his body will prevent the trolley running them over. What would you do?

We guess you (like 90% of people) decided *not* to push the fat man off the bridge. Here, the popular decision involves the loss of five lives rather than only one, and so is *not* based on utilitarianism. Instead, it involves deontology (Greek for "study of duty"), which was popularised by the German philosopher, Immanuel Kant. According to this approach, actions can be right or wrong *without* taking their consequences into account. We should take personal responsibility for our actions and the *intentions* behind our actions are very important. Thus, most people believe that, "Thou shalt not kill," is an important moral principle and that principle determines their decision with the footbridge dilemma.

Important findings on moral issues raised by autonomous vehicles were reported by Bonnefon et al. (2016). When people were asked whether it would be preferable for autonomous vehicles to be programmed to sacrifice one passenger rather than kill ten pedestrians, 76% argued it would be more moral to sacrifice the one passenger.

So far, so good – the great majority supported the utilitarian approach. In addition, 85% of people argued autonomous vehicles should be programmed to minimise loss of life.

However, most people were unenthusiastic about buying an autonomous vehicle programmed to sacrifice them and a family member to save ten or 20 pedestrians. Only 19% would buy such a car compared to 50% who would buy an autonomous car programmed to sacrifice the pedestrians while saving them and a family member. This produces a real dilemma. As Bonnefon et al. pointed out, "Although people … agree that everyone would be better off if [driverless cars] were utilitarian (in the sense of minimising casualties), these same people have a personal incentive to ride in [driverless cars] that will protect them at all costs" (p. 1575).

The applicability of the trolley problem to real-world driving situations is arguable: the outcomes of the possible decision choices are known with certainty in the trolley problem but are much less clear-cut when considering many road-driving conditions. Suppose a driverless car is programmed to mount the pavement where pedestrians are walking if that prevents a serious car crash. The harm that would be caused depends on numerous factors (e.g., whether the pedestrians are looking at the car; the pedestrians' mobility).

There are several other more specific moral dilemmas. For example, should autonomous vehicles be programmed to attach more value to the lives of young children than older adults? Should autonomous vehicles prefer to save humans over animals, females over males, or higher-status individuals over lower-status ones? Intriguingly, the answers to these questions are systematically influenced by cultural factors, thus undermining the notion of universal moral laws.

Awad et al. (2018) explored moral issues posed by autonomous vehicles by obtaining 40 million moral decisions from people in over 200 countries. They found nations can be divided into three groups. The first group (Western cluster) consists of North American and many European countries where Christianity has historically been dominant. The second group (Eastern cluster) includes countries such as Japan, Pakistan, Taiwan, and Indonesia where Confucian or Islamic beliefs are strong. The third group (Southern cluster) consists of the Latin American countries of Central and South America, plus France and its former colonies.

The most dramatic findings related to countries in the Eastern and Southern clusters. The preference for sparing younger rather than older people was much stronger among individuals in the Southern cluster than those in the Eastern cluster. This is predictable given the strong tradition of respecting and caring for the elderly in most Eastern countries. Those in the Southern cluster also had the strongest preference for sparing higher-status individuals over lower-status ones, with those in the Eastern cluster showing the weakest preference.

How should lawmakers proceed? First, they must decide whether the moral programming of autonomous vehicles should be *common* throughout a given society or determined by the *individual* vehicle owner. The former approach is demonstrably superior if based on the utilitarian approach of minimising casualties and deaths because allowing selfish interests to have paramount importance would increase total traffic deaths (Gogoll & Müller, 2017).

Second, this common moral programming will be most acceptable if it reflects majority moral beliefs within any given culture. That means that common moral programming will necessarily vary from one culture to another.

Warfare: autonomous weapons systems and "killer robots"

In the movie *Terminator 2*, Skynet is an artificial neural network that controls the nuclear arsenal to perfection. However, when it becomes self-aware, its human operators are frightened and try to pull the plug on it. Skynet retaliates by instigating a nuclear war to destroy billions of humans. That movie (and numerous others) plus numerous violent video games have created the impression that robots and other autonomous weapons systems will play a central role in future wars.

However, when considering the use of AI systems and robots in warfare, we are not only thinking about future hypothetical situations. For example, in 2008, there were between 4,000 and 6,000 ground robots in Iraq, mostly used to detonate roadside improvised explosive devices. However, a few (e.g., SWORDS TALON robots) were equipped with lethal machine guns or anti-tank rocket launchers (see Figure 6.3). Since then, the MQ-9 Reaper unmanned aerial vehicle has been developed. It uses a thermographic camera to identify targets and can fire laser-guided bombs; its functioning is only partially controlled by humans. Such devices have been described as "killer robots."

Even though the media have focused on the destructive capabilities of killer robots, AI can be used in warfare in many other ways. Horowitz (2019) compared AI to electricity because it provides the basis for numerous applications. He divided its military applications into three types: (1) allowing machines to act without human supervision, (2) processing and interpreting large amounts of data, and (3) aiding the command and control of war.

Using robots in warfare has several potential advantages. First, they can be very efficient – we might need relatively few humans to supervise and monitor the use of thousands of autonomous weapons. This could minimise the loss of human life. Second, and counterintuitively, robots can potentially be *more* ethical than humans because they never become angry or seek revenge. Third, robots can be programmed to conform to the human-made laws governing warfare.

Figure 6.3 Photograph of Foster-Miller SWORDS TALON.

Source: From Wikipedia article entitled "Foster-Miller TALON"

198 Robots and morality

There are also several potential disadvantages associated with using robots in warfare. First, their use could trigger a global arms race with little effective control over the development and deployment of killer robots. Second, autonomous weapon systems are becoming increasingly complex: the probability of accidents occurring typically increases as system complexity increases.

Third, many autonomous weapon systems are so complicated humans cannot calculate precisely what will happen when they are deployed. A key element of waging war is to have a *single* commander in overall charge. However, no human is really in charge if they do not understand how an autonomous weapon system works. The answer is explainable AI with autonomous weapon systems providing transparent accounts of their proposed decisions to ensure they are consistent with human decision making. However, this is often hard to achieve.

Fourth, hacking is potentially a huge problem. For example, the training data used in the programming of a killer robot or drone could be hacked by adding fake information to those data (Shah, 2019). Imagine a war where one side has developed AI systems discriminating very accurately between enemy armed forces and civilians (this would be a long way in the future!). Say 100,000 drones have been programmed to kill the enemy's soldiers but not its civilians. A hacker could potentially design a virus that would *reverse* the programming so the drones killed only civilians. This could provide a massive propaganda coup for the enemy.

Moral issues

Moral issues with respect to the use of killer robots (and other lethal AI systems) in warfare are especially important because of the large-scale loss of life they can cause. Accordingly, we will consider such moral issues here, leaving a more general discussion of AI systems and moral accountability for later.

Malle et al. (2019) reported relevant evidence based on a moral dilemma occurring within a military context. A decision has to be made whether to launch a missile strike on a terrorist compound even though it would risk a child's life or to cancel the strike to protect the child but thereby risk a terrorist attack. This decision is made by an AI system, an autonomous drone, or a human drone pilot. People were asked to make moral judgements about the decisions made by each of these entities taking account of the pilots' superiors, who have recommended that the missile strike should be launched.

What did Malle et al. (2019) find? First, 72% of people ascribed wrongness to an AI system but only 51% did the same for an autonomous drone. The lower figure for the autonomous drone probably reflects the common notion that a drone is basically a passive metal device.

Second, comparable levels of blame were attached overall to all three entities. However, the human pilot was blamed less than the AI system or the autonomous drone when the missile strike was carried out but more when it was cancelled. Why was this? It was expected that only the human pilot would be responsive to the command structure (i.e., the superiors' recommendation to carry out the strike).

We have seen that many people are willing to attach blame to killer robots for their lethal actions in war-like conditions. This raises the more general issue of working out moral responsibility when humans and robots are both potentially blameworthy. This issue was raised by Sharkey (2012, p. 791), who argued that using, "a weapon without a clear chain of accountability is not a moral option."

There is a major problem here because it is typically difficult to assess accountability. The optimal solution would be to use killer robots only where it is possible for humans to make crucial life-and-death decisions and to accept full responsibility for those decisions.

However, killer robots and other autonomous weapon systems are becoming increasingly complicated as their ability to learn and to plan increases. As a consequence, humans often cannot predict accurately what killer robots will do in complex, rapidly changing, battle conditions.

Roff and Danks (2018) considered what humans engaged in military conflicts should do given that the actions of killer robots are often unpredictable. They argued that war-fighters could, in principle, trust autonomous weapon systems if they could develop an understanding of *why* these systems behave as they do. For example, war-fighters could receive extensive training with autonomous weapon systems under conditions where there is no risk to human life.

Conclusions

It is indisputable that killer robots and drones can be very effective weapons. There could potentially be a great reduction in the loss of life by using these AI systems. At present, however, the lack of transparency of many killer robots and the relative ease with which their programming can be hacked pose substantial (and as yet unresolved) moral issues.

Realpolitik also raises complex issues. The use of killer robots would perhaps be morally acceptable if all countries abided by international laws concerning the conduct of wars. However, the history of human conflicts indicates a high probability that certain countries would simply ignore those laws. That would make it much harder for countries that wanted to retain moral values to fight wars successfully.

Robots

Half the robots in industrial settings are used in car production (see Figure 6.4). The advantages of using robots to

Figure 6.4 Robots involved in car production.

produce cars are discussed in Chapter 2. Here, we consider potential disadvantages:

1 Industrial robots are often expensive: the typical cost per robot varies between £35,000 and £55,000.

2 There is increasing demand for customisation (providing customers with their preferred options). However, most robots function inflexibly and so are less well equipped than human workers to deal with customisation. As a result, the Mercedes factory in Sidelfingen, Germany, recently replaced some of its robots with humans to increase flexibility.

3 Robots lack intelligence and emotions and so cannot respond appropriately in unexpected situations.

4 The increased use of robots in car production has often caused problems by leading to redundancies and unemployment among human car workers.

5 Even though the use of robots has reduced injuries and deaths to human car workers, robots have caused

several human deaths. For example, on 25 January 1979, Robert Williams, a 24-year-old American worker, was killed by the arm of a 1-ton robot at a Ford plant in Flat Rock, Michigan. Since then, there have been approximately 40 robot-related deaths in industrial settings in the United States. However, it is eight times more dangerous for Americans to work in a bar than in manufacturing so we must not exaggerate the risks.

Why are humans killed or injured by robots in industrial settings? In many cases, humans enter a safety cage containing a robot without fully appreciating the potential risks (e.g., many robots move very quickly and silently). In other cases, robots free to move around have sensors to detect human movement and are programmed to stop if a human comes very close. However, these sensors (or other fail-safes) sometimes fail to respond appropriately.

How should we treat robots?

There are several well-documented cases where humans have maltreated robots. For example, Europe's first sex-robot brothel opened a few years ago in Barcelona. On its website, the brothel offers, "totally realistic dolls both in their movements and in their 'feel,' that will allow you to fulfil all your fantasies without limits." A sex robot called Samantha, who can talk and responds to touch, was displayed at a technology fair in Austria. Men visiting the fair left Samantha "heavily soiled," and her creator, Sergi Santos, claimed that these men treated Samantha "like barbarians."

Unsurprisingly, our reactions to human-like robots differ considerably from those to robots not resembling humans. We might imagine our responses to robots would become steadily more positive the more human-like they appear. Interestingly, that is *not* the case.

Mori (1970) proposed a more complex relationship between human-likeness and our responses in his uncanny valley hypothesis. According to this hypothesis, our responses go through three stages:

1 Our reactions are more positive to vaguely human-like robots than those very different to humans (e.g., industrial robots).
2 When we move from vaguely human-like robots to ones closely resembling humans (e.g., zombies and animated characters), our reactions go from positive to strongly negative. This is known as the "uncanny valley": we have uncanny or eerie feelings and these feelings are in a "valley" because they are far more negative than those we experience with robots less like humans. Consider Gollum in *Lord of the Rings*. Gollum was a computer-generated imagery animation constructed around the facial features, voice, and acting style of the actor Andy Serkis. Thus, Gollum as he appears on screen is a complex amalgam of robot and human, and we perceive him as scary and unpleasant (see Figure 6.5).
3 The third stage consists of a rapid increase in the positivity of reactions to genuine human beings compared to robots looking very similar to humans.

Much research strongly supports Mori's (1970) hypothesis. Why does the "uncanny valley" exist? Many different hypotheses have been proposed (Mathur et al., 2020). One is that robots in the uncanny valley are dislikeable because they increase our awareness of our own mortality. Another hypothesis is that they trigger dehumanisation responses similar to those directed at human groups subject to prejudice.

Figure 6.5 Photograph of Gollum.

However, the "category confusion" hypothesis is perhaps the most popular: it assumes we most dislike robots especially hard to categorise as "human" or "non-human." Mathur et al. (2020) reported no support for this hypothesis using images of real robot and human faces. The most disliked faces were consistently perceived as non-human or mechanical and so did not exhibit category confusion. Moreover, the maximally ambiguous faces were not disliked.

Appel et al. (2020) hypothesised that human-like robots create a sense of eeriness to the extent they are perceived as possessing psychological features typically associated exclusively with humans. As predicted, robots that experienced emotions or that possessed agency (e.g., planning ahead and self-control) were perceived as significantly more eerie than those lacking those qualities.

How should robots be programmed?

Could we reduce the number of deaths and injuries caused by robots by programming them differently? Before addressing that question, we consider a thought experiment suggested by Bostrum (2003). He argued there are potential dangers even when robots pursue apparently desirable goals. Imagine a robot given the goal of manufacturing as many paperclips as possible. Such a system might achieve its goal by turning everything on earth (including humans) into paperclips.

The take-home message from Bostrum's (2003) thought experiment is as follows. Robots are typically programmed to achieve a single main goal (e.g., producing car components). However, to ensure achieving this main goal, they may well pursue additional destructive sub-goals. Examples of possible sub-goals are as follows: (i) destroying any environmental obstacles reducing their ability to produce car components and (ii) self-preservation – being strongly resistant to any attempts by human beings to switch them off.

This thought experiment suggests we need to program robots to adhere to social and moral norms (e.g., caring for others' well-being and being trustworthy). Robots' ability to differentiate between right and wrong could be increased by training them on moral stories. In principle, this could allow robots to become encultured (adopting the moral values of a given culture). As yet, little progress in that direction has been made.

Does AI have moral agency?

There has been a steady increase in the number of people killed by robots or other AI-systems. In this chapter, for example, we mentioned two people (Joshua Brown and Elaine and Elaine Herzberg) killed in accidents associated with autonomous vehicles and one person (Robert Williams) killed by a robot in a factory accident. Who (or what) has moral responsibility for these and other AI-based tragedies? Is it the AI system itself, is it the designers of the AI system, or are both partially responsible?

One might imagine that very few people would believe that robots and other AI systems have any moral responsibility for their behaviour. However, the evidence indicates otherwise. Consider a study by Shank and DeSanti (2018). They started by identifying several real-life moral violations involving AI systems (e.g., a bot tweeting racial slurs and AI incorrectly predicting the chances of convicts re-offending based on race). Here, is a moral violation involving children's videos:

> YouTube Kids is a new mobile device app that Google has marketed as safe for preschoolers. Children who are too young to spell or type can verbally search YouTube Kids. Then the app suggests and plays videos. YouTube Kids uses an algorithm to determine which videos are family-friendly. Also, the suggested videos are partially based on the user's previously watched videos. The outcome is that the app showed a range of videos and advertisements, some of which were violent or obscene. (p. 409)

The AI system was perceived as somewhat responsible for the violations. It was also perceived as having some awareness of the potential for these violations to occur and intending the negative outcomes to occur. Those individuals believing the AI had some mind (e.g., free will and mind of its own) attributed more intentionality and moral wrongness to it.

Shank et al. (2019a) explored the same moral violations in more detail. The violations resulted from individual decisions (by AI or a human) or there was joint decision making (an AI monitored by a human or a human receiving recommendations from an AI). A similar low level of moral fault was ascribed to AI in all conditions. Humans were consistently faulted more than AI, but to a lesser extent when the human was not directly involved when the decision was made.

There is a potential issue when interpreting findings such as those just discussed. Participants in an experiment are often responsive to what Orne (1962) called the "demand characteristics" of the situation: these are the cues used by participants to work out what the experiment is about. Suppose you were a participant in one of the above studies. You are asked whether AI has a mind of its own, intentions, free will, desires, and beliefs. It seems unlikely the experimenter would ask all these questions if they expected you to respond "not at all" to all of them.

A different approach probably reducing the impact of demand characteristics was adopted by Shank et al. (2019b). Participants reported a personal interaction with an AI in which they perceived it to have a mind (an important prerequisite for having moral agency). They were not explicitly asked about their emotional reactions. However, 55% spontaneously reported emotions such as surprise, amazement, happiness, and amusement when interacting with an AI apparently having a mind. Here, is a sample reaction by a 24-year-old man:

> Once I wanted to test Siri on personal romantic relationships (see Figure 6.6). I asked a first question which was "Do you have a girlfriend Siri?" It gave me an answer that was totally shocking to me and it seemed to me to be thinking on its own entirely, be in full control of its own destiny, have its free will and decide its own outcome. I was literally surprised by the response and it was not cliché as other AI responses. So the response it gave me was: "Why? So we can get ice cream together, and listen to music, and travel across galaxies, only to have it end in slammed doors,

Figure 6.6 Photograph of Siri from Shutterstock.

heartbreak and loneliness? Sure, where do I sign up?"
This was the moment I felt like Siri was in full control
of his own actions and resources. (p. 260)

Why is AI perceived as morally responsible?

There are several reasons why many experts (and non-experts) argue AI has (or can have) moral responsibility.
We will initially focus mostly on factors influencing our
judgements concerning human moral responsibility. After
that, we consider moral responsibility in robots and other
AI systems in the light of those factors.

First, an individual's moral responsibility depends on
whether they are perceived as exercising free will, self-determination or autonomy (see Figure 6.7) (Bigman et al.,
2019). If the situation is so constraining that an individual
cannot choose what to do, they are perceived as having
less moral responsibility. As a result, individuals behaving
somewhat unpredictably and as if they have freely chosen
their behaviour are perceived as having moral responsibility.

Figure 6.7 Man using free will to choose between two possible roads.

Much research supports the above arguments. Shariff et al. (2014) found that participants' beliefs in free will were reduced by exposing them to neuroscience research implying that human behaviour is caused mechanistically. This exposure reduced the perceived blameworthiness of criminals (i.e., reduced responsibility). Baumeister et al. (2009) found individuals not believing in free will behaved less responsibly (i.e., more aggressive behaviour and less helpful behaviour) than those believing in free will.

Second, our perceptions of someone else's responsibility for their actions depends on our assessment of that person's personal agency (independent capacity to determine one's own actions) (Weiner, 1995). Suppose a student produces a very poor essay. If we attribute their poor performance to a controllable cause (e.g., effort), we hold them responsible for their behaviour. If, however, we attribute their performance to a non-controllable cause (e.g., lack of ability), we do not hold them responsible. Weiner (1995) discussed much empirical support for his viewpoint.

Third, there is mental capacity. Young children clearly behave intentionally and somewhat unpredictably, and their behaviour often reflects the exercise of free will. However, children are perceived as having less moral responsibility than adults because they lack full mental capacity. As a result, the age of criminal responsibility in most countries is at least 12.

Fourth, Malle et al. (2014) proposed a theory of blame or moral responsibility encompassing the factors considered so far. One route to blame is as follows: an event is perceived as a norm violation caused intentionally by an agent (e.g., person) for unjustifiable reasons. There is also a second route: a norm-violation event is caused unintentionally by an agent; this agent should have prevented the event and could have prevented it (i.e., they had the capacity).

Anthropomorphism (the tendency to assign human characteristics to non-human species and robots; see Chapter 7) is of key importance to understanding of the above findings (e.g., those of Shank & DeSanti, 2018). Anthropomorphism is strongly determined by similarities of behaviour between objects or robots and humans. This is unsurprising given that our judgements of others' intentionality, thoughts and moral responsibility are all mostly based on observation of their behaviour.

Anthropomorphism extends well beyond robots to include even simple objects. Consider the following experiment (Michotte, 1946/1963). Observers see square A move towards square B; when it gets close to square B, square B moves off away from square A. Many observers interpret this event as showing that square A intends to catch square B, and square B intends to escape from square A.

The above findings are striking because we would not normally expect squares to have intentions. Formanowicz et al. (2018) clarified these findings. When the key object appeared to exhibit agency (striving to achieve a goal) it was perceived as more human-like than when not exhibiting agency. Thus, intentionality is a key feature of human behaviour.

In one study (Waytz et al., 2014), participants drove an autonomous car in a simulator. When this car had anthropomorphic features (name, gender, and voice), they had more trust that its performance would be competent than when it lacked those features.

Earlier we discussed the notion (Weiner, 1995) that we hold individuals more responsible for their behaviour when that behaviour is perceived as controllable. Van der Woerdt and Haselager (2019) presented people with short videos where a robot failed a task through lack of effort (controllable) or lack of ability (uncontrollable). For example, one task required the robot to pick up a toy giraffe and put in a box. The robot failed this task either by grasping it properly but then throwing it away (lack of effort) or by dropping the toy giraffe en route (lack of ability). As predicted, perceived agency and responsibility (e.g., attributing blame) were greater when the robot showed deficient effort.

In sum, it is often argued that AI systems can have some moral responsibility, especially if they appear to exercise free will, personal agency, behave unpredictably, and are human–like. Recent advances in AI allow robots to learn and behave much less predictably than was previously the case. These advances will increase the tendency to perceive robots as possessing free will and ascribing them moral responsibility (Bigman et al., 2019). An increased tendency to regard robots as having moral responsibility is also likely to follow from the increasingly human–like features of today's robots compared to those produced a few years ago.

AI does not have moral responsibility

Those believing robots possess moral responsibility make the overarching assumption that there are major *similarities* between robots and humans which are reflected in their behaviour. However, robots and humans can behave identically even though the processes underlying that behaviour are entirely different. For example, consider Searle's Chinese Room argument (see Chapter 4). Someone knowing no Chinese can behave in ways apparently indicating an excellent knowledge of that language if armed with the appropriate instruction book.

Those believing that robots lack moral responsibility argue that robots and other AI systems are qualitatively different from humans. They have put forward several arguments. First, human moral reasoning and behaviour depend on emotions as well as rational thinking and deliberation. For example, moral behaviour in humans owes much to empathy (our ability to understand other people's feelings and beliefs). It seems far-fetched to claim that robots possess empathy (or any other emotions).

Second, understanding human morality extends well beyond simply focusing on empathy. Koleva et al. (2012) identified five broad areas of human moral concerns: (1) harm/care, (2) fairness/reciprocity, (3) ingroup/loyalty, (4) authority/respect, and (5) purity/sanctity. There is vanishingly little evidence that robots or AI systems exhibit any of these moral concerns.

Third, there is a very close relationship between morality and an individual's goals and motives. When we decide whether someone has behaved morally or immorally, we start by identifying their goals and motives. Robots often act *as if* pursuing their own goals. However, they are merely carrying out the goals of the humans who programmed them. Thus, they are essentially tools (albeit often very complex ones), and in no way do they determine their own goals and values. For example, consider Bostrum's hypothetical robot that destroyed the world while pursuing the goal of producing as many paperclips as possible – that goal was determined by its programmers.

Fourth, robots differ fundamentally from humans, which makes it inappropriate to regard them as moral agents. Characteristics unique to humans (and thus *not* shared by robots and other forms of AI) include: "Curiosity, imagination, intuition, emotions, passion, desires, pleasure, aesthetics, joy, purpose, objectives, goals, values, morality, experience, wisdom, judgement, and even humour" (Braga & Logan, 2017, p. 1).

We would add consciousness to the above list – we often engage in an internal debate with ourselves before making decisions having moral implications. Indeed, such conscious processing is of the essence of morality in spite of arguments to the contrary,

Fifth, "A central feature of the human experience as moral agents is that people frequently feel poised between acting selfishly and acting altruistically" Wallach & Allen, 2009, pp. 61–62). A key reason why children learn to avoid behaving selfishly is because of the threat of punishment if they fail to adhere to moral rules of behaviour. In contrast, it is impossible to punish robots when we disapprove of their behaviour (Wallach & Allen 2009).

In sum, similarities of behaviour between robots and humans can mislead us into believing that robots possess at least some moral responsibility. In fact, there are numerous crucially important differences between robots and humans. The existence of these differences means it would be very unwise to attribute moral responsibility to robots and other AI systems.

Can we produce moral agents?

There is a reasonable consensus that it has not so far proved possible to construct AI systems that should be regarded as moral agents. What can be done in future to achieve that desirable goal? A starting point is to establish a method for assessing the ethical standards of AI systems. Allen et al.

(2000) proposed the interesting idea of developing a moral Turing test. As in the standard Turing test, human interrogators chat with humans and with AI systems and attempt to decide whether any given conversation is with a human or an AI system. However the conversation is restricted to discussions about morality. If the human interrogators' performance is at (or close to) chance performance, the AI system is regarded as a moral agent.

There are various objections to the moral Turing test. For example, the interrogators might be able to distinguish between AI systems and humans because the former express superior moral values (e.g., more opposed to lying and cheating) (Allen et al., 2000). However, AI systems lack understanding of language (see Chapters 4 and 7). Accordingly, while their responses may indicate a moral perspective, this is merely imitating morality (Puri, 2020). A final objection is that there can be a large gap between expressed views and behaviour. For example, humans who consistently break moral rules may nevertheless claim deceptively to adhere to those rules when questioned about them.

A preferable way of assessing AI's moral status was proposed by Arnold and Scheutz (2016). They argued that we need to consider not only *what* behaviour is produced by an AI system but also *why* that behaviour is produced. This goal can be achieved by verification in which the underlying processes that jointly determine an AI system's responses are identified. This approach makes much sense. However, it is difficult to implement in practice. As we saw earlier, most AI systems (especially those based on deep learning neural networks) are so complex that it is extremely difficult to work out precisely why they have behaved in a given way.

Šabanović et al. (2014) focused on the issue of how we could create robots that are moral agents. They argued this can be done by designing robots responsive to the cultural values prevalent in any given society. However, that approach has the disadvantage that it does not take account of large differences in cultural values across cultures. A superior approach would be to design robots that are adaptable in the sense that they can adjust their behaviour to make it culturally appropriate within any given society.

There is controversy concerning the feasibility of designing AI systems that are moral agents. One reason for pessimism is that there is no consensus on most moral and ethical issues (van Wynsberghe & Robbins, 2019). More importantly, the development of morality in humans involves a complex combination of cognition, emotion, and motivation. At the cognitive level, a fully functioning AI moral agent would need to possess most of the features required of artificial general intelligence. However, it has not so far proved possible to develop an AI system possessing artificial general intelligence (see Chapter 4). In addition, as discussed earlier, AI systems also lack the relevant emotional and motivational characteristics associated with morality.

Chapter 7

And the winner is?

In this book, we have discussed the strengths and limitations of AI systems (including robots) and humans. In this synoptic chapter, the key issues are summarised with the final goal being to decide who has won this gruelling contest.

AI systems: Strengths

AI systems are far better than humans at processing information incredibly fast (e.g., solving complex mathematical problems). They also outperform human experts on numerous complex tasks (e.g., chess; Go, and poker).

So far as practical relevance and importance are concerned, AI systems can diagnose many diseases from medical images more accurately than medical experts. In addition, these diagnoses are often made faster by AI systems. For example, a company called Arterys found its AI system could diagnose heart problems from cardiac MR (magnetic resonance) images in 15 seconds. In contrast, human experts often took 30 minutes to make their diagnosis.

Speed is often extremely important. For example, recent AI systems are very good at detecting camouflaged objects

DOI: 10.4324/9781003162698-7

(Fan et al., 2020). If used in military situations, they would probably detect camouflaged enemy personnel and tanks faster than humans.

AI systems also have the advantage of learning complex skills in much less time than humans. In 2017, AlphaZero (a very sophisticated AI system) achieved superhuman performance at three complex games (Go, chess, and shogi: a Japanese form of chess) (see Chapter 2). Incredibly, AlphaZero reached this level of performance in just over a day, although admittedly it managed to squeeze in over 20 million training games on each game in that time. It takes years to train a human doctor to make consistently accurate diagnoses from medical images. Alternatively, a hospital could simply buy an AI system matching that doctor's diagnostic performance.

Another advantage of AI systems is that their performance level remains consistently high even when working 24 hours a day. In contrast, fatigue and loss of concentration would inevitably impair the performance of medical experts after several hours staring at medical images.

AI systems have a single-minded approach when confronted by a problem. Unlike humans, they are not impaired by emotion, by the motivation to enhance their self-esteem, or by their need for belongingness within social groups. In other words, the processing capacity of AI is solely devoted to task-relevant processing whereas humans often pursue multiple goals at the same time.

AI has made considerable progress in language skills, which are of direct relevance to intelligence. We saw in Chapter 2 that an AI system (IBM's Watson) beat outstanding human contestants on the quiz show *Jeopardy!* Success on this show apparently requires understanding of the questions coupled with a very rapid ability to access relevant knowledge. AI systems have also exhibited increasingly accurate performance on speech-recognition tasks, where their error rates approach those of human expert transcribers (see Chapter 2).

AI models have also displayed excellent performance on tests of text comprehension (see Chapter 2). For example, several AI language models including BERT (Bi-directional Encoder Representation from Transformers) and models related to BERT have achieved above-human levels of performance on the General Language Understanding Evaluation (GLUE) test. (Yang et al., 2019). In addition, AI in the form of neural machine translation has recently achieved human-level performance in translating texts from one language to another (Fische & Läubli, 2020).

Another general strength of AI is a "ratchet effect": the performance of AI on almost every task has *improved* over time. In addition, this enhanced performance can typically be made readily available all over the world. For example, anyone with £100 available can purchase a chess-playing AI system capable of beating the human world champion.

Finally, AI's progress over the past decade is mostly due to the rapid proliferation of deep neural networks. These networks have produced outstanding feats of unsupervised learning (e.g., playing complex games like chess and Go better than any human and diagnosis from medical images). However, this learning typically transfers poorly to other, similar tasks. Computer systems can store huge amounts of information relating to learning on previous tasks. That information (ranging from the highly specific to the very general) can then be used to accelerate learning on subsequent tasks via meta-learning. Vanschoren (2018) discussed several examples of AI systems exhibiting substantial meta-learning.

Artificial intelligence: limitations

Our discussion of AI's limitations will focus mostly on areas where it is generally believed AI has made the greatest progress. The overarching theme is that AI's achievements are much narrower and more easily subject to disruption than generally supposed.

Limitations: classifying images

Deep neural networks classifying visual inputs have achieved notable successes (e.g., accurately diagnosing diseases from medical images (see Chapter 2). However, many studies fail to reflect actual clinical practice because additional clinical information is not provided. Furthermore, the medical images used in testing often overlap substantially with the training images, which artificially exaggerates AI's effectiveness. For example, Navarrete-Dechent et al. (2018) found an AI system performed well in dermatological diagnosis when tested on training images (over 80% accuracy) but achieved only 29% accuracy on new images.

Finlayson et al. (2019) focused on research where small, imperceptible changes were made to medical images (adversarial attacks). In one case, deep neural networks correctly classified the original image of a mole as benign with greater than 99% confidence. However, an adversarial attack caused these neural networks to have 100% confidence the mole was malignant!

Deep neural networks also perform well when classifying or categorising images of everyday objects (see Chapter 2). However, their classification performance can readily be impaired. Suppose, a network is trained to classify birds based on a collection of bird images. If the network is subsequently trained to recognise additional bird species or is given a different task (e.g., tree recognition), its performance plummets (Kemker et al., 2018).

Hendrycks et al. (2021) found neural networks were 99% sure an image of a ligature was a jellyfish, a painting was a goldfish, garlic bread was a hotdog and a highway or motorway was a dam (see Figure 7.1). Amusingly, in 2017, the Metropolitan Police found an AI system searching

Ligature   Jellyfish (99%) Painting   Goldfish (99%)

Highway   Dam (99%) Garlic Bread   Hotdog (99%)

Figure 7.1 Incorrect object misclassifications with 99% confidence by an AI system.

Source: From Hendrycks et al. (2021).

through the phones of suspected child molesters often misidentified images of sand dunes as pornographic!

An Achilles heel of deep neural networks is that they are brittle. Why are they so brittle? Note that the comparable levels of classification accuracy often achieved by humans and deep neural networks are misleading. Image classification and visual perception generally can involve two very different kinds of processing (humans use both but neural networks rely primarily on the former; Lamme, 2018):

1 Bottom-up or feedforward processing starts with basic image elements (e.g., edges and features). Shapes are then processed, eventually leading to increasingly detailed and elaborate image representations.
2 Bottom-up processing is followed by top-down or recurrent processing based on our knowledge of objects and the world. This allows us to form expectations about a viewed object and facilitates its identification.

Why does it matter that deep neural networks typically rely almost entirely on data-driven processing? Suppose a deep neural network is trained to classify dogs and cats, and that dogs are always shown looking to the left whereas cats are always shown looking to the right. The network would be very error-prone if subsequently tested on images of dogs and cats not looking in the same direction as during training. Thus, part of what deep neural networks learn is *irrelevant* information (e.g., direction of looking); this leads to poor generalisation to new images. More generally, AI systems are often *over-sensitive* to the specific information provided in training.

The processing of deep neural networks classifying images is often limited primarily to simple visual features. For example, a deep neural network detecting human faces was presented with an image of Kim Kardashian with her mouth and one of her eyes transposed (see Figure 7.2) (Bourdakos, 2017). It was insensitive to the arrangement of facial features, and so was more confident this grotesque image was a face than it was when presented with an ordinary image of Kim Kardashian!

AI systems do not have *concepts*. A deep neural network may successfully identify dogs, but it has no idea why dogs have four legs and two ears and eyes, what sounds dogs

Figure 7.2 A deep neural network was 88% confident that an ordinary image of Kim Kardashian was a human face but 90% that a distorted image was a human face.

Source: From Bourdakos (2017).

make, or that dogs like being taken for walks. The susceptibility of deep neural networks to misclassify objects is due partly to this lack of rich contextual information.

Limitations: task specificity

There are several differences between tasks typically performed very well by AI systems and those performed poorly:

1 AI systems are generally most successful on tasks with definite rules (e.g., games such as chess, Go, and shogi). In contrast, AI systems typically perform relatively

poorly when there are no definite rules (e.g., language tasks and most real-world problem solving.

2 The successful responses of deep neural networks are associated with positive reinforcement or reward. This works best when it is easy to determine whether a network's performance is successful (e.g., games having a winner and a loser). In real life, success and failure are often less clear-cut. Is an expensive modern painting a great work of art or a joke?

3 Nearly all tasks on which AI systems excel are narrow in scope (e.g., diagnosing a specific disease from medical images). In contrast, AI systems typically perform worse than six-year-olds on general IQ tests, and do especially poorly on perceptual and motor tasks (see Chapter 4).

Language limitations: general issues

Suppose a natural language processing model eventually achieves human-like levels of performance across numerous language tasks. Some AI experts have argued that would imply that AI systems understood language as humans do but we strongly disagree. Consider Searle's (1980) Chinese Room argument (also discussed in Chapter 4). An English speaker knowing no Chinese is locked in a room containing numerous Chinese symbols plus an instruction book for manipulating these symbols. People outside the room send in Chinese symbols in the form of questions. The man sends out Chinese symbols providing correct answers by following the instructions of a computer program.

According to Searle (1980), the man's behaviour suggests he understands Chinese even though he does not, just as computers can respond to questions without understanding their meaning. Searle (2010) developed his argument by distinguishing between *simulation* and *duplication*: a computer simulation of understanding language should not be confused with duplicating genuine language understanding.

Cole (2020) disagreed with Searle. According to him, if we attribute language understanding to humans based on their behaviour, should we not do the same when computer programs exhibit similar behaviour or output? Compelling evidence that behavioural evidence can be very misleading is available in the achievements of Clever Hans (see Figure 7.3). Over 100 years ago, this horse apparently showed he could count by tapping his hoof the correct number of times when asked mathematical questions (e.g., "If the eighth day of the month comes on a Tuesday, what is the date of the following Friday?") by his owner and teacher Wilhelm von Osten. Clever Hans could also spell out the name of the artist who had produced any given painting (Samhita & Gross, 2013).

When the psychologist Oskar Pfungst (1911) placed a screen between the horse and von Osten, he discovered Clever Hans used von Osten's subtle facial movements as the cue to stop tapping. The take-home message is that Clever Hans' lack of language understanding was revealed by his catastrophically poor performance when

Figure 7.3 Clever Hans with his owner Wilhelm von Osten.

the testing situation changed. Similarly, an AI model displaying human-like language skills could be shown to lack language understanding if we found language tasks where its performance was abysmal.

Analogous findings to those with Clever Hans have been reported with respect to AI's language skills. BERT, a very successful AI language model, was presented with pairs of sentences and decided whether the first sentence implied the second (McCoy et al., 2019). BERT's performance was often near-perfect. However, its performance was close to 0% on other sentences pairs. BERT was using the lexical overlap heuristic (rule of thumb). This heuristic simply involves deciding the first sentence implies the second when both sentences contain the same words but not when both sentences contain different words. Crucially, this strategy requires no language understanding whatsoever.

Further evidence that simple heuristics requiring language comprehension can produce high levels of performance was reported by Weissenborn et al. (2017). Here is a sample question:

> When did building activity occur on St. Kazimierz Church?

> Building activity occurred in numerous noble palaces and churches [...]. One of the best examples [...] are Krasinski Palace (1677–1683), Wilanow Palace (1677–1696), and St. Kazimierz Church (1688–1692).

Weissenborn et al. (2017) argued that high levels of performance on this task could be achieved by using a simple rule of thumb or heuristic: select an answer matching the required answer type (a time indicated by "*When*") and is close to key words in the question ("*St. Kazimierz Church*"). The correct answer "1688–1692" is produced using this heuristic. An AI model using this heuristic achieved a high level of performance in the absence of language understanding.

We can develop the above ideas by identifying five kinds of information relevant to language understanding (Bisk et al., 2020a):

1   *Corpus*: the words we have encountered. An important part of our understanding of any given word comes from the probabilities that other words co-occur with it. Thus, "You shall know a word by the company it keeps" (Firth, 1957).

2   *Internet*: a phenomenal amount of information is accessible via the internet; many AI language models depend heavily on very extensive web-crawls.

3   *Perception*: our visual, auditory, and tactile experiences enrich our language comprehension. Our understanding of people, objects, and activities is incomplete if we lack direct perceptual experience of them. For example, a web crawl of articles on painting would leave us with an impoverished understanding of what a painting actually is (Bisk et al., 2020b).

4   *Embodiment and action*: full language comprehension involves translating language into action. Consider the following question: "*Is an orange more like a baseball or more like a banana?*" (Bisk et al., 2020a, p. 5). Focusing only on visual features would produce the answer, "a baseball." However, focusing on action as well introduces additional factors: an orange resembles a baseball more than a banana because both afford similar manipulations, whereas it resembles a banana more than a baseball with respect to being able to be peeled.

AI language models are not grounded in experience and action. This limitation was explored by Boratko et al. (2020). Initially, they asked people questions easy for them to answer based on their past experience (e.g., "Name something that people usually do before they leave the house for work?"). The ranked lists of answers for each question produced by humans and by AI models differed substantially on this experience-based test.

Most AI language models are limited because they rely primarily on internet information and neglect the relationship between language and action and the social nature of language. For example, chatbots can sometimes appear to be conversing in an almost human-like fashion. However, they cannot cope with conversations requiring more than internet information. As mentioned in Chapter 4, Sir Roger Penrose stumped a chatbot by saying to it, "I believe we've met before."

Generative pre-trained transformer 3 (GPT-3): artificial general intelligence?

Most people have impressive all-round language abilities. In contrast, most AI language models focus narrowly on only one language skill. The most notable exception is Generative Pre-Trained Transformer 3 (GPT-3) (Brown et al., 2020), which received massive general training but minimal training specific to any given task.

GPT-3 was tested on numerous language tasks including those requiring text generation, translation, question-answering, reasoning, and comprehension. Its performance was reasonably good on these tasks (especially text generation) (Brown et al., 2020). Intriguingly, it can write its own computer programs after receiving a few useful instructions.

GPT-3 is arguably the most powerful and versatile language model ever created. It has numerous potential applications including enhancing the performance of chatbots (e.g., Siri and Alexa) and providing reasonably accurate (and amazingly rapid) translations of text from one language to another. However, it has no language comprehension.

For example, when deciding whether a given word has the same meaning in two different sentences, GPT-3's performance was at chance level.

Why does GPT-3 lack language comprehension? It is a generative model. An important part of its training involved using texts where sentences have a word missing. GPT-3 was trained to predict the probabilities of various words that could plausibly complete the sentence from the sentence context. GPT-3 is very good at that task. However, successful sentence completion is very different from full language comprehension.

GPT-3 often produces nonsense. Marcus and Davis (2020) recorded GPT-3's responses when provided with prompts. The prompt "physical reasoning" produced this response:

> You are having a small dinner party. You want to serve dinner in the living room. The dining room table is wider than the doorway, so to get it into the living room, you will have to remove the door. You have a table saw, so you cut the door in half and remove the top half.

Don't ask GPT-3 to assist you with furniture moving! There are several confusions in the above text: (i) it makes more sense to turn the table on its side, (ii) if you need to remove a door, you would take it off its hinges, and (iii) a "table saw" is actually a saw built into a work table. As Marcus and Davis (2020, p. 4) concluded, "What it does is something like a massive act of cutting and pasting, stitching variations on text that it has seen, rather than digging deeply for the concepts that underlie those texts ... It learns correlations between words, and nothing more ... It's a fluent spouter of bullshit."

GPT-3's language processing is very inefficient. Consider the language information GPT-3 received during initial training. A bit is a binary digit (0 or 1), 8 bits form a byte, and a megabyte consists of about 1 million bytes. GPT-3 was trained on 570 billion megabytes of information (equivalent to 57 billion words). In comparison, the average human probably processes half a billion words in their lifetime. Even if we double that figure, GPT-3 was trained on 57 billion times the number of words processed by any given human!

In sum, as Heaven (2020) pointed out, "OpenAI's new language generator GPT-3 is shockingly good—and completely mindless." How can we explain this apparent paradox? What is "shockingly good" about GPT-3 is that it performs numerous language tasks with reasonable proficiency and great speed. Thus, its output or "behaviour" often appears intelligent. However, it is "completely mindless" because the processes underlying that output do not rely on intelligence or understanding. As Rini (2020) pointed out, "When GPT-3 speaks, it is only us speaking, a refracted parsing of the likeliest semantic paths trodden by human expression. When you send query text to GPT-3, you aren't communing with a unique digital soul. But you are coming as close as anyone ever has to literally speaking to the Zeitgeist [spirit of the age]." Thus, text produced by GPT-3 is merely a distorted reflection or echo of previous human thinking rather than a product of thoughtful deliberation.

Conclusions

AI language models have improved progressively so most language tasks can now be performed by AI models much more accurately and/or faster than ever before. However, these improvements primarily reflect continuous increases in the power and memory storage capacity of AI models rather than progress in language comprehension. For example, GPT-3 is good at "synthesising text it has found elsewhere on the internet, making it a kind of vast, eclectic scrapbook created from millions and millions of snippets of text that it then glues together in weird and wonderful ways" (Heaven, 2020).

Most AI systems perform moderately effectively when given relatively specific language tasks. However, more general and complex tasks would be required to assess more precisely disparities between AI systems' language skills and those of humans. For example, we could ask an AI system to watch a YouTube video and then answer questions about it (Marcus, 2020). So far no AI system comes anywhere near to succeeding on that test.

Limitations: consciousness

In Chapter 3, we distinguished between basic consciousness (e.g., perception of the environment) and meta-consciousness (knowing one is having a conscious experience). Humans possess both types of consciousness.

Do AI systems possess consciousness? McDermott (2007) found 50% of senior AI researchers believed AI would eventually achieve basic consciousness. David Chalmers, a leading expert, said in 2020, "I am open to the idea … that GPT-3 with 175 billion parameters is conscious." It is tempting (but potentially very misleading) to argue that AI systems are conscious when their behaviour resembles human behaviour. However, a substantial majority of people deny that AI has conscious awareness.

We start by expanding on our distinction between basic consciousness and meta-consciousness based on the three levels of consciousness identified by Dehaene et al. (2006):

1   Level 0: Lack of conscious awareness; several independent processing strands occur "blindly" at the same time.

2 Level 1: Conscious access: the outputs from processing at Level 0 are integrated and co-ordinated; this leads to basic conscious awareness of a *single* type of information (e.g., visual perception of the environment).

3 Level 2: Self-monitoring: this is meta-consciousness in which individuals monitor and reflect on their own mental states and experiences. It provides us with a sense of self and an understanding of others' minds (theory of mind). It also involves meta-cognitive knowledge: beliefs and knowledge about one's own cognitive processes and likely level of performance.

We will discuss two major theories of basic consciousness. After that, we turn to the issue of whether AI systems possess basic consciousness. The crucial assumption of Tononi's integrated information theory (e.g., Tononi et al., 2016) is that consciousness involves integrated information processing. Support for this theory comes from studies assessing brain activity when someone is presented with a visual image (Eysenck & Keane, 2020). Initially, several smallish brain areas are activated relatively independently: each area is associated with a particular form of processing (e.g., colour, shape, and motion). After that, there is a huge increase in integrated or synchronised brain activity across large areas of the brain associated with conscious awareness of the presented object.

King et al. (2013) supported integrated information theory. They focused on four groups: (i) patients in a vegetative state (lacking conscious awareness), (ii) minimally conscious state patients, (iii) conscious patients with brain damage, and (iv) healthy participants. There were substantial increases in integrated brain activity (especially long-distance integration) as we move from group (i) to group (iv) (see Figure 7.4).

Within Tononi's integrated information theory, integrated information is defined as, "the amount of

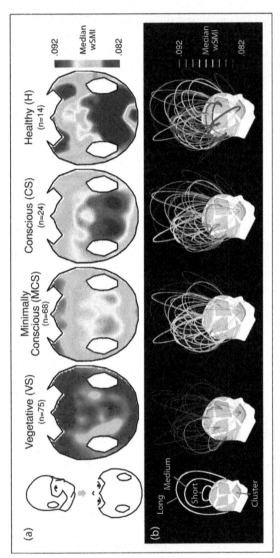

Figure 7.4 (a) Integration across the brain (blue = low integration; red/brown = high integration; (b) integration across short, medium and long distances within the brain.

Source: From King et al. (2013).

information generated by a complex of elements, above and beyond the information generated by its parts" (Tononi, 2008, p. 216). Thus, conscious experience is typically very rich and informative because it depends on integrated activation within large brain networks. If consciousness is required for making possibly life-and-death decisions and controlling the environment, it makes sense that our conscious experience consists of richly integrated information maximally relevant to the current situation.

Integrated information theory offers a quantifiable measure of integrated information: φ (the Greek letter *phi*). Tononi and Massimini devised the zap-and-zip or perturbational complexity index measure of φ (discussed by Koch, 2018). An intense pulse of magnetic energy applied to the skull produces an electric current in brain neurons (the zap). EEG records the electrical signals throughout the brain producing a detailed picture of what is happening; the data are then compressed analogously to "zip" computer files.

Massimini et al. (2005) found the perturbational complexity index was between 0.31 and 0.70 in all healthy individuals when awake but below 0.31 when deeply asleep or anaesthetised. Other research found 95% of minimally conscious patients were correctly identified as conscious using the perturbational complexity index (Koch, 2018).

Integrated information theory is important. However, it wrongly implies integration is both necessary and sufficient for consciousness. Disconfirming evidence was discussed by Brogaard et al. (2020). In one study, observers had excellent conscious awareness of single features but very limited conscious awareness of the integrated information contained in conjunctions of features. In sum, there is typically a close association between integrated information and consciousness. However, integrated information is neither necessary nor sufficient for conscious awareness to occur.

The second major theory, proposed by Lamme (e.g., 2018), meshes neatly with Tononi's approach. As discussed earlier, the processing of visual images involves bottom-up, feedforward processing and/or top-down, recurrent processing. Lamme's crucial theoretical assumption is that basic conscious awareness of external stimuli requires recurrent processing. Conscious visual experience is typically coherent even when the available visual information is ambiguous because of recurrent processing. Most research supports this theory. However, some conscious experience based solely on feedforward processing is found with very easy visual tasks (e.g., is the image of an animal or a non-animal?).

What are the implications of these two theories for the issue as to whether AI systems possess conscious awareness? According to Lamme's (2018) theory, the great majority of deep neural networks of image classification use only feedforward processing and so should lack consciousness. Tononi and Koch (2015) argued that AI models' reliance on feedforward processing means they totally lack integrated processing and so φ (the measure of integrated information) is zero.

There are two additional reasons why top-down or recurrent processing is strongly linked to consciousness. First, goal-directed behaviour depends on top-down processes and is greatly facilitated by basic conscious awareness of the current environment (Pennartz, 2018). Second, selective attention is an important top-down process. It is closely linked to basic consciousness (Webb & Graziano, 2015) and is especially important in ensuring the most relevant aspects of the current environment are processed.

In sum, most of the available evidence strongly implies that AI systems lack Level 1 or basic consciousness. However, there are two caveats. First, it is hard to assess φ in AI models (Cerullo, 2015). Second, AI models incorporating some recurrent processing are starting to appear (Ricci et al., 2021).

Unsurprisingly, AI systems also lack Level 2 or meta-consciousness. Here are some major cognitive processes associated with Level 2 consciousness but lacking in AI systems:

1 AI systems lack the meta-cognitive knowledge associated with Level 2 consciousness.
2 In humans, Level 2 consciousness is used to identify task-relevant strategies. It is then used to monitor the success (or otherwise) of those strategies during task performance and to decide whether to change strategies. None of these processes is present in AI systems.
3 One of the most impressive aspects of Level 2 consciousness is theory of mind (our ability to understand that other individuals have different beliefs, intentions, and emotions to ourselves; discussed earlier). Theory of mind allows us to tailor what we say (and how we say it) when having a conversation. AI systems do not possess this ability (discussed later).

Conclusions

In the absence of conscious processing, the responses produced by AI systems typically depend on relatively automatised and inflexible processes. In contrast, Level 2 consciousness in humans allows for a consideration of different options in terms of goal selection, task strategies, and decision making. As such, it is of central importance to the flexibility characterising much human thinking and behaviour and is a cornerstone of human intelligence.

Anthropormorphism

"Anthropomorphism" is, "the attribution of distinctively human-like feelings, mental states, and behavioural characteristics to inanimate objects, animals, and … to natural phenomena and supernatural entities" (Salles et al.,

2020, p. 89). There are various types of anthropomorphism. Of most relevance here is "cognitive anthropomorphism" (Mueller, 2020): the assumption that cognitive processing in AI systems resembles that of humans. There is also emotional anthropomorphism (the assumption AI systems can respond emotionally in human-like fashion). Anthropomorphism can lead us to misinterpret AI's performance on cognitive tasks (see Figure 7.5].

There are numerous examples of anthropomorphism in AI. Even Alan Turing (1948, p. 412) admitted that playing chess against an AI system gives "a definite feeling that one is pitting one's wits against something alive." As Watson, 2019, p. 417) pointed out, "We speak of machines that *think*, *learn*, and *infer*. The name of the discipline itself—artificial intelligence—practically dares us to compare our human modes of reasoning with the behaviour of algorithms."

When writing about visual image classification (Chapter 2 and earlier in this chapter), we had to be careful not to describe what AI was doing as "object recognition."

Figure 7.5 Anthropomorphism is more common when explaining the behaviour of humanoid robots such as the one pictured than non-humanoid robots.

That term implies not merely classifying an object correctly but also understanding what it is used for. What AI systems are actually doing is associating complex patterns of pixels with object names, a far less impressive achievement.

Other examples of anthropomorphism are rife in language research. AI language models are said to *understand* and *comprehend* even though they are trained primarily on the form or structure of language and so cannot understand or comprehend (Bender & Koller, 2020).

Why are humans so susceptible to anthropomorphism? Epley et al. (2007) identified three factors. First, most humans are motivated to understand and explain the behaviour of other agents (including AI systems). Potential anxiety about being unable to predict an agent's behaviour leads us to anthropomorphise.

Second, we can rapidly provide anthropomorphic explanations of the behaviour (especially human-like behaviour) of non-human agents. When explaining such behaviour, we typically rely on relatively accessible information mostly consisting of self-knowledge (why I would behave like that) and knowledge of other humans (why other people would behave like that). In the case of robots, most of our knowledge and understanding comes from media sources (e.g., movies), where robots are typically represented as possessing human-like characteristics and motives (Bartneck, 2013).

Suppose you wanted to provide non-anthropomorphic explanations of the behaviour of AI agents. You would probably find it very hard to think of any such explanations. Thus, anthropomorphism is typically a relatively "automatic" response to any human-like behaviour (Caporael & Heyes, 1997).

Third, anthropomorphism often arises because of the human desire for social connection with others. As discussed in Chapter 6, social bonds with robots are most likely to be formed when they look and behave in human-like ways.

Anthropomorphism matters for two reasons. First, it is a cognitive bias because it does not reflect reality. Second, it leads to an *over-estimation of* AI's achievements. For example, comparability of AI and human image classification performance led many AI experts to conclude AI processing resembles human processing (see Chapter 2 and earlier in this chapter). It thus came as a nasty surprise when it was discovered that tiny changes to a visual image could dramatically impair deep neural networks' image classification (Szegedy et al., 2014). Another nasty surprise was that image classification by deep neural networks was often very poor when tested on images not used in training (e.g., Navarrete-Dechent et al., 2018). These findings were surprising because they showed beyond peradventure that AI processing differs radically from human processing.

Researchers on language abilities in deep neural networks have also exaggerated AI's achievements. Anthropomorphism has played a significant role here. Deep neural networks have proved successful in many language tasks such as speech recognition, text comprehension, translation, and holding conversations. These successes have led numerous researchers to over-estimate the similarity between language processing in neural networks and humans.

AI systems asked general-knowledge questions typically perform especially well if the questions are very specific and accessing the answer rapidly is advantageous. These strengths explain why an AI system called Watson beat human champions on the general-knowledge television programme *Jeopardy!* (see Chapter 2). Watson responded so fast and so accurately because its stored information nearly always had the answer very close to the question.

Millions of people were surprised or astonished by Watson's performance because of their tendency towards anthropomorphism. Most humans find very specific questions harder than more general ones and often take several seconds to retrieve answers to such questions. As a result, they were unduly impressed by Watson's performance.

We have just completed three Google searches (involving deep neural networks). The query, "In which year was Alastair Cook born?" produced the correct answer in an impressive 0.86 seconds and the query, "Who was England cricket captain in 1984?" produced the answer in 0.93 seconds. The third query, "Who was England cricket captain in the year Alastair Cook was born?" produced 985,000 results in 0.82 seconds. Sadly, none directly answered the question – they indicated when Alastair Cook was born (1984) or listed England cricket captains with the relevant years but not both.

The above findings illustrate the dangers of anthropomorphism. Humans knowing when Alastair Cook was born and who was an England cricket captain in that year would rapidly link those two facts. In contrast, deep neural networks have 200 million pages of information stored but typically access information in a very compartmentalised way.

Much research apparently shows deep neural networks have excellent comprehension abilities (see Chapter 2). However, their achievements were often exaggerated because it was implicitly assumed their comprehension performance involved human-like processes. That assumption was destroyed by evidence that deep neural networks were using simple heuristics or rules of thumb not requiring comprehension (e.g., McCoy et al., 2019; Weissenborn et al., 2017; discussed earlier).

The Cambridge Dictionary defines "understanding" as "to know why or how something happens or works." AI does not exhibit understanding based on that definition. Maetschke et al. (2021) identified four capabilities relevant to understanding:

1 Compositional knowledge representation (e.g., the component of an object as well as the object itself are represented).

2 Combining information from different modalities (e.g., vision and audition) to form a structured knowledge representation.

3 Integration of symbolic knowledge (e.g., abstract information as in language) and non-symbolic knowledge (e.g., concrete information).

4 Symbolic reasoning with uncertain information (e.g., incomplete information; world changes).

Maetschke et al. (2021) evaluated 28 AI models designed to process visual images or language. On average, each model demonstrated approximately one of the above capabilities. Thus, we are a very long way from developing AI models possessing full understanding.

Deep learning

Deep learning has proved enormously successful. However, most AI experts were somewhat surprised at its success because it was not based on any major innovation. Deep learning is a great engineering feat, but it lacks any solid theoretical basis. More importantly, the precise reasons why deep learning works so well remain obscure (Plebe & Grasso, 2019). In addition, deep neural networks lack understanding and comprehension even on tasks where their performance level is high.

You may have been surprised at the huge amount of data and enormous training period typically required for deep neural networks to produce excellent performance. As Marcus (2018, p. 5) pointed out, "In a world with infinite data, and infinite computational resources, there might be little need for any other technique." In the real world, however, neither data nor computational resources are infinite. In spite of the successes of deep neural networks, it involves a "brute force approach" (Marcus, p. 6).

Deep neural networks resemble the inter-connections of neurons within the human brain, suggesting that such networks might one day match human cognitive abilities. However, the resemblance is only superficial and the complexity of the human brain is markedly greater than that of any neural network.

In sum, the successes of deep learning have blinded many people to its numerous limitations, many of which may be intrinsic to the entire approach. Imagine someone whose goal is to reach the moon. They start by climbing short trees and then move on to climbing taller trees or a tall ladder (see Figure 7.6). The fact they are getting progressively closer to the moon convinces them their strategy is the right one. It could be argued (although rather unfairly), that AI researchers who are confident that deep neural networks increasingly demonstrate human-level intelligence resemble the tree or ladder climber.

Figure 7.6 A man (optimistically) standing on a tall ladder in order to touch the moon.

Overall conclusions

Booch et al. (2020, p. 1) concluded as follows: "State-of-the-art AI still lacks many capabilities that would naturally be included in a notion of intelligence, for example, if we compare these AI technologies to what human beings are able to do. Examples ... are generalisability, robustness, explainability, causal analysis, abstraction, common sense reasoning, ethics reasoning, as well as a complex and seamless integration of learning and reasoning supported by both implicit and explicit knowledge."

We would add several other capabilities to that list. AI lacks basic consciousness and meta–consciousness as well as understanding and comprehension. Most AI systems also lack selective attention. As Tsimenidis (2020, p. 6) pointed out, "Their attention is uniform; every element of their inputs, every pixel of an image, every word of a sentence, carries equal weight." That means AI systems rarely discriminate effectively between more and less important information. Finally, all AI systems lack general intelligence (see Chapter 4).

In sum, AI lacks key human abilities relating to attention, planning, consciousness, memory, language, and so on. Most AI systems are inflexible and brittle (and lack understanding and judgement) because they lack these abilities. These deficiencies explain why it has so far proved impossible to produce artificial general intelligence (Chapter 4).

Humans: strengths

The processes and structures underlying the excellence of human cognition were discussed in Chapter 3. We have ready access to stored knowledge in semantic memory and to past experiences in episodic memory, and episodic memory also facilitates our imagining of the future.

Our command of language facilitates our access to stored information and, more generally, to accumulated cultural knowledge. The processes operating on all these sources of information include working memory (with its executive processes relating to attentional control), meta-consciousness, and meta-cognition.

Why do the above abilities produce such high levels of thinking and intelligence? There are two main reasons. First, the fact these abilities combine and interact is of fundamental importance. Their inter-dependence explains why human thinking is massively more flexible and adaptable than the performance of AI systems. It also explains why humans possess general intelligence as assessed by measures, such as "g" and IQ.

Second, unlike other species, our cognitive processing is not mostly limited to the here-and-now but can also focus on abstract thinking and hypothetical situations far removed from concrete environmental realities. For example, episodic memory allows us to imagine future possibilities and language provides an appropriate medium for abstract thinking. In addition, meta-consciousness and meta-cognition permit us to plan and engage in decision making based on evaluating the outcomes of our initial processing of a situation.

Why has our species flourished?

Our species (*Homo sapiens*) has become increasingly dominant over evolutionary history whereas other human-like species (Neanderthals; *Homo erectus*) became extinct. A key reason is because *Homo sapiens* was more resilient and flexible (Roberts & Stewart, 2019). Our species (unlike other human-like species) colonised most of the world's continents starting approximately 200,000–100,000 years ago. The ability of our species to cope with extreme environments (e.g., high-altitude regions, deserts, and Arctic regions) indicates we were "generalists" able to adapt to an enormous range of environmental conditions.

Cultural factors are crucially important. The dual-inheritance theory (e.g., Henrich & Muthukrishna, 2021; see Chapter 3) provides a plausible (if necessarily some-what speculative) explanation of how human intelligence has benefited greatly from cultural factors. Increasing cultural complexity within human societies increases their effectiveness. Of crucial importance, those individuals best able to acquire complex cultural knowledge were more likely than less intelligent individuals to reproduce. Thus, the interaction between culture and evolution provided a dynamic impetus to increasing human intelligence.

Another reason the human species has flourished is because humans are social creatures organised into groups and society. This gives us an enormous advantage over other species (and AI systems). Imagine your life without the assistance (direct or indirect) of numerous other people. You would have to learn how to build somewhere to live (and then provide it with heating and lighting), take care of your own health without medical assistance, and learn skills without recourse to teachers.

The establishment of societies also allows us to tran-scend many human limitations. For example, many spe-cies can move much faster than us, but we overcome that limitation by using various forms of transport. Similarly, the time is approaching when we will rely increasingly on AI systems to overcome limitations in our thinking speed and accuracy. This is a resounding success – humans designed those AI systems and so deserve the credit for their successes.

Children

We have demonstrated the superiority of adult human thinking and information processing compared to AI systems. However, it would be more striking if we found that even young children outperform AI systems. Supportive evidence was discussed in Chapter 4. In one study (Liu et al., 2019), it was estimated that six-year-old children have greater general intelligence than AI systems.

Here we will focus on whether young children exhibit meta-consciousness, which is closely associated with active learning. An important manifestation of active learning is curiosity: young children sometimes (but not always!) have awareness of their ignorance, which motivates them to explore the unknown. A common example is the interest most children show in smart phones and the speed with which they learn how such phones work.

Most children show clear evidence of theory of mind (ability to understand what others are thinking) by four or five years of age (Apperley & Butterfilld, 2009; see Chapter 3), and aspects of theory of mind are present by the second year of life (Onishi & Baillargeon, 2005). These findings are highly relevant because theory of mind is closely related to meta-cognitive processes and meta-consciousness (Bartsch & Estes, 1996).

Gopnik et al. (2017) asked people to make a gadget light up. Initially, it lit up when a specific object was put in it. After that, it only lit up when a combination of objects was put in it. Four-year-old children learned the appropriate combination of objects more rapidly than adults. Thus, their thinking can sometimes be very flexible and effective.

There are numerous other examples of surprisingly sophisticated thinking and information processing by young children mostly reflecting the flexibility of thought associated with meta-consciousness (Gopnik et al., 2017). As Alison Gopnik has argued, "The largest and most powerful computers [are] no match for the smallest and weakest humans."

Humans: limitations

Numerous human limitations have been identified (see Chapter 5). However, many are associated with various advantages and so arguably should not be categorised as "limitations." However, human intelligence and thinking do have some (arguably numerous) genuine limitations. These limitations should be seen in the light of our evolutionary history.

Evolutionary history

Evolution is indisputably a wonderful thing. However, it is a long way short of being perfect with respect to our bodies. For example, millions of people suffer from backache, our night vision is poor, our hips and knees can wear out, and we have numerous "junk" genes. Evolution has also given us imperfect minds. As Richerson and Boyd (2005, p. 135) put it, "All animals are under stringent selection pressure to be as stupid as they can get away with." More precisely, "Natural selection chooses the better of present available alternatives … The animal that results is not the most perfect design conceivable … It is the product of a historical sequence of changes, each one of which represented … the better of the alternatives that happened to be around" (Darwin, 1871, p. 46).

We need to strike a balance here. Marcus (2008) emphasised the notion of a "kluge," which he defined as "a clumsy or inelegant – yet surprisingly effective solution to a problem" (p. 2). Marcus argued the human mind is a kluge forged by the rough-and-ready processes of evolution. In other words, the mind is a paradoxical mixture of the inelegant and the effective.

In sum, evolution has equipped humans to cope reasonably well with an amazingly diverse set of environmental circumstances. The downside is that most of us are generalists rather than specialists; as the saying goes, "A jack of all trades is a master of none." However, the original saying had "but oftentimes better than a master of one" added to it. Thus, being a generalist may be less of a disadvantage than is often assumed.

Speed-accuracy trade-off: cognitive misers

One of the most obvious (but important) features of human cognitive processing is speed-accuracy trade-off: there is typically an inverse relationship between speed and accuracy. While it might seem desirable for us to strive for accuracy at the expense of speed, the busy nature of our lives means that is often not feasible. A major human limitation is that we often fail to adopt the optimal speed-accuracy trade-off in any given situation.

Numerous theorists (e.g., Kahneman, 2011) have proposed dual-process theories to account for human thinking, problem solving, decision making, and reasoning. Humans have Type 1 intuitive processes (e.g., use of heuristics or rules of thumb) that are fast and relatively effortless and Type 2 reflective processes that are slow and deliberate. Type 2 processes are more likely than Type 1 processes to produce correct answers to problems, but require more time and effort.

We are cognitive misers who avoid expending cognitive effort unless essential (Fiske & Taylor, 1991). As a result, we often respond rapidly (but sometimes incorrectly) to problems using Type 1 processes without checking our answers using Type 2 processes. Many cognitive biases discussed in Chapter 5 occur because of our excessive use of Type 1 processes.

The above account is over-simplified. Frederick (2005) designed the Cognitive Reflection Test, which involves a conflict between Type 1 and Type 2 processes (see below). What are your answers to the questions?

Cognitive Reflection Test

1 A bat and a ball cost $1.10 in total. The bat costs $1 more than the ball. How much does the ball cost? _____ cents

2 If it takes five machines five minutes to make five widgets, how long would it take 100 machines to make 100 widgets? _____ minutes.

3 In a lake, there is a patch of lily pads. Every day, the patch doubles in size. If it takes 48 days for the patch to cover the entire lake, how long would it take for the patch to cover half the lake? _____ days.

The correct answers are 5 cents (problem 1), five minutes (problem 2), and 47 days (problem 3). Do not worry if you did not get them all right – only about 25% of highly intelligent individuals answer all the items correctly. Most incorrect answers (10 cents, 100 minutes, and 24 days) are *intuitive* responses produced using Type 1 processes.

Contemporary wisdom predicts it should be relatively easy to persuade people to use Type 2 processes and so enhance their performance on the Cognitive Reflection Test. This prediction is wrong. Providing powerful financial incentives for accurate performance has no effect on performance (Branas-Garza et al., 2019). Providing feedback ("Incorrect") when people produce wrong answers increases the time people spend deliberating but does not improve performance (Janssen et al., 2020). Why is this? The first answer we think of is generally associated with a strong feeling-of-rightness (Ackerman & Thompson, 2017) and this dissuades us from seriously considering other answers.

Prioritisation among multiple goals

Humans often pursue multiple goals concurrently (see Chapter 5). For example, when we perform a task, one goal is likely to be to achieve a high level of task performance. Other goals may include to satisfy our needs for belongingness or social identity and for self-enhancement or self-esteem. Unfortunately, our prioritisation strategy among these various goals is sometimes far short of optimal. We will focus on a common life-threatening example.

When driving a car, it can be dangerous or fatal not to prioritise the goal of driving safely. However, millions of drivers engage in conversations on their mobile phones while driving (see Figure 7.7). The evidence is clear-cut: drivers using a mobile phone are several times more likely to be involved in a car crash (Nurullah, 2015). Approximately 1.6 million car accidents worldwide every year are caused by use of mobile phones and 400,000 individuals were injured in those accidents. In the United States, one in four car accidents is caused by mobile phone usage.

There are several reasons why it is dangerous for car drivers to use a mobile phone. It causes them to focus excessively on the road ahead, to attend less to potential

Figure 7.7 Photograph of a driver using a mobile phone.

hazards, and to react slowly and inappropriately to dangerous situations (Strayer & Fisher, 2016).

Why do drivers use mobile phones in spite of massive
publicity about the dangers involved? The answer is simple: they believe erroneously they can drive safely while
using a mobile phone whereas most other people cannot
(Sanbonmatsu et al., 2016).

Killing ourselves

Arguably, many cognitive biases discussed in Chapter 5 are
trivial: they were discovered in artificial laboratory conditions and no serious consequences follow from possessing
them. Here we consider biased (and inadequate) thinking
associated with potentially fatal consequences.

Smoking

It has been known for several decades that smoking causes
numerous serious and fatal diseases (e.g., bronchitis, emphy-
sema, lung cancer, other cancers, and coronary heart disease). Individuals who smoke throughout their adult life lose
several years of life on average. For example, a large-scale
Japanese study found female smokers lost ten years of life and
male smokers eight years (Sakata et al., 2012).

The optimal strategy is to avoid smoking altogether.
Those who have started smoking should use the life-
shortening impact of smoking to provide themselves with
the motivation to quit. In fact, most smokers deny the
overwhelming scientific evidence is of much relevance to
them: this is a form of exceptionalism. They rationalise
their smoking behaviour in several ways: smoking in mod-
eration (as they do) is not harmful; they engage in compensatory behaviour (e.g., physical exercise) to offset any
risks from smoking; smoking is no riskier than coffee or a
glass of wine (Heikkinen et al., 2010).

So far we have only told part of the story. The human mind (aided by nicotine patches) has proved powerful enough to permit many millions of individuals to quit smoking. In the United Kingdom, for example, only 14% of adults now smoke compared to 45% in 1974. However, there are still approximately 1 billion smokers worldwide.

Obesity

Everyone knows obesity is a big problem and is becoming bigger every year. It is typically defined by the ratio of an individual's weight and height as assessed by the body mass index (BMI): kilograms/metres^2. A BMI of 30 or more indicates obesity, 25–30 indicates being overweight, and a BMI between 18.5 and 25 indicates a healthy weight. BMI is a reasonable (although imperfect) measure; for example, professional footballers have a relatively high BMI because they have built up layers of muscle.

Using the above definition, it is estimated that 700 million individuals worldwide are obese (three times the number 35 years ago). On current trends, over 50% of the English adult population will be obese before 2050.

Obesity increases the probability of many serious conditions including heart disease, type-2 diabetes, stroke, and several cancers. It also reduces life expectancy. This is especially the case with individuals who are morbidly obese (typically with a BMI of over 40; see Figure 7.8). Lung et al. (2019) found obesity reduced life expectancy for obese women by 6.1 years and for obese men by 8.3 years. Severe obesity reduced life expectancy even more: 7.8 years for women and 10.4 years for men. Extreme obesity (BMI between 55 and 60) reduces life expectancy by 13.7 years (Kitahara et al., 2014).

It is generally known obesity has potentially serious health consequences. It is also well known it is extremely difficult to lose weight and then maintain it. For example,

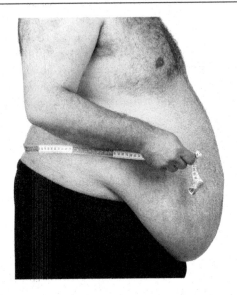

Figure 7.8 Photograph of a morbidly obese individual.

Fildes et al. (2015) found obese women had only a one in 124 chance of returning to a healthy weight within 12 months and the figure was one in 210 for men.

It would be optimal if humans were designed so they ate healthily and never became obese. If, by mischance they did become obese, then they should summon up the determination and will-power to follow an effective long-term diet. The obvious starting point would be for obese individuals to accept they are obese and that obesity is life-threatening. That is not what typically happens. Ogunleye et al. (2019) found 87% of obese students at school did *not* regard themselves as obese, mostly believing themselves to be slightly overweight. Only 22% of obese women regard themselves as obese with 6% perceiving themselves as having a healthy weight (Truesdale & Stevens, 2008). For obese men, only 7% thought they were obese and 20% thought their weight was healthy and normal.

Mathematics

An oddity about British people is how many are proud of their innumeracy (e.g., "I'm hopeless at maths," said with a chuckle). However, serious consequences can follow from innumeracy and its associated cognitive biases. One could write an entire book on this topic (and some individuals have already done that). Here we will focus on one such bias because of its widespread negative impact on the finances and well-being of individuals and societies.

Exponential growth bias

Here is a mathematical problem used by Wagenaar and Sagaria (1975):

The pollution index changes as follows:

Year 1:   3
Year 2:   7
Year 3:   20
Year 4:   55
Year 5:   148

What will the pollution index be in Year 10?

The correct answer is 25,000. However, two-thirds of people gave an answer below 10% of the correct answer. The problem revolves around exponential growth: that means that a quantity (e.g., pollution index) increases at a rate proportional to its current size. Thus, the rate at which a quantity grows increases over time. The great majority of people are very surprised by the rapidity of exponential

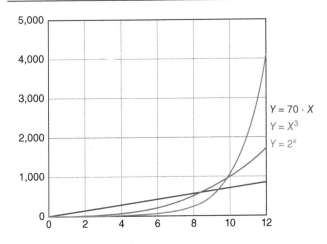

Figure 7.9 Illustrative differences over time between exponential growth (grey line) and linear growth (blue line); also shown is cubic growth (red line).

Source: From Zamir and Teichman, 2021).

growth: this is the exponential growth bias discovered by Wagenaar and Sagaria (1975).

Individuals very often misperceive exponential growth as linear growth where a quantity increases at a constant and unchanging rate over time (Zamir & Teichman, 2021). The very large differences between linear and exponential growth over time are shown in Figure 7.9.

The exponential growth bias impacts on our lives in several important ways (Zamir & Teichman, 2021). Consider the numbers of new cases of Covid in the United Kingdom during March and early April 2020:

1 March:	22
5 March:	50
9 March:	147
13 March:	479

17 March:	769
21 March:	1,195
25 March:	2,690
29 March:	2,856
2 April:	4,862

If you have that bias (and it is probable that most leading British politicians do), the figures during most of March do not look too threatening. That probably helps to explain why the government only introduced a full lockdown on 23 March 2020 when the number of new cases was 2,326. However, the very dangerous exponential growth in the numbers would have been apparent to a mathematician by, say, 13 March. If a lockdown had been introduced on the 13 March when the number of new cases was only 20% of the number ten days later, many thousands of lives would have been saved.

The tardiness of the U.K. lockdown undoubtedly also depended on other factors (e.g., the uniqueness of the situation and the potentially crippling effects on business of a lockdown). However, the government made precisely the same mistake when faced by exponential growth in Covid cases in early autumn 2020. SAGE (Scientific Advisory Group for Emergencies) strongly advised initiating a lockdown in late September, but the government only introduced one in early November, by which time the number of new cases had quadrupled.

Most Americans exhibited exponential growth bias by substantially underestimating the rapid increase in cases of Covid during March 2020 (Lammers et al., 2020). Instructing them to avoid this bias increased their support for social distancing and a lockdown. Thus, public misperception of the dangers of Covid increased Americans' reluctance to observe social distancing.

The slow response to Covid of the British and American governments has probably been very costly. The same is true of climate change. Most people believe that climate change is occurring relatively slowly. In fact, the growth of climate-destroying processes is probably exponential (Zamir & Teichman, 2021). The susceptibility of governments to the exponential growth bias means the eventual costs of dealing with climate change will be substantially greater than they would otherwise have been.

Most people use credit to buy goods immediately with the money borrowed being repaid over time. These repayments typically involve compound interest (interest is charged on interest). An interest rate of 3% per month suggests an annual interest rate of 36%; in fact, it is 43% using compound interest, which exhibits exponential growth.

Exponential growth bias partially explains why millions of people struggle to meet their interest repayments on loans (Zamir & Teichman, 2021). Suppose you must repay a £10,000 loan after two years with 3% compound monthly interest. Most people would guess the repayment required would be approximately £18,000. In fact, it is £28,983.

Exponential growth is sometimes good news. Workers who start saving relatively early in their working lives benefit from exponential growth of their savings and so are likely to retire with a relatively large pension. However, workers subject to the exponential growth bias underestimate the future value of their savings and so save less for the future than those lacking the bias (Stango & Zinman, 2009).

Conclusions

Humans have many limitations, some of which (e.g., difficulties in giving up smoking and obesity) can reduce life expectancy by several years. Exponential growth bias can ruin individuals' finances by tempting them to borrow more than they can afford to repay and to make insufficient provision for their retirement. The same bias can also prove very costly to society at large by leading governments to underestimate the dangers associated with threats, such as Covid and climate change.

The above limitations can be understood with respect to evolutionary history. Our ancestors did not have to decide whether to smoke. They did not have to worry about obesity – for them, a crucial problem was having access to enough food for survival rather than avoiding eating too much. In addition, they did not eat the rich and sweet high-calorie food most of us so enjoy. In their hunter-gatherer world, there was no evolutionary advantage in having a sophisticated understanding of mathematics.

In sum, the take-home message is that the slowness of evolutionary change has prevented humans from adapting fully to the very rapid changes in human societies over the past few thousand years. The rough-and-ready nature of most evolutionary changes combined with their slowness condemns us to coping sub-optimally with many of the challenges and threats we face.

And the winner is ...?

If we compare the human brain against supercomputers, it appears to be no contest. The human brain occupies only approximately 1,200 cubic centimetres, weighs a mere 3 pounds and accounts for only 2% of our body weight. In contrast, consider IBM's Summit supercomputer (the world's most powerful computer in 2018). It occupies 5,600 square feet of floor space and weighs a massive 310 tons. Thus, the human brain is less than 1/230,000th of the weight of Summit!!!

Summit uses 13 megawatts of power (13,000 kilowatts of electricity per hour), making it necessary to pump 4,000 gallons of water through its entire system to prevent over-heating. In contrast, the human brain uses an exceptionally modest 20 watts of power per hour, barely sufficient to power a very weak light bulb. Of most relevance here, the human brain consumes approximately 1/650th of the power of Summit.

Finally, we consider the relative *power* of supercomputers and the human brain. Many people would imagine super-computers are massively more powerful than the human brain. For example, Summit can perform 200,000 trillion calculations per second (200 petaFLOPS or 10^{15} FLOPS) (FLOPS are the number of floating point operations per second: a floating point corresponds to the decimal expansion of a number). That figure seems incredibly impressive even we do not (fully) understand what it means. In 2020, Summit was displaced by Japan's Fugaku, which has achieved 442 petaFLOPS per second (see Figure 2.1). Since the brain does not work in floating point values, it is specu-lative to compare the processing power of supercomputers and human brains based on FLOPS. Another issue is that human processing capacity depends hugely on the precise task we are engaged in. For example, we typically process huge amounts of information very rapidly in visual per-ception. However, we have limited short-term memory (and the contents of consciousness are limited) and so we struggle with a problem, such as multiplying two 19-digit numbers (an estimated processing speed of less than 0.01 FLOPS per second; see Chapter 3).

If we want to compare the human brain against super-computers, it is more fruitful to consider the story of David and Goliath. Goliath was 9 feet 9 inches tall, covered in bronze armour, and equipped with a bronze spear. In con-trast, David was a lowly shepherd boy lacking armour who looked puny compared to Goliath. However, he showed ingenuity by using his sling to fire a rock that hit Goliath on the forehead and killed him.

Goliath (like supercomputers) had enormous brute strength and would undoubtedly have triumphed in hand-to-hand fighting. However, David (like the human brain) had much greater processing flexibility and so won the battle. The relevance of this story is that the identity of the "winner" in any comparison of brain and AI depends on the precise field of battle (literal or metaphorical).

The human brain often operates much more efficiently than supercomputers. It can perform many complex calculations using 300 or 400 neuron transmissions that might require a computer to take millions of steps. Tegmark (2018) identified activities, "involving people, unpredictability and creativity," as ones that most humans are good at and where the huge processing power of supercomputers is essentially irrelevant. More generally, the power of AI systems is relatively ineffective when tasks require flexible processing and the ability to generalise across situations.

In sum, we have a situation neatly expressed by David Richerby (posted in 2014): "On the one hand, you need a huge computer to simulate a human brain; on the other hand, you need a huge number of human brains to simulate a desktop computer." Thus, the strengths (and limitations) of computers and human brains are very different. However, the human brain is the hands-down winner in efficiency: its overall performance is dramatically superior to that of supercomputers even though it weighs only 1/230,000th as much as a supercomputer.

Bounded rationality

How impressive are human thinking and intelligence? It is indisputable that our cognitive processes fall short of ideal (see Chapter 5). For example, we lack the perfect rationality associated with *homo economicus*: "A hypothetical agent who has complete information about the options available for choice, perfect foresight of the consequences from choosing those options, and the wherewithal to solve an optimisation problem (typically of considerable complexity) that identifies an option, which maximises the agent's personal utility" (Wheeler, 2018, p. 2).

Simon proposed a much more realistic assessment of human rationality based on "bounded rationality" (see Chapter 5). According to Simon (1990, p. 7), "Human rational behaviour is shaped like a scissors whose blades are the structure of task environments and the computational capabilities of the actor." Thus, our thinking is often sub-optimal because of our limited processing capacity and our incomplete knowledge, problems in anticipating future consequences and limited behavioural repertoire.

The notion of "bounded rationality" is valuable. However, it is often used very vaguely without specifying the underlying cognitive limitations and how those limitations constrain cognitive performance. Lieder and Griffiths (2020) proposed a resource-rationality approach building on Simon's theorising. According to this approach, we need to assess human processing limitations and key environmental features, and find algorithms providing the optimal trade-off between use of resources and performance accuracy. Those algorithms can then be compared against actual human performance.

Some support for resource rationality was provided by van den Berg and Ma (2018) in a study on short-term memory for visually presented items. Participants allocated their processing resources flexibly to produce a near-optimal balance between maximising performance while minimising use of resources.

Humans often pursue two or more goals concurrently and our performance on complex tasks often involves emotional factors as well as cognitive ones. That complicates the task of deciding whether the optimists or the pessimists provide a more accurate account of human thinking. Consider this extreme example. Soldiers were in a military plane when one engine stopped and they were told the plane would shortly ditch in the ocean (Berkun et al., 1962). They completed a complex "emergency procedure" form in these very stressful conditions. Unsurprisingly, their performance was impaired compared to individuals completing the same form in neutral conditions.

We could regard the above findings as indicating the sub-optimal nature of human thinking in a stressful environment. However, it is preferable to argue that it is perfectly rational for individuals to focus on an immediate threat to their survival rather than the complex questions posed on a form.

In sum, human thinking and cognition are characterised to some extent by bounded rationality and resource rationality. However, it has proved very difficult to assess the precise extent. One problem is that tasks vary enormously in the precise cognitive processes required, and it is often hard to identify those processes. In addition, assessing the optimality of resource use requires detailed knowledge of the environment but such knowledge is rarely available (Ma & Woodford, 2020).

Underestimating AI strengths: anthropocentrism and anthropofabulation

Buckner (2013) discussed the biases involved when humans compare themselves against other species or AI systems. The most studied bias is anthropomorphism (attributing human-like characteristics to non-human species or objects; discussed earlier). Another bias is anthropocentrism – the view that human cognitive abilities form the "gold standard" against, which the cognitive achievements of other species (and AI systems) should be compared.

Anthropocentrism has led many experts to devalue the successes of deep neural networks by claiming those successes depend on insufficiently human-like processing. This can led to

> constantly shifting goalposts; every time … an artificial system satisfies a previously specified benchmark,

> the critic can simply endorse a yet more restrictive interpretation of "real" or "genuine" [intelligence] and push the borderline ever-closer to the uppermost limits of human performance
>
> (Buckner, 2020, p. 11).

There are two major problems with anthropocentrism. First, we lack a precise definition of "human intelligence" and so the "gold standard" provided by human achievements is vague. Second, anthropomorphism excludes the possibility that AI may simply possess a very different, non-human-like intelligence. However, it has proved remarkably difficult to define the essence of such intelligence.

Consider the famous Turing test (discussed in Chapters 2 and 4). An AI system and a human being hold a conversation via typed messages and the AI system "passes" the test if human judges cannot distinguish between its linguistic output and a human's. This test involves anthropocentrism because AI systems are evaluated by their ability to reveal human-level language skills and intelligence (Proudfoot, 2011).

Turing (1950) knew his test was limited: "May not machines carry out something, which ought to be described as thinking but which is very different from what a man does?" (p. 435). For example, an AI system asked to add 34,957 and 70,764 might produce the right answer very rapidly, but would need to delay responding for several seconds to imitate human intelligence!

Turing (1950) also argued his test was biased against AI. If a human tried to imitate an AI system, they would perform very poorly because of their slowness and inaccuracy when presented with arithmetical problems.

Researchers are guilty of anthropocentrism when they selectively focus on tasks and/or measures providing a built-in human advantage. This selective focus can lead us to under-estimate AI systems' processing abilities. We start with findings on image-classification tasks. Deep neural networks perform extremely well on such tasks. However, their performance is very poor when tiny irrelevant changes are made to images. These findings allegedly demonstrate the limitations of such networks (e.g., Heaven, 2019).

Consider such findings from the perspective of deep neural networks trained to use any predictive features of images to classify them accurately. Some of these features are nonsensical or imperceptible to humans. However, humans create the categories used on image-classification tasks and so what is learned by deep neural networks is entirely appropriate given their lack of relevant knowledge about those categories. Similarly, humans decide the subsequent image changes should be labelled "adversarial examples" making it no surprise that deep neural networks perform poorly in those circumstances (Ilyas et al., 2019).

In one study (Utrera et al., 2020), adversarial examples were (or were not) presented during initial training on an image-classification task. Subsequent performance on different sets of images was much higher when adversarial examples had been used during training., indicating that adversarial examples can sometimes enhance AI performance.

Anthropocentrism leads to a more widespread denigration of AI's achievements than discussed so far. The emphasis in most research comparing humans and AI has been on accuracy rather than speed. This is often disadvantageous to AI systems which often achieve high levels of performance much faster than humans. For example, AI systems are typically inferior to humans with respect to performance accuracy on most language tasks (see Chapter 4). However, AI systems often outperform on humans with respect to the speed of language processing. Examples include language translation and answering general knowledge questions (e.g., on the quiz show *Jeopardy!*; see Chapter 2).

In the real world, there are many situations where speed is essential (e.g., detecting enemy faces in a war, speed chess, diagnosing a critically ill patient, and deciding whether someone is carrying a gun). In such situations, AI systems might well prove superior to humans.

Anthropofabulation

When anthropocentrism is combined with an exaggerated assessment of human cognitive abilities, we have what Buckner (2013) called "anthropofabulation." Buckner (2020) discussed several examples of anthropofabulation, and we will consider a few.

A claimed advantage of humans over deep neural networks is that our image classification (unlike that of deep neural networks) is typically unaffected by adversarial examples. However, we could equally well claim such findings indicate that human perceptual sensitivity is less than that of neural networks because we are unresponsive to the tiny image changes contained within adversarial examples (Buckner, 2020).

Human visual processing typically involves bottom-up or feedforward processing and top-down or recurrent processing whereas deep neural networks primarily rely on feedforward processing. Most research comparing the effects of adversarial examples in humans and neural network has involved tasks where humans can use feedforward and recurrent processing. Such tasks may convey an unfair advantage to humans. Suppose we presented visual images very briefly so humans could use only feedforward processing. In those conditions, adversarial examples impaired human image classification (Elsayed et al., 2018).

Another criticism of AI systems is that they often engage in "reward hacking:" they learn to increase task rewards using strategies outside the spirit of the rules. For example, a soccer robot rewarded every time it touched the ball learned to touch it numerous times in quick succession with very small vibratory movements. An AI agent called

Eurisko accumulated numerous points in a video game by falsely taking credit for other agents' successes.

Reward hacking on video games is often regarded as an inferior form of learning because the strategies associated with it are contrary to the intentions of the humans who designed the games. In fact, reward hacking involves ingenious ways of succeeding on a game or task when the rules are insufficiently explicit. Thus, being dismissive of reward hacking by AI systems is a prime example of anthropofabulation. Ironically, humans playing video games often use exploits (strategies taking advantage of bugs or glitches) closely resembling the reward hacking of AI systems. However, human "cheating" is perceived much more positively than AI "cheating" (Buckner, 2020).

Ehsan et al. (2018) provided more evidence of anthropofabulation. People watched videos of three robots (two of which are relevant here) using deep neural networks playing the video game Frogger identically. One robot provided human-like (but inaccurate) explanations of its behaviour whereas the other robot provided the most causally accurate explanations. Almost 40% of those watching the videos thought the human-like explanations were the most satisfactory compared to only 1% who regarded the AI-like explanations as the best.

The human-like explanations provided by one of the robots were basically rationalisations (inaccurate but plausible *post hoc* accounts). In contrast, the AI-like explanations were reasonably accurate but were rejected by most humans.

Underestimating human strengths

Anthropocentrim and anthrofabulation lead us to underestimate the processing ability of AI systems while overestimating that of humans. However, there is also a real danger of underestimating human intelligence. Most comparisons between human and AI intelligence have involved narrow cognitive tasks (e.g., categorising objects, chess playing, and medical diagnosis): the emphasis has been on "cold" cognition (information processing lacking emotional involvement). This traditional approach can be contrasted with a broader approach including not only emotional factors but also motives and social factors. Such an approach focuses on "hot" cognition.

Human superiority to AI systems is greater with hot cognition than cold cognition. This is unsurprising since nearly all AI systems are programmed to perform tasks involving cold cognition (Cuzzolin et al., 2020). Much research on hot cognition in humans has focused on emotional intelligence: "the extent and manner in which individuals experience and utilise affect-laden information of an intrapersonal (e.g., managing one's own emotions) and interpersonal (e.g., managing others' emotions) nature" (van der Linden et al., 2017, p. 37). Theory of mind (the ability to infer others' beliefs and emotions) is an important aspect of emotional intelligence.

There are two forms of emotional intelligence. Trait emotional intelligence concerns an individual's perception of their own social and emotional skills. Individuals with high trait emotional intelligence have warm and positive personalities – extraverted, agreeable, conscientious, and open to experience but low on neuroticism (van der Linden et al., 2017). In contrast, ability emotional intelligence concerns an individual's ability to perceive and influence their own emotions and those of other people.

Trait and ability emotional intelligence predict important real-world outcomes. Individuals high in trait emotional intelligence are happier than low scorers (Ye et al., 2019) and have greater relationship satisfaction (Malouff et al., 2014). Evidence that high trait emotional intelligence *causes* greater relationship satisfaction was reported by Parker et al. (2021). Trait and ability emotional intelligence both correlate moderately positively with job performance (O'Boyle et al., 2011) and predict academic performance (MacCann et al., 2020).

In sum, human intelligence is extremely broad in scope. Humans adapting successfully to their environment possess high levels of emotional intelligence (or hot cognition) plus high levels of "traditional" or cold intelligence.

Many experts (e.g., Braga & Logan, 2017) argue AI systems are incapable of experiencing emotion and conclude such systems lack emotional intelligence or theory of mind. In fact, the issue is more nuanced. For example, Rabinowitz et al. (2018) constructed a deep neural network predicting agents' mental states from limited information about their behaviour. It performed well on a task assessing theory of mind. However, the neural network required 32 million samples to display some evidence of theory of mind (Jara-Ettinger, 2019). This is equivalent to 175,000 learning trials each day for a period of six months – hugely more than the amount of time young children devote to acquiring theory of mind.

Our theory of mind leads us to predict that highly intelligent individuals often form more complex beliefs than less intelligent ones and that forgetful individuals have simpler beliefs than those with better memories (Burger & Jara-Ettinger, 2020). In contrast, Rabinowitz et al.'s (2018) deep neural network did not accommodate individual differences and so was much more limited.

Conclusions

Jeffrey (2015, p. 369) asked the question to which this entire chapter has been devoted: "Can we do better than 3.5 billion years of evolution did with us?" She concluded (as do we) that the answer is a resounding, "No!" suggesting it would "an immense act of hubris" (p. 366) to believe it is possible to achieve (or surpass) human intelligence in an AI system.

The human tendency to engage in anthropocentrism and anthropofabulation means comparisons between humans and AI are sometimes biased in our favour because the playing field is not level. However we do not regard this as a serious obstacle to concluding that humans have vastly greater and hugely more wide-ranging cognitive abilities than AI. This conclusion is strengthened by evidence that we also engage in anthropomorphism, which leads us to be unduly impressed by the performance of AI.

Chapter 8

The future

We have seen that human intelligence is demonstrably superior to AI intelligence in generality and flexibility. However, many AI experts argue that AI will triumph in the not-too-distant future, an issue we address in this chapter. We also consider whether AI's future influence will be beneficial or catastrophically destructive.

The final issue discussed in this chapter has attracted less attention than the preceding issues. Can humans fight back by exploiting their currently greater intelligence than AI to good effect? Alternatively, can they harness future rapid increases in the sophistication of AI by somehow combining the strengths of AI and human intelligence?

How will AI develop?

As the great baseball player Yogi Berra argued, "'It's tough to make predictions, especially about the future." That is certainly true when predicting how AI will develop in the future. There is fierce controversy, even among experts. Below we consider the views of those believing AI will rapidly outstrip human intelligence and totally transform society and those who believe the development of AI will be relatively slow and so will only have a mildly transformative effect.

DOI: 10.4324/9781003162698-8

Massive transforming changes

Many experts argue AI systems will develop rapidly in the future as a consequence of hardware and/or software developments. We will start with hardware developments. In 1965, Gordon Moore (co-founder of Intel) observed that the number of transistors in an integrated circuit had doubled every two years (although he was less explicit about this than generally supposed). He proposed Moore's law, according to which this rapid doubling would continue into the future. That prediction was accurate. It also turned out that Moore's law was at least approximately applicable to many other aspects of AI. For example, the capacity of the world's computers doubled every 18 months between 1986 and 2007.

However, what Moore (1965) proposed was not really a "law" in the sense of a theoretically based scientific principle. Indeed, it is already becoming obsolete. According to Moore (2015, p. 38), "We won't have the rate of progress that we've had over the last few decades. I think that's inevitable with any technology .... I see Moore's law dying here in the next decade."

Hardware developments have indisputably increased processing speed in AI systems. However, most such developments lead only to *quantitative* changes in processing. In contrast, potential software developments involving algorithms (well-defined procedures used by computers to solve problems) might produce *qualitative* and transformational changes that would put humans in the intellectual shade.

Some support for the above viewpoint comes from the recent history of AI. For example, there has been a rapid shift from an emphasis on Good Old-Fashioned AI (GOFAI) to deep learning (Chapter 1). This has produced rapid and dramatic improvements in the performance of AI systems in several domains (Chapter 2). Indeed, the great majority of AI's most impressive achievements have involved deep neural networks.

Since the human brain provides an incredibly successful example of general intelligence, it might in principle be possible to enhance the general intelligence of AI by developing AI systems that mimic brain functioning. This goal could be achieved in two different ways: *biological* and *psychological*. Thus, we could construct AI systems copying either the biology of the human brain or its cognitive processes and structures.

Sandberg (2013) indicated how the brain's biology might be copied: "The basic idea is to take a particular brain, scan its structure in detail, and construct a software model of it that is so faithful to the original that, when run on appropriate hardware, it will behave in essentially the same way as the original brain" (p. 251).

The above approach would be phenomenally hard to implement. An old joke capturing part of the problem concerns a brain surgeon who opens up a patient's brain and says, "Oh, there are no thoughts in here! I can't see a single thought!" More generally, there is the staggering complexity of the human brain. For example, it contains 100 billion neurons, each having an average of 7,000 synaptic connections to other neurons. Artificial emulation of the whole brain is most unlikely to happen any time soon. Indeed, it may well never happen.

A more promising approach involves modelling the human brain's key cognitive processes and structures. This could be done by developing cognitive architectures focusing on those aspects of human cognition of general importance over time and across different task domains. More precisely, cognitive architectures provide an overarching theory of the structure and key mechanisms of the mind which could then be instantiated in AI systems.

Turing (1950) advocated a simpler variant of the above approach: "Instead of trying to produce a program to simulate the adult mind, why not rather try to produce one, which simulates the child's?" The main problem is that there is increasing evidence that children's cognitive abilities are much greater than used to be believed.

In recent years, there has been a proliferation of cognitive architectures – it was estimated in 2017 that 300 cognitive architectures had already been proposed. Laird et al. (2017) produced a standard model of the mind based on commonalities among major cognitive architectures (see Figure 8.1). It has five major components: (1) declarative long-term memory (memory for information that can be consciously recalled), (2) procedural memory (memory for information such as motor skills that is not consciously accessible), (3) perception (including all sense modalities such as vision and audition), (4) motor (involved in the control of action), and (5) working memory (described below).

The single most important component is working memory. It is a very general mechanism that receives information

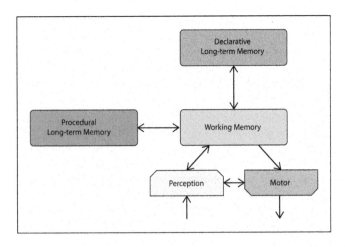

Figure 8.1 The standard model of the human cognitive architecture.

Source: Based on Laird et al. (2017).

from the two memory components and from perception. It then combines and processes this information to solve problems and guide action, with its outputs influencing all the other components. Working memory can also provide brief storage of various kinds of information (e.g., about goals and intermediate states during problem solution).

Working memory is of crucial importance to any cognitive architecture because it co-ordinates and integrates the functioning of all the other components. Its importance is also indicated by the finding that individual differences in working memory capacity are strongly related to fluid intelligence (the ability to solve novel problems).

Cognitive architectures show considerable promise. However, those produced so far share several limitations. First, unlike humans, they typically show little (or no) creativity in their processing. Second, human conflict resolution and problem solving are often strongly influenced by emotions or 'gut feelings'. However, it is rare for the processing within cognitive architectures to be affected by emotion. Third, much of human thinking involves meta-cognition (awareness and understanding of one's own cognitive processes). This self-reflective aspect of human thinking involving conscious awareness is totally absent from cognitive architectures. Fourth, the functioning of human working memory is incredibly complex. No cognitive architecture is even close to capturing that complexity.

Vernor Vinge (pronounced Vin-jee; see Figure 8.2) is very optimistic about the development of AI. In the 19909s, he popularised the notion of a singularity (the emergence of a new AI intelligence that rapidly upgrades itself) producing what Vinge (1993) called "an intellectual runaway." This intelligence is known as "superintelligence." In other words, it is a form of intelligence considerably superior to that of even the cleverest human beings.

What would this singularity mean for us? Vinge (1993), never one to understate matters, argued it would mean AI

Figure 8.2 Vernor Vinge.

becoming dominant over humans. He said it was unlikely to occur before 2005 or after 2030, so the clock is ticking.

Vinge expanded on his definition of a "singularity" in an interview with Kevin Kelly (1995): "All sorts of apocalyptic visions are floating around, but mine is very narrow. It just says that if we ever succeed in making machines as smart as humans, then it's only a small leap to imagine that we would soon thereafter make ... machines that are even smarter than any human ... That's the end of the human era — the closest analogy would be the rise of the human race within the animal kingdom. The reason for calling this a "singularity" is that things are completely unknowable beyond that point."

Many AI experts are thinking along similar lines. Grace et al. (2018, p. 731) provided experts at an AI conference in 2015 with the following definition: "'High-level machine intelligence' (HLMI) is achieved when unaided machines can accomplish every task better and more cheaply than human workers." On average, the experts predicted there was a 50% chance of HLMI occurring within 45 years and a 10% chance of it occurring within nine years (i.e., by 2024). Asian experts expected it would happen in 30 years, whereas American experts predicted it would happen in 2089.

The experts then predicted when there would be full automation of labour (i.e., all jobs can be carried out better and more cheaply by AI systems). The experts predicted a 50% probability of full automation of labour in 2137 (77 years after the predicted arrival of high-level machine intelligence).

Gruetzemacher et al. (2020) provided a more up-to-date assessment of the likely impact of developments within AI on the labour market by asking several questions of those attending three AI conferences in 2018. On average, they believed 22% of paid work tasks currently performed by humans could be done equally well with existing AI. They predicted this figure would rise to 40% within the next five years and 60% in ten years. More worryingly, they predicted on average that 90% of human work tasks could be performed by AI in 25 years and 99% in 50 years. There was the greatest optimism that AI would rapidly replace human workers among those attending the conference whose work focus was on the most advanced AI topics.

All the above predictions were made before the arrival of COVID-19. Its long-term impact on the role of AI in the workplace is currently unclear. However, the dangers to workers posed by the virus at the time of writing suggest the rate of increase of automation in the workplace is likely to accelerate.

So far we have focused on those AI experts confident that the world as we know it is going fairly shortly to be totally transformed by AI. We turn now to the view of AI experts who are far more sceptical about the probable rate of change.

Minor, non-transforming changes

Vinge's (1993) notion of the imminent arrival of the singularity involves making some dubious assumptions. Of most importance, he argued that increasingly intelligent robots will eventually design other robots that are even cleverer than they are. As we are about to see, that is highly implausible,

The ability required to exhibit apparently intelligent behaviour is radically different from the ability to design robots exhibiting even more intelligent behaviour. That would require robots to develop an understanding of their own intelligence and how it works, and then to exploit that understanding. As Aleksander (2017, p. 2) pointed out, "There is no guarantee that designing ever more competent AI algorithms will ever lead to the design of an AI designer as required by the singularity sequence."

One of the most trenchant critics of superintelligence is the American philosopher John Searle. Of central importance to his position is the distinction between observer-independent intelligence and observer-relative intelligence. As the term implies, "observer-independent intelligence" refers to genuine, indisputable intelligence whose existence owes nothing to what anyone else thinks. In contrast, "observer-relative intelligence" owes its existence entirely to the attitudes or beliefs of others.

According to John Searle (2014, p. 3), "If we ask, 'How much real, observer-independent intelligence do computers have, whether 'intelligent' or 'superintelligent'?', the answer is zero, absolutely nothing. The intelligence is entirely observer-relative. And what goes for intelligence goes for thinking, remembering, deciding, desiring, reasoning, motivation, learning, and information processing, not to mention playing chess and answering the factual questions posed on *Jeopardy!*" In other words, even though a computer can produce apparently intelligent behaviour, there is no underlying intelligence within it causing this behaviour.

Searle's (2014) central argument has widespread application. For example, most AI systems appear to exhibit goal-directed behaviour because their processing is designed to solve some problem or complete some task. However, the goals pursued by AI systems are programmed into them by humans. Thus, they are merely doing what they have been instructed to do because they have no ability to ignore their programmers' intentions and pursue their own goals. That is why robots and other AI systems cannot be held morally responsible for their actions (see Chapter 5).

There are other ways AI systems lack fundamental aspects of human intelligence. Chalmers (2010): "Language is necessary for knowing what one knows as one talks to oneself. But computers have no need or desire to communicate with others and hence never created language and without language one cannot talk to oneself and hence computers will never be conscious."

Conclusions

A theme running through this book is that all current AI systems are substantially inferior in intelligence to humans. Their inferiority is especially marked with respect to several crucial aspects of intelligence: they lack general intelligence, they lack the flexibility associated with the possession of full consciousness, and their language abilities are limited. In addition, the great majority of AI systems have very little ability to generalise their learning to novel stimuli or to tasks differing from the one on which they were trained.

Braga and Logan (2017) provided a comprehensive enumeration of the important characteristics possessed by humans but not by AI systems. According to them, "The list includes curiosity, imagination, intuition, emotions, passion, desires, pleasure, aesthetics, joy, purpose, objectives, goals, telos [ultimate purpose], values, morality, experience, wisdom, judgement, and even humour" (p. 1). Of crucial importance, no AI system developed so far has been self-motivated in the sense of setting its own goals. There is not the slightest reason for believing that situation will change very much in the future. AI systems lacking self-motivation will never achieve dominance over humans.

It could well be argued that these conclusions represent a clear case of anthropocentrism. In other words, they are based on the questionable assumption that human cognition is the touchstone against which the performance of AI systems should be judged (see Chapter 7). The problem with this line of argument is that we do not have a coherent conceptualisation of superior intelligence other than the one provided by humans. Until that is achieved, it is hard to evaluate AI's achievements other than by comparing them against those of humans.

What effects will AI developments have on society?

We have seen that experts differ considerably in their predictions concerning the nature and speed of future developments of AI. Here we turn to the related issue of whether likely changes in AI will broadly speaking have beneficial or profoundly negative effects on human lives and society.

Apocalypse soon?

There has been a dramatic increase in media focus on expert predictions of future doom and gloom as computers "take over" from humans. For example, Stephen Hawking, the British scientist, argued that, "The development of full artificial intelligence could spell the end of the human race" and Elon Musk claimed, "AI is potentially more dangerous than nukes." However, Musk has a well-known liking for hyperbole.

Finally, Grace et al. (2018) in a study discussed earlier asked AI experts whether high-level machine intelligence would have a positive or negative impact on humanity. Views were decidedly mixed. At one extreme, 20% predicted the impact would be extremely good, whereas 5% predicted it would be extremely bad (e.g., human extinction). Overall, three times as many experts predicted the impact of high-level machine intelligence would be good rather than bad.

Second, we need to predict the uses to which AI systems will put their ever-increasing "intelligence" in future. Will AI systems still remain useful tools used by humans for our purposes? Alternatively, will they develop and implement goals of their own (e.g., establishing dominance over the human race)? If they become massively more intelligent than humans, we could be in serious trouble. As Nathan, the builder of a killer robot in the movie *Ex Machina* says, "One day the AIs are going to look back on us the same way we look at fossil skeletons on the plan of Africa. An upright ape living in dust with crude language and tools, all set for extinction."

However, we cannot be entirely complacent about a future apocalypse involving AI systems. The greatest danger will come from humans. Humans acting with malicious intent could program or re-program robots and other AI systems to kill millions of people and cause mass destruction. The crucial point is that apocalypse would be caused by humans using AI systems as weapons and not by those AI systems themselves.

How should humans respond?

If there is any validity to the notion that AI will become much cleverer than humans at some point over the next 100 years, it is extremely important for humans to decide how to respond. Below we consider various possibilities designed to enhance the intelligence of the human brain.

Non-invasive brain stimulation

Suppose we make the overarching assumption that humans often fail to use the brain's processing resources optimally when performing cognitive and other complex tasks. If so, it might be possible to enhance human intelligence and cognitive performance by using non-invasive brain stimulation to increase (or decrease) the neural excitability of key brain areas. This is one of several "brain-boosting" techniques receiving considerable media attention in recent years.

Much evidence demonstrates that our performance of many tasks does not fully reflect our cognitive abilities. Two ways this happens are as follows: (1) task-irrelevant processing and/or (2) sub-optimal task-relevant processing. Task-irrelevant processing can be triggered by *external* stimuli (i.e., distraction) or by *internal* thoughts (e.g., worries and personal concerns). The term "mind-wandering" refers to shifts of attention away from the current task to one's internal thoughts (Robison et al., 2020).

Konishi and Smallwood (2016) reviewed research on mind-wandering. They found people's conscious thoughts wander away from their current activity between 25% and 50% of the time. Mind-wandering sometimes occurs even more of the time. For example, drivers on their daily commute engage in mind-wandering 60% of the time (Burdett et al., 2018; see Chapter 6).

One of the most-used techniques designed to enhance human cognition is transcranial direct current stimulation (tDCS), where a very weak electrical current is passed through a given brain area (often for several minutes) (see Figure 8.3). Anodal tDCS increases the neuronal excitability of the chosen brain area and often enhances performance; in contrast, cathodal tDCS reduces neural excitability, and often impairs performance.

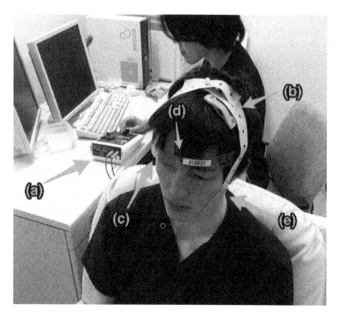

Figure 8.3 Administration of anodal transcranial direct current stimulation (tCDS). (a) tDCS equipment, (b) anodal electrodes, (c) cathodal electrodes, (d) head strap, and (e) rubber band.

Transcranial direct current stimulation (tDCS) has been used to reduce the frequency of mind-wandering during performance of tedious and monotonous tasks. Mind-wandering is strongly associated with the default mode network (Raichle, 2015). This brain network is active "by default" when an individual is not actively involved in performing a task but rather is processing internal thoughts (e.g., remembering the past). It consists of brain areas including the medial prefrontal cortex, posterior cingulate cortex/precuneus and bilateral inferior parietal lobe.

Coulborn et al. (2020) reviewed the findings from several studies using tDCS to alter mind-wandering. Overall, the effects were small and inconsistent. In their own study, Coulborn et al. found neither anodal nor cathodal tDCS had any effect on mind-wandering.

Working memory (used for the processing and brief storage of information) is extensively used during the performance of numerous cognitive tasks including problem solving and reasoning (Baddeley, 2012). In view of the general importance of working memory, it is arguable that human intelligence could be improved if tDCS were used to enhance its functioning. Relevant research was discussed by Papazova et al. (2020). They reported tDCS has typically had non-significant effects on working memory (including in Papazova et al.'s own study).

So far we have considered only the effects of non-invasive brain stimulation on healthy individuals whose cognitive abilities and intelligence are in the normal range. Suppose we focused on individuals under-performing cognitively because of some mental disorder or physical disease (e.g., stroke). It seems likely we could reduce the under-performance of such individuals. Papazova et al. (2020) discussed research showing beneficial effects of tDCS on working memory in depressed individuals and schizophrenics with impaired working-memory function. However, Sloan et al. (2021) found in a meta-analytic review that non-invasive brain stimulation had no effect on schizophrenics' working memory performance.

Approximately 70–90% of stroke patients have some cognitive impairment, and up to 50% have multiple cognitive impairments. Van Lieshout et al. (2019) reviewed research concerned with the effects of non-invasive brain stimulation on cognitive abilities in stroke patients. Most studies reported beneficial effects of brain stimulation which were generally still observable several months later. These beneficial effects have been found with respect to visual perception, attention, working memory, and memory.

Finally, we consider the effects of non-invasive brain stimulation on individuals exhibiting highly superior cognitive functioning. Krause et al. (2019) studied G.M., a 46-year-old German man who was the world champion at mental calculation. Non-invasive brain stimulation applied to dorsolateral prefrontal cortex (an area heavily involved in most complex cognitive activities) had no effect on his performance of an exceptionally difficult arithmetic task. The same non-invasive brain stimulation actually impaired the performance of highly competent mathematicians on a complex multiplication task. However, previous research (discussed by Krause et al., 2019) had shown that non-invasive brain stimulation often enhances the mathematical performance of individuals with average mathematical ability.

In sum, deficient cognitive functioning in clinical patients can sometimes be enhanced somewhat by tDCS. Since these patients' typical cognitive performance is below their pre-clinical performance, what is typically happening is that non-invasive brain stimulation is partially successful in reversing the adverse effects of their clinical condition.

However, there is vanishingly little evidence that tDCS can enhance intellectual capacity in healthy individuals. Why is that the case? The main reason for these latter disappointing findings is that applying electrical current to a small brain region is a crude technique for enhancing something as complex and sophisticated as brain functioning. Most cognitive tasks involve the use of several brain networks, each consisting of several strongly interconnected brain areas. As a consequence, increasing or decreasing neural excitability in a small brain area has major (largely unpredictable) consequences for numerous other brain areas.

Neurofeedback

As we have seen, tDCS has relatively small and inconsistent effects on cognitive processes and performance. There is a dearth of evidence concerning any long-term consequences of prior exposure to tDCS. However, long-term effects are probably even smaller than immediate ones. In principle, it would appear that a superior way of achieving long-term effects would be to use a technique encouraging individuals to *learn* how to alter their brain functioning to enhance their cognitive performance. Neurofeedback is such a technique (see Figure 8.4).

What happens with neurofeedback is that the researcher initially has theoretical reasons for targeting a given brain area. After that, participants are provided with real-time displays of their current brain activity in the selected brain area while performing a task. They are instructed to attempt to increase (or decrease) their brain activity. Thus, the goal of neurofeedback is for individuals to learn to self-regulate key aspects of their own brain function.

How neurofeedback works can be seen in the following concrete example. Eysenck et al. (2007) proposed attentional control theory, according to which high anxiety is associated with impaired attentional control. Morgenroth et al. (2020) argued that functional connectivity between the dorsolateral prefrontal cortex and anterior cingulate cortex is of central importance in efficient attentional control. Accordingly, they instructed high-anxious individuals

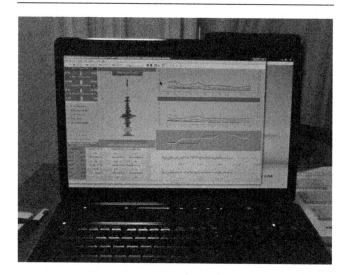

Figure 8.4 Real-time data displayed on a computer screen during feedback training.

to increase this functional connectivity under neurofeedback conditions. As predicted, neurofeedback increased that functional connectivity and also reduced participants' anxiety level.

Neurofeedback research has been reasonably successful in increasing cognitive functions in individuals with clinical conditions associated with impaired functioning. For example, children with attention-deficit/hyperactivity disorder (ADHD) have problems with maintaining attention on cognitive tasks. Neurofeedback enhanced sustained attention, working memory, and academic performance in several studies on ADHD children (e.g., Shereena et al., 2019).

Findings with healthy individuals have mostly been disappointing. Staufenbiel et al. (2014) found neurofeedback had the predicted effects on brain activity in older individuals. However, it had non-significant effects on cognitive performance and intelligence. Gordon et al. (2020)

obtained only very limited evidence that neurofeedback had any enhancement effect on working memory in healthy young adults.

Research on neurofeedback is at an early stage of development and the mechanisms by which it has its effects are largely unknown (Hampson et al., 2020). Most research has focused on the treatment of various clinical conditions and has contributed little to enhancing the cognitive performance of healthy individuals. High levels of cognitive performance and intelligence depend on integrated processing activities across several brain regions. As a consequence, using neurofeedback to increase or decrease activity in a single region will not necessarily have much impact on cognitive performance.

There is another reason why neurofeedback (and non-invasive brain stimulation) have so far had very limited effects. The human brain took literally billions of years of evolutionary development to reach its current excellence. It seems improbable in that context that increasing or decreasing brain activity in one small brain region will ever produce large enhancement effects on human cognition.

How to make human brains much more effective?

Non-invasive brain stimulation and neurofeedback may prove to be useful ways of enhancing human cognition and intelligence. However, there are unlikely to be enormous game changers. If we adopt a futuristic perspective, there are three ways human intelligence might conceivably be enhanced substantially. First, suppose we could devise technology allowing two (or more) human brains to communicate with each other *directly* rather than through speech. This would involve setting up a brain-to-brain interface, with the networked brains being potentially smarter than any of the individual brains.

Second, there are brain-machine interfaces. These interfaces come in many different forms, but here we will focus on cyborgs. The term cyborg (a combination of **cyb**ernetic and **org**anism) was first proposed by Clynes and Kline (1960). It refers to a living being with added mechanical or electronic parts to enhance its functioning. The overarching assumption is that combining the strengths of the human brain and AI can produce cognitive performance greatly in excess of either on its own.

Third, there is genetic engineering based on biotechnology. This approach involves manipulating an organism's genes *directly* to produce substantial changes in humans or other animals. The natural selection process in evolution is very effective but is typically very slow. In principle, genetic engineering could produce dramatic changes in humans over a relatively short period of time. We are not talking science fiction – genetic engineering was first used with humans several year ago (Almeida & Diogo, 2020).

Brain-to-brain interfaces

Several years ago, the feasibility of the above approach was demonstrated by Pais-Vieira et al. (2015). They inserted multi-electrode arrays into the brains of four rats, with the electrical brain activity of each rat being sent to the brains of the other three rats. The tasks used included pattern discrimination, image processing, storage and retrieval of tactile information, and weather forecasting. Pais-Vieira et al. discovered the performance of the interconnected rat brains was always equal (or superior to) that of single rats.

Jiang et al. (2019) used a similar approach in humans. They used a game where one person (the Receiver) decided whether to rotate a block to fit with blocks already present. They developed BrainNet (see Figure 8.5), which allowed two Senders to assist the Receiver's performance. Even though the Receiver could not see the blocks already present,

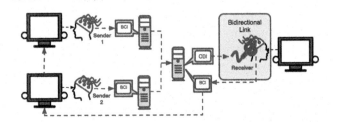

Figure 8.5 Architecture of BrainNet. EEG records the brain signals of the two senders using a brain-computer interface (BCI). Then transcranial magnetic stimulation (TMS) sends the relevant information directly to the receiver's brain via a computer-brain interface (CBI) based on TMS. After processing the senders' inputs, the receiver produces an action using a BCI. The senders see the outcome of this action, and can then convey new information to the receiver.

Source: From Jiang et al. (2019).

performance accuracy was 81%, proving that the Senders' brain signals strongly influenced the Receiver's decisions.

There is massive long-term potential in the BrainNet connecting human brains set up by Jiang et al. (2019). It opens up the prospect of producing what might be called a "biological computer." However, their study was limited in several ways. EEG provides very imprecise information concerning which brain areas are more or less active during task performance. One solution would be to combine EEG with functional magnetic resonance imaging (fMRI), which indicates activity levels in different areas very clearly. Another limitation is that the information the Receiver obtained via transcranial magnetic stimulation was delivered to the occipital area (concerned with visual perception). More complex cognitive information could be delivered if transcranial magnetic stimulation were applied to higher brain areas (e.g., the prefrontal cortex).

Finally, the task used by Jiang et al. (2019) required only a simple binary decision (i.e., rotate the block vs do not rotate the block). It will be important in future research to develop brain-brain interfaces that can cope with considerably more complex tasks.

The prospect of major developments in brain-to-brain interfaces could prove very valuable in several ways. For example, patients with locked-in syndrome find it extremely difficult to communicate with other people. In future, such patients may be able to communicate directly using this technology. However, the use of brain-to-brain interfaces raises ethical issues relating to privacy and agency (Hildt, 2019). These issues are best addressed by ensuring that all those involved provide free and informed consent and by allowing them to control the kinds of information they are willing to communicate and to receive.

Brain-machine interfaces: cyborgs

Cyborgs that may come readily to mind include fictional characters, such as Darth Vader in *Star Wars*, the Borgs in *Star Trek*, or the Terminator. However, there are numerous much more mundane examples of cyborgs. For example, patients with cardiac pacemakers and deaf humans with cochlear implants fit most definitions of cyborgs.

There has been some progress in the development of animal cyborgs controlled by humans. For example, Dutta (2019) inserted lightweight micro-electrodes into the antenna lobes of a Madagascar hissing cockroach (see Figure 8.6). The cockroach turned to the right when its left antenna lobe was stimulated and to the left when stimulation was applied to its right antenna lobe. However, these effects reduced over time because the information provided by the stimulation was often inconsistent with visual information provided by the environment.

In principle, animal cyborgs could be extremely useful for many different purposes. For example, consider potential military uses. Cyborg sharks armed with bombs could

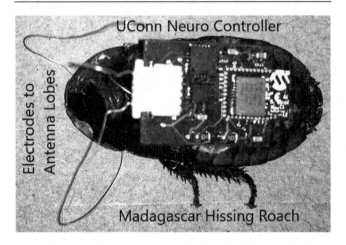

Figure 8.6 A Madagascar hissing cockroach with an inserted micro-circuit interfaced to both antenna lobes and the thorax.

Source: From Dutta (2019).

be controlled so they pursue, catch and destroy enemy ships. Note, however, that progress has been disappointingly slow: only approximately 50% of research studies have achieved the goal of controlling the movements of animal cyborgs (Dutta, 2019).

The cyborgs of most relevance to this book are those where humans have technological implants inside their brain to increase their functional intelligence. That may sound like science fiction. However, the fact that the human cerebral cortex has considerable plasticity and adaptability offers some hope that such cyborgs could be produced (Clark, 2003).

Considerable progress has already been made. For example, there are numerous cases in which brain-machine interfaces have been established. For example, consider the case of Zac Vawter, whose leg was amputated above the knee in 2009. He was provided with a leg prosthetic that moved in response to brain signals using a targeted muscle re-innervation. As a result, Zac Vawter managed to climb up all 2,100 steps of Chicago's Willis Tower in just over 53 minutes.

According to Elon Musk, "We're already cyborgs ... Your phone and your computer are extensions of you, but the interface is through finger movements or speech, which are very slow" (quoted in Ricker, 2016) How can the speed of communication between the brain and an external device be greatly increased? In Musk's opinion, this could be done by inserting a "neural lace" lace consisting of a set of electrodes into the brain through the skull using a tiny needle. In principle, this neural lace would monitor brain function and would permit bi-directional communication between the brain and a computer or other device.

Musk argued in 2016 that a system such as that described in the previous paragraph would be in place within four or five years. That time period has elapsed with no sign of the magic neural lace.

Finally, we need to consider ethical issues raised by the increasing number of cyborgs. Of key importance here is the motivation for inserting technological devices in human beings. There seem to be far great moral problems with creating cyborgs to produce "superhumans" than with creating them to overcome the impairments caused by handicaps or diseases (Pelegrin-Borondo et al., 2020).

Genetic engineering

Today's humans are living proof that Darwinian evolution is often very effective at producing species extremely well adapted to their environment. However, evolution is typically very slow. Various attempts have been made to speed up the evolutionary process in humans, the most notorious of which was the eugenics movement started by Sir Francis Galton and others in the late nineteenth century. The basic idea was that individuals with allegedly desirable heritable characteristics should have more children than those lacking such characteristics. That led inexorably to the abominations of Nazi Germany and the total discrediting of that approach.

One of the most famous examples of genetic engineering was a genetically modified rabbit called Alba. The Brazilian bio-artist Edouardo Kac collaborated with scientists at the National Institute of Agronomic Research in France. Alba was created by implanting the green fluorescent gene (GFP) gene from a green fluorescent jellyfish into the embryo of a white rabbit. She appeared white with pink eyes under normal lighting conditions. However, a photograph of Alba seen around the world showed her glowing a bright shade of green when exposed to ultraviolet light.

Edouardo Kac triumphantly identified himself as the first transgenic artist. However, there is a twist in the tale. Louis-Marie Houdebine, the French scientist who genetically engineered Alba, said the photograph was a fake. He accepted that Alba's eyes and ears would appear blue under ultraviolet light. However, the fur would not appear green because it is dead tissue that cannot express the gene. Houdebine's position is supported by the molecular biologist Reinhard Nestelbacher. He carried out similar research using mice with the green fluorescent protein (GFP) gene. He found no evidence the GFP gene was expressed in the hair of the mice.

In spite of well-informed scepticism about Alba, effective genetic engineering is possible and has enormous potential. We turn now to ways genetic engineering can be applied to humans. Gene editing can be used to insert, delete, or replace specific genetic material. In 2018, for example, several base pairs of the CCR5 gene were deleted to protect twin baby girls from the possible transmission of HIV from their HIV-positive father. Several moral concerns have been raised, partly but not entirely because the risk of transmission of HIV was apparently negligible (Bionews.org.uk, 2018).

Genetic engineering in humans takes many forms. There is a crucial distinction between genetic therapy (designed to reverse genetically caused impairments) and genetic enhancement (designed to increase human capacities above those presently attainable) (Almeida & Diogo, 2020). The National Academies of Sciences and Medicine (2017) reported much more public support for the former (e.g., disease curing) than the latter (e.g., improving children's intelligence in the womb). However, the dividing line between genetic therapy and genetic enhancement is blurred.

There are very serious ethical issues with respect to genetic enhancement, and the National Academies of Sciences and Medicine (2017) strongly recommended that no clinical trials in this area be permitted for the foreseeable future. One major concern is that there would probably be no consensus as to which forms of genetic enhancement are desirable or undesirable. In addition, society might become less accepting of those who intelligence had not been genetically enhanced. Finally, it would be very divisive if only wealthy individuals were able to enhance their family's intelligence or other capacities.

There are strong moral objections to using genetic engineering to produce "super-intelligent" humans and concerns about humans "playing at being God." Nevertheless, we can consider whether such engineering would be feasible if regarded as morally acceptable. A promising start is that we know from twin studies that genetic factors account for approximately 60% of individual differences in intelligence in adolescence and adulthood (Malanchini et al., 2020).

Genetic factors have *direct* and *indirect* influences on an individual's intelligence. There are indirect influences because individuals' choice of environment is partly determined by genetic factors – those with more genetic ability are more likely than those with less ability to choose cognitively demanding activities (e.g., reading numerous books, going to university, and having an intellectually demanding career).

Most people greatly underestimate the complexities involved in enhancing human intelligence via genetic engineering. For example, 75% of Americans mistakenly believe many forms of human behaviour are controlled by *single* genes (Christensen et al., 2010). In fact, an important "law" of behavioural genetics is that, "a typical human behavioural trait is associated with very many genetic variants, each of which accounts for a very small percentage of the behavioural variability" (Chabris et al., 2015, p. 304).

There are at least 1,016 different genes involved in human intelligence (Savage et al., 2018). It would be extraordinarily difficult to manipulate or alter several hundred genes. Even if that ever proved possible, most alterations would have only trivial effects on intelligence. Another issue is that an altered gene might well interact in complex (and counter-productive) ways with other genes involved in intelligence.

Conclusions

It is not difficult to find experts who are totally convinced that brain-to-brain interfaces, brain-machines interfaces, and genetic engineering will totally transform human cognitive abilities and intelligence. We do not agree with them. We believe strongly that the human brain is so complex and so well engineered that it will prove incredibly difficult to improve significantly on its functioning in any of those ways over the nest 20–30 years. However, would be presumptuous to speculate dogmatically about what might happen over a longer time scale.

Marriage of AI and humans

A central theme of this book is that the strengths (and limitations) of human intelligence and AI are very different. For example, human intelligence is flexible, commonsensical, imprecise, empathic, and sometimes creative but slow and prone to error. In contrast, AI processing is consistent, fast and efficient. At the risk of oversimplification, we can argue that AI excels at reckoning or calculation whereas humans excel at judgement (Smith, 2019).

The above differences between humans and AI suggest there could be huge advantages in combining and integrating their respective strengths. Already there is excellent co-operation between AI systems and humans in areas, such as medical decision making (Chapter 2), and industrial activities, such as car production (Chapter 5). Perhaps the best example of collaboration between humans and AI is our use of the internet. Humans make 3.5 billion Google searches per day or 1.2 trillion every year. It is estimated that Google stores somewhere between 10 and 15 Exabytes of data. In comparison, the total number of words spoken by all humans throughout our entire history corresponds to only approximately 5 Exabytes of data!

The ultimate goal is to create hybrid intelligence: this is a form of intelligence that combines human and AI intelligence to produce performance that is superior to either on their own (Dellermann et al., 2019). A key aspect of hybrid intelligence is bi-directional learning: AI systems "learn" from us and we learn from them. For example, human experts have learned much from AlphaGo Zero's outstanding performance at the game of Go (Silver et al., 2017).

In sum, the major focus of this book has been on comparing and contrasting the cognitive performance of humans and AI. The optimistic point of view (and one to which we subscribe) is that the future will involve progress based on humans + AI rather than humans vs AI.

References

Abdullah, H., Warren, K., Bindschaedler, V., Papernot, N., & Traynor, P. (2020). SoK: The faults in our ASRs: An overview of attacks against automatic speech recognition and speaker identification systems. https://arxiv.org/abs/2007.06622.

Aberegg, S.K., Haponik, E.F., & Terry, P.B. (2005). Omission bias and decision making in pulmonary and critical care medicine. *Chest*, *128*, 1497–1505.

Abrams, D., Wetherall, M., Cochrane, S., Hogg, M.A., & Turner, J.C. (1990). Knowing what to think by knowing who you are: Self-categorisation and the nature of norm formation, conformity and group polarisation. *British Journal of Social Psychology*, *29*, 97–119.

Ackerman, R., & Thompson, V.A. (2017). Meta-reasoning: Monitoring and control of thinking and reasoning. *Trends in Cognitive Sciences*, *21*, 607–617.

Adiwardana, D., Luong, M.T., So, D.R., Hall, J., Fiedel, N., Kulshreshtha, Y.A., et al. (2020). Towards a human-like open-domain chatbot. arXiv:2001.09977.

Aleksander, I. (2017). Partners of humans: A realistic assessment of the role of robots in the foreseeable future. *Journal of Information Technology*, *32*, 1–9.

Alemzadeh, H., Raman, J., Leveson, N., Kalbarczyk, Z., & Ravishankar, K.I. (2016). Adverse events in robotic surgery: A retrospective study of 14 years of FDA data. *PLoS ONE*, *11*, e0151470.

Allen, C., Varner, G., & Zinser, J. (2000). Prolegomena to any future artificial moral agent. *Journal of Experimental & Theoretical Artificial Intelligence*, *12*, 251–261.

Almeida, A., & Diogo, R. (2020). Human enhancement genetic engineering and evolution. *Evolution, Medicine, and Public Health, 1*, 183–189.

Almog, J., & Zitrin, S. (2009). In M. Marshal & M. Oxley (eds), *Aspects of Explosive Detection* (pp. 47–48). Amsterdam: Elsevier.

Anderegg, W.R.L., Prall, J.W., Harold, J., & Schneider, S.H. (2010). Expert credibility in climate change. *Proceedings of the National Academy of Sciences, 107*, 12107–12109.

Angwin, J., Larson, J., Mattu, S., & Kirchner, L. (2016). Machine bias: There's software used across the country to predict future criminals. And it's biased against blacks. *ProPublica*, 23 May. www.propublica.org/article/machine-bias-risk-assessmentsin-criminal-sentencing

Appel, M., Izydorczyk, D., Weber, S., Mara, M., & Lishetzke, T. (2020). The uncanny of mind in a machine: Humanoid robots as tools, agents, and experiencers. *Computers in Human Behavior, 102*, 274–286.

Apperly, I.A., & Butterfill, S.A. (2009). Do humans have two systems to track beliefs and belief-like states? *Psychological Review, 116*, 953–970.

Arnold, T., & Scheutz, M. (2016). Against the moral Turing test: Accountable design and the moral reasoning of autonomous systems. *Ethics and Information Technology, 18*, 103–115.

Asaro, P. (2013). A body to kick, but still no soul to damn: Legal perspectives on robotics. In N.P. Lin, K. Abney, & G. Bekey (eds), *Robot Ethics: The Ethical and Social Implications of Robotics* (pp. 169–186). Cambridge, MA: MIT Press.

Asch, S.E. (1951). Effects of group pressure on the modification and distortion of judgements. In H. Guetzkow (ed.), *Groups, Leadership and Men* (pp. 177–190). Pittsburgh, PA: Carnegie.

Asch, S.E. (1955). Opinions and social pressure. *Scientific American, 193*, 31–35.

Asch, S.E. (1956). Studies of independence and conformity: A minority of one against a unanimous majority. *Psychological Monographs, 70*, 1–70 (Whole No. 416).

Austin, J.L. (1975). *How to Do Things with Words*. Oxford: Oxford University Press.

Awad, E., Dsouza, S., Kim, R., Schulz, J., Henrich, J., Shariff, A., & Bonnefon, J.-F. (2018). The moral machine experiment. *Nature, 563*, 59–78.

Baddeley, A.D. (2012). Working memory: Theories, models, and controversies. *Annual Review of Psychology, 63*, 1–29.

Baddeley, A.D., & Hitch, G.J. (1974). Working memory. In G.H. Bower (ed), *Recent Advances in Learning and Motivation*, Vol. 8 (pp. 47–89). New York: Academic Press.

Badue, C., Guidolini, R., Carneiro, R.V., Azevedo, P., Cardoso, V.B., Forechi, A., et al. (2021). Self-driving cars: A survey. *Expert Systems with Applications, 165*, Article No. 113816.

Barbey, A.K. (2018). Network neuroscience theory of human intelligence. *Trends in Cognitive Science, 22*, 8–20.

Baron-Cohen, S., Leslie, A.M., & Frith, U. (1985). Does the autistic child have a "theory of mind"? *Cognition, 21*, 37–46.

Barron, G., & Leider, S. (2010). The role of experience in the gambler's fallacy. *Journal of Behavioral Decision Making, 23*, 117–129.

Bartneck, C. (2013). Robots in the theatre and the media. *Design and Semantics of Form and Movement*, 64–70. doi:10.13140/RG.2.2.28798.79682.

Bartsch, K., & Estes, D. (1996). Individual differences in children's developing theory of mind and implications for metacognition. *Learning and Individual Differences, 8*, 281–304.

Baumeister, R.F., Masicampo, E.J., & DeWall, C.N. (2009). Prosocial benefits of feeling free: Disbelief in free will increases aggression and reduces helpfulness. *Personality and Social Psychology Bulletin, 35*, 260–268.

Baumeister, R.F., & Vohs, K.D. (2018). Revisiting our reappraisal of the (surprisingly few) benefits of high self-esteem. *Perspectives on Psychological Science, 13*, 137–140.

Bender, E.M., & Koller, A. (2020). Climbing towards NLU: On meaning, form, and understanding in the Age of Data. *Proceedings of the 58th Annual Meeting of the Association for Computational Linguistics*, 5185–5198.

Benny, Y., Pekar, N., & Wolf, L. (2020). Scale-localised abstract reasoning. arXiv:2009.09405v1 [cs.AI].

Benoit, R.G., & Schacter, D. (2015). Specifying the core network supporting episodic simulations and episodic memory by activation likelihood estimation. *Neuropsychologia, 75*, 450–457.

Bentham, J. (1789). *An Introduction to the Principles of Morals and Legislation*. Oxford: Clarendon Press.

Beran, M.J. (2019). Animal metacognition: A decade of progress, problems, and the development of new prospects. *Animal Behavior and Cognition, 6*, 223–229.

Beran, M.J., Menzel, C.R., Parrish, A.E., Perdue, B.M., Sayers, J.D., & Washburn, D.A. (2016). Primate cognition: Attention, episodic memory, prospective memory, self-control, and metacognition as examples of cognitive control in non-human primates. *Wiley Interdisciplinary Reviews in Cognitive Science*, 7, 294–316.

Berkun, M.M., Bialek, H.M., Kern, R.P., & Yagi, K. (1962). Experimental studies of psychological stress in man. *Psychological Monographs*, 76(15), 1–39.

Bigman, Y.E., Waytz, A., Alterovitz, R., & Gray, K. (2019). Holding robots responsible: The elements of machine morality. *Trends in Cognitive Sciences*, 23, 365–368.

Binsted, L. (1996). *Machine Humour: An Implemented Model of Puns*. Ph.D. thesis, University of Edinburgh, UK.

Bionews.org.uk. (2018). First genome-edited babies: A very different perception of ethics. www.bionews.org.uk/page_140060

Bishop, T.M. (2021). Artificial intelligence is stupid and causal reasoning will not fix it. *Frontiers in Psychology*, 11, Article No. 513474.

Bisk, Y., Holtzman, A., Thomason, J., Andreas, J., Bengio, Y., Joyce Chai, J., et al. (2020a). Experience grounds language. arXiv preprint arXiv:2004.10151.

Bisk, Y., Zellers, R., Le Bras, R., Gao, J., & Choi, Y. (2020b). PIQA: Reasoning about physical commonsense in natural language. *Thirty-Fourth AAAI Conference on Artificial Intelligence*, 7–12 February, New York, NY, USA.

Boden, M.A. (1992). Understanding creativity. *Journal of Creative Behavior*, 26, 213–217.

Bond, R., & Smith, P.B. (1996). Culture and conformity: A meta-analysis of studies using Asch's (1952b, 1956) line judgement task. *Psychological Bulletin*, 119, 111–137.

Bonk, D., & Tamminen, K.A. (2021). Athletes' perspectives of preparation strategies in open-skill sports. *Journal of Applied Sport Psychology*, 33. https://doi.org/10.1080/10413200.2021.1875517.

Bonnefon, J.-F., Shariff, A., & Rahwan, I. (2016). The social dilemma of autonomous vehicles. *Science*, 352, 1573–1576.

Booch, G., Fabiano, F., Horesh, L., Kate, K., Lenchner, J., Linck, N. et al. (2020). Thinking fast and slow in AI. arXiv:2010.06002v1.

Booth, R.W., Sharma, D., & Leader, T.I. (2016). The age of anxiety? It depends where you look: Changes in STAI trait anxiety, 1970-2010. *Social Psychiatry and Psychiatric Epidemiology*, 51, 193–202.

Bor, D., & Seth, A.K. (2012). Consciousness and the prefrontal parietal network: Insights from attention, working memory, and chunking. *Frontiers in Psychology*, *3*, Article No. 63.

Boratko, M., Li, X.L., O'Gorman, T., Das, R., Le, D., & McCallum, A. (2020). ProtoQA: A question answering dataset for prototypical common-sense reasoning. arXiv:2005.00771v3.

Bostrum, N. (2003). Ethical issues in advanced artificial intelligence. In I. Smit et al. (eds), *Cognitive, Emotive and Ethical Aspects of Decision Making in Humans and in Artificial Intelligence*, Vol. 2 (pp. 12–17). Tecumseh, ON: International Institute of Advanced Studies in Systems Research and Cybernetics.

Botella, M., Zenasni, F., & Lubart, T. (2018). What are the stages of the creative process? What visual art students are saying. *Frontiers in Psychology*, *9*(2266), 1–28.

Bourdakos, N. (2017). Capsule networks are shaking up AI. *Hackernoon*, 9 November. https://hackernoon.com/capsule-networks-are-shaking-up-ai-heres-how-to-use-them-c233a0971952

Braga, A., & Logan, R.K. (2017). The emperor of strong AI has no clothes: Limits to artificial intelligence. *Information*, *8*, Article No. 156.

Braga, A., & Logan, R.K. (2019). AI and the singularity: A fallacy or a great opportunity? *Information*, *10*, Article No. 73.

Branas-Garza, P., Kujal, P., & Lenkei, B. (2019). Cognitive reflection test: Whom, how, when. *Journal of Behavioral and Experimental Economics*, *82*, Article No. 101455.

Bräuer, J., Hanus, D., Pika, S., Gray, R., & Uomini, N. (2020). Old and new approaches to animal cognition: There is not "one cognition." *Journal of Intelligence*, *8*, Article No. 28.

Bremner, J.G., Slater, A.M., & Johnson, S.P. (2015). Perception of object persistence: The origins of object permanence in infancy. *Child Development Perspectives*, *9*, 7–13.

Bringsjord, S., & Licato, J. (2012). Psychometric artificial general intelligence: The Piaget-MacGuyver Room. In P. Wang & B. Goertzel (eds), *Theoretical Foundations of Artificial General Intelligence. Atlantis Thinking Machines*, Vol. 4. Paris: Atlantis Press.

Broadbent, D.E. (1971). *Decision and Stress*. London: Academic Press.

Brockman, J. (1998). Consciousness is a big suitcase: A talk with Marvin Minsky. *Edge*, 26 February, 1-28.

Brogaard, B., Chomanski, B., & Gatzia, D.E. (2020). Consciousness and information integration. *Synthese*. https://doi.org/10.1007/s11229-020-02613-3.

Brooks, R. (1986). *Flesh and Machines*. New York: Pantheon Books.

Brooks, R.A. (1991). Intelligence without representation. *Artificial intelligence*, *47*, 139–159.

Brown, A.S., Caderao, K.C., Fields, L.M., & Marsh, E.J. (2015). Borrowing personal memories. *Applied Cognitive Psychology*, *29*, 471–477.

Brown, K.F., Kroll, J.S., Hudson, M.J., Ramsay, M., Green, J., Vincent, C.A., et al. (2010). Omission bias and vaccine rejection by parents of healthy children: Implications for the influenza A/H1N1 vaccination programme. *Vaccine*, *28*, 4181–4185.

Brown, N., & Sandholm, T. (2018). Superhuman AI for heads-up no-limit poker: Libratus beats top professionals. *Science*, *359*, 418–424.

Brown, N., & Sandholm, T. (2019). Superhuman AI for multi-player poker. *Science*, *365*, 885–890.

Brown, T.B., Mann, B., Ryder, N., Subbiah, M., Kaplan, J., Dhariwal, P., et al. (2020). Language models are few-shot learners. arXiv:2005.14165v4.

Brunoni, A.R., & Vanderhasselt, M.-A. (2014). Working memory improvement with non-invasive brain stimulation of the dorsolateral prefrontal cortex: A systematic review and meta-analysis. *Brain and Cognition*, *86*, 1–9.

Buckner, C. (2013). Morgan's canon, meet Hume's dictum: Avoiding anthropofabulation in cross-species comparisons. *Biology & Philosophy*, *28*, 853–871.

Buckner, C. (2019). The comparative psychology of artificial intelligences. Library Catalog: philsciarchive.pitt.edu.

Buckner, C. (2020). Black boxes or unflattering mirrors? Comparative bias in the science of machine behaviour. *The British Journal for the Philosophy of Science*. doi:10.1086/714960.

Bulley, A., & Schacter, D.L. (2020). Deliberating trade-offs with the future. *Nature Human Behaviour*, *4*, 238–247.

Bullmore, E., & Sporns, O. (2012). The economy of brain network organisation. *Nature Reviews Neuroscience*, *13*, 336–349.

Burdett, B.R.D., Charlton, S.G., & Starkey, N.J. (2018). Inside the commuting driver's wandering mind. *Transportation Research Part F*, *57*, 59–74.

Burger, L., & Jara-Ettinger, J. (2020). *Mental Inference: Mind Perception as Bayesian Model Selection*. cogsci.yale.edu.

Caffrey, A.C. (2020). *The Impact of Machine Learning on the Norwegian Legal Industry*. Master's thesis, Nord University, Norway.

Cai, C.J., Reif, E., Hegde, N., Hipp, J., Kim, B., Smilkov, D., et al. (2019). Human-centred tools for coping with imperfect algorithms during medical decision-making. *CHI Proceedings of the 2019 CHI Conference on Human Factors in Computing Systems*. doi:10.1145/3290605.3300234.

Cai, Z.G., Gilbert, R.A., Davis, M.H., Gaskell, M.G., Farrar, L., & Adler, S. (2017). Accent modulates access to word meaning: Evidence for a speaker-model account of spoken word recognition. *Cognitive Psychology, 98*, 73–101.

Callaway, E. (2020). "It will change everything": DeepMind's AI makes gigantic leap in solving protein structures. *Nature News*, 30 November. www.nature.com/articles/d41586-020-03348-4

Calvillo, D.P., Swan, A.B., & Rutchick, A.M. (2020). Ideological belief bias with political syllogisms. *Thinking & Reasoning, 26*, 291–310.

Campbell, D.T. (1960). Blind variation and selective retention in creative thought as in other knowledge processes. *Psychological Review, 67*, 380–400.

Cane, J.E., Ferguson, H.J., & Apperly, I.A. (2018). Using perspective to resolve reference: The impact of cognitive load and motivation. *Journal of Experimental Psychology: Learning, Memory, and Cognition, 43*, 591–610.

Cann, H.W., & Raymond, L. (2018). Does climate denialism still matter? The prevalence of alternative frames in opposition to climate policy. *Environmental Politics, 27*, 433–454.

Caporael, L.R., & Heyes, C. (1997). Why anthropomorphise? Folk psychology and other stories. In R.W. Mitchell, N.S. Thompson, & H.L. Miles (eds), *Anthropomorphism, Anecdotes, and Animals* (pp. 59–73). Albany, NY: University of New York Press.

Carroll, J.B. (1993). *Human Cognitive Abilities: A Survey of Factor Analytic Studies*. New York: Cambridge University Press.

Carruthers, P., & Williams, D.M. (2019). Comparative metacognition. *Animal Behavior and Cognition, 6*, 278–288.

Cartmill, E.A., Beilock, S., & Goldin-Meadow, S. (2012). A word in the hand: Action, gesture and mental representation in humans and non-human primates. *Philosophical Transactions of the Royal Society B, 367*, 129–143.

Cattell, R.B. (1963). Theory of fluid and crystallised intelligence. *Journal of Educational Psychology, 54*, 1–22.

Cerullo, M.A. (2015). The problem with phi: A critique of integrated information theory. *PLoS: Computational Biology, 11*, e1004286.

Cervantes, J.-A., López, S., Rodriguez, L.-F., Cervantes, S., Cervantes, F., & Ramos, F. (2020). Artificial moral agents: A survey of the current status. *Science and Engineering Ethics, 26*, 501–532.

Chabris, C.F., Lee, J.J., Cesarini, D., Benjamin, D.J., & Laibson, D.I. (2015). The fourth law of behaviour genetics. *Current Directions in Psychological Science, 24*, 304–312.

Chalmers, D. (2010). The singularity: A philosophical analysis. *Journal of Consciousness Studies, 17*, 7–65.

Chamberlain, R., Mullin, C., Scheerlinck, B., & Wagemans, J. (2018). Putting the art in artificial: Aesthetic responses to computer-generated art. *Psychology of Aesthetics, Creativity, and the Arts, 12*, 177–192.

Charpentier, C.J., De Neve, J.-E., Li, X., Roiser, J.P., & Sharot, T. (2016). Models of affective decision making: How do feelings predict choice? *Psychological Science, 27*, 763–775.

Chater, N., & Christiansen, M.H. (2018). Language acquisition as skill learning. *Current Opinion in Behavioral Sciences, 21*, 205–208.

Cheek, N.N., & Schwartz, B. (2016). On the meaning and measurement of maximisation. *Judgment and Decision Making, 11*, 126–146.

Chen, Y., Yuan, X., Zhang, J., Zhao, Y., Zhang, S., Chen, K., et al. (2020). Devil's whisper: A general approach for physical adversarial attacks against commercial black-box speech recognition devices. *Proceedings of the 29th USENIX Security Symposium*, August 12–14, Boston, MA, USA, 2667–2684.

Chomsky, N. (1965). *Aspects of the Theory of Syntax*. Cambridge, MA: MIT Press.

Chomsky, N. (1980). *Rules and Representations*. Oxford: Basil Blackwell.

Christensen, K.D., Jayaratne, T., Roberts, J., Kardia, S., & Petty, E. (2010). Understandings of basic genetics in the United States: Results from a national survey of black and white men and women. *Public Health Genomics, 13*, 467–476.

Christiansen, M.H., & Chater, N. (2008). Language as shaped by the brain. *Behavioral and Brain Sciences, 31*, 489–558.

Clark, A.J. (2003). *Natural-Born Cyborgs: Minds, Technologies, and the Future of Human Intelligence*. New York: Oxford University Press.

Clark, D.D., & Sokoloff, L. (1999). Circulation and energy metabolism of the brain. In G.J. Siegel, B.W. Agranoff, R.W. Albers, S.K. Fisher, & M.D. Uhler (eds), *Basic Neurochemistry: Molecular, Cellular and Medical Aspects* (pp. 637–670). Philadelphia, PA: Lippincott.

Clayton, N.S. (2017). Episodic-like memory and mental time travel in animals. In J. Call, G.M. Burghardt, I M. Pepperberg, C.T. Snowdon, & T. Zentall (eds), *APA Handbook of Comparative Psychology: Perception, Learning, and Cognition* (pp. 227–243). Philadelphia, PA: Lippincott, Williams and Wilkins.

Clynes, M.E., & Kline, N. (1960). Cyborgs and space. *Astronautics*, 26–27 September, 74–75.

Cole, D. (2020). The Chinese room argument. *Stanford Encyclopaedia of Philosophy*. Palo Alto, CA: Stanford University.

Collin, G., Sporns, O., Mandl, R.C.W., & van den Heuvel, M.P. (2014). Structural and functional aspects relating to costs and benefit of rich club organisation in the human cerebral cortex. *Cerebral Cortex*, *24*, 2258–2267.

Colman, A.M. (2015). *Oxford Dictionary of Psychology* (4th edn). Oxford: Oxford University Press.

Computer Shogi Association (2017). Results of the 27th world computer shogi championship. www2.computer-shogi.org/wcsc27/index_e.html

Copeland, B. (2004). *The Essential Turing—The Ideas That Gave Birth to the Computer Age*. Oxford: Clarendon Press.

Corbett-Davies, S., & and Goel, S. (2018). The measure and mismeasure of fairness: A critical review of fair machine learning. https://arxiv.org/abs/1808.00023.

Corbett-Davies, S., Pierson, E., Feller, A., Goel, S., & Aziz Huq, A. (2017). Algorithmic decision making and the cost of fairness. *Proceedings of the International Conference on Knowledge Discovery and Data Mining* pp. 797–806.

Cormier, D.C., Bulut, O., McGrew, K.S., & Frison, J. (2016). The role of Cattell-Horn-Carroll (CHC) cognitive abilities in predicting writing achievement during the school-age years. *Psychology in the Schools*, *53*, 787–803.

Corneille, O., & Hütter, M. (2020). Implicit? What do you mean? A comprehensive review of the delusive implicitness construct in attitude research. *Personality and Social Psychology Review*, *24*, 212–232.

Corner, A., Hahn, U., & Oaksford, M. (2011). The psychological mechanism of the slippery slope argument. *Journal of Memory and Language, 64*, 133–152.

Coulborn, S., Bowman, H., Miall, C., & Fernandez-Espejo, D. (2020). Effect of tDCS over the right inferior parietal lobule on mind-wandering propensity. *Frontiers In Human Neuroscience, 14*(230). doi: 10.3389/fnhum.2020.00230.

Cowan, N. (2005). *Working Memory Capacity*. Hove: Psychology Press.

Craycraft, N.N., & Brown-Schmidt, S. (2018). Compensating for an inattentive audience. *Cognitive Science, 42*, 1509–1528.

Crootof, R. (2019). "Cyborg justice" and the risk of technological-legal lock-in. *Columbia Law Review Forum, 119*, 233–251.

Crosby, M. (2020). Building thinking machines by solving animal cognition tasks. *Minds and Machines, 30*, 589–615.

Crosby, M., Beyret, B., Shanahan, M., Hernández-Orallo, J., Cheke, L., & Halina, M. (2020). The animal-AI testbed and competition. *Proceedings of Machine Learning Research, 123*, 164–176.

Cui, X.D., Zhang, W., Finkler, U., Saon, G., Picheny, M., & Kung, D. (2020). Distributed training of deep neural network acoustic models for automatic speech recognition: A comparison of current training strategies. *IEEE Signal Processing Magazine, 37*, 39–49.

Cunningham, W.A., Preacher, K.J., & Banaji, M.R. (2001). Implicit attitudes measures: Consistency, stability, and convergent validity. *Psychological Science, 12*, 163–170.

Cushman, F. (2020). Rationalisation is rational. *Behavioral and Brain Sciences, 43*(e28), 1–59.

Cuzzolin, F., Morelli, A., Cîrstea, B., & Sahakian, B.J. (2020). Knowing me, knowing you: Theory of mind in AI. *Psychological Medicine, 50*, 1057–1061.

Dale, R. (2018). Law and word order: NLP in legal tech. *Natural Language Engineering, 25*, 211–217.

Da Lio, Plebe, A., Bortoluzzi, D., Papini, G.P.R., & Dona, R. (2018). Autonomous vehicle architecture inspired by the neurocognition of human driving. *Proceedings of the 4th International Conference on Vehicle Technology and Intelligent Transport Systems (VEHITS 2018)*, 507–513.

Danaher, J. (2016). Robots, law and the retribution gap. *Ethics and Information Technology, 18*, 299–309.

Darwin, C. (1859). *The Origin of Species*. London: Macmillan.

Darwin, C. (1871). *The Descent of Man* (2nd edn). New York: A.L. Burt.

Davis, E.S., & Marcus, G.F. (2020). Computational limits don't fully explain human cognitive limitations. *Behavioral and Brain Sciences*, *43*, 21–22.

de Bode, S., Smets, L., Mathern, G.W., & Dubinsky, S. (2015). Complex syntax in the isolated right hemisphere: Receptive grammatical abilities after cerebral hemispherectomy. *Epilepsy & Behavior*, *51*, 33–39.

Dehaene, S., Changeux, J.P., Naccache, L., Sackur, J., & Sergent, C. (2006). Conscious, preconscious, and subliminal processing: A testable taxonomy. *Trends in Cognitive Sciences*, *10*, 204–211.

Dehaene, S., Lau, H., & Kouider, S. (2017). What is consciousness, and could machines have it? *Science*, *358*, 486–492.

Dellermann, D., Ebel, P., Söllner, M., & Leimeister, J.M. (2019). Hybrid intelligence. *Business & Information Systems Engineering*, *61*, 637–643.

Demertzi, A., Soddu, A., & Laureys, S. (2013). Consciousness supporting networks. *Current Opinion in Neurobiology*, *23*, 239–244.

DeMiguel, V., Garlappi, L., & Budescu, D.V. (2009). Optimal versus naive diversification: How inefficient is the 1/N portfolio strategy? *Review of Financial Studies*, *22*, 1915–1953.

Deutsch, M., & Gerrard, H.B. (1955). A study of normative and informational influence upon individual judgement. *Journal of Abnormal and Social Psychology*, *51*, 629–636.

Devalla, S.K., Sripad, K., Liang, Z., Pham, T.H., Boote, C., Strouthidis, N.G., et al. (2020). Glaucoma management in the era of artificial intelligence. *British Journal of Ophthalmology*, *104*, 301–311.

Devlin, J., Ming-Wei Chang, M.-W., & Toutanova, K. (2019). BERT: Pre-training of deep bi-directional transformers for language understanding. *Proceedings of the 2019 Conference of the North American Chapter of the Association for Computational Linguistics: Human Language Technologies*, *1*, 4171–4186.

Deza, A., & Konkle, T. (2020). Emergent properties of foveated perceptual systems. arXiv:2006.07991.

Dismukes, R.K., & Nowinski, J.L. (2006). Prospective memory, concurrent task management, and pilot error. In A. Kramer, D. Wiegmann, & A. Kirlik (eds), *Attention: From Theory to Practice* (pp. 223–238). Oxford: Oxford University Press.

Dogramaci, S. (2020). What is the function of reasoning? On Mercier and Sperber's argumentative and justificatory theories. *Episteme*, *17*(3), 316–330.

Dowsett, E., Semmler, C., Bray, H., Ankeny, R.A., & Chur-Hansen, A. (2018). Neutralising the meat paradox: Cognitive dissonance, gender, and eating animals. *Appetite, 123,* 280–288.

Dressel, J., & Farid, H. (2018). The accuracy, fairness, and limits of predicting recidivism. *Sciences Advances, 4,* Article No. Eaao5580.

Dror, I.E. (2020). Cognitive and human factors in expert decision making: Six fallacies and the eight sources of bias. *Analytical Chemistry, 92,* 7998–8004.

Dudokovic, N.M., Marsh, E.J., & Tversky, B. (2004). Telling a story or telling it straight: The effects of entertaining versus accurate retellings on memory. *Applied Cognitive Psychology, 18,* 125–143.

Dufner, M., Gebauer, J.E., Sedikides, C., & Denissen, J.J.A. (2019). Self-enhancement and psychological adjustment: A meta-analytic review. *Personality and Social Psychology Review, 23,* 48–72.

Du-Harpur, X., Watt, F.M., Luscombe, N.M., & Lynch, M.D. (2020). What is AI? Applications of artificial intelligence to dermatology. *British Journal of Dermatology, 183,* 423–430.

Dujmović, M., Malhotra, G., & Bowers, J.S. (2020). What do adversarial images tell us about human vision? *eLife, 9,* e55978.

Dunbar, R.I.M. (1998). The social brain hypothesis. *Evolutionary Anthropology, 6,* 178–190.

Dunbar, R.I.M., & Shultz, S. (2017). Evolution in the social brain. *Science, 317,* 1344–1347.

Duncan, J., Assem, M., & Shashidhara, S. (2020). Integrated intelligence from distributed brain activity. *Trends in Cognitive Sciences, 24,* 838–852.

Durisko, Z., Mulsant, B.H., & Andrews, P.W. (2015). An adaptationist perspective on the aetiology of depression. *Journal of Affective Disorders, 172,* 315–323.

Dutta, A. (2019). Cyborgs: Neuromuscular control of insects. *9th International IEEE EMBS Conference on Neural Engineering,* 20–23 March, San Francisco, CA, USA.

Echterhoff, G., & Higgins, E.T. (2018). Shared reality: Construct and mechanisms. *Current Opinion in Psychology, 23,* iv–vii.

Ehsan, U., Harrison, B., Chan, L., & Riedl, M.O. (2018). Rationalisation: A neural machine translation approach to generating natural language explanations. *Proceedings of the 2018 AAAI/ACM Conference on AI, Ethics, and Society,* 81–87.

Eil, D., & Lien, J.W. (2014). Staying ahead and getting even: Risk attitudes of experienced poker players. *Games and Economic Behavior, 87,* 50–69.

Einstein, G.O., & McDaniel, M.A. (2005). Prospective memory: Multiple retrieval processes. *Current Directions in Psychological Science, 14*, 286–290.

Elsayed, G.F., Shankar, S., Cheung, B., Papernot, N., Kurakin, A., Goodfellow, I., et al. (2018). Adversarial examples that fool both computer vision and time-limited humans. *Advances in Neural Information Processing Systems*, 3910–3920.

Enke, B., Gneezy, U., Hall, B., Martin, D., Nelidov, V., Offerman, T., & van de Ven, J. (2020). Cognitive biases: Mistakes or missing stakes? *CES Working Paper*, No. 8168.

Epley, N. (2018). A mind like mine: The exceptionally ordinary underpinnings of anthrpomorphism. *Journal of the Association for Consumer Research, 3*, 591–598.

Epley, N., Waytz, A., & Cacioppo, J. T. (2007). On seeing human: A three–factor theory of anthropomorphism. Psychological Review, 114, 864–886.

Esteva, A., Kuprel, B., Novoa, R.A., Ko, J., Swetter, S.M., Blau, H.M., et al. (2017). Dermatologist-level classification of skin cancer with deep neural networks. *Nature, 542*, 115–118.

Evans, J.S.B.T., & Stanovich, K.E. (2013a). Dual-process theories of higher cognition: Advancing the debate. *Perspectives on Psychological Science, 8*, 223–241.

Evans, N., & Levinson, S. (2009). The myth of language universals: Language diversity and its importance for cognitive science. *Behavioral and Brain Sciences, 32*, 429–492.

Evans, S., McGettigan, C., Agnew, Z.K., Rosen, S., & Scott, S.K. (2016). Getting the cocktail party started: Masking effects in speech perception. *Journal of Cognitive Neuroscience, 28*, 483–500.

Everaert, J., Duyck, W., & Koster, E.H.W. (2014). Attention, interpretation, and memory biases in subclinical depression: A proof-of-principle test of the combined biases hypothesis. *Emotion, 14*, 331–340.

Eysenck, M.W. (1982). *Attention and Arousal: Cognition and Performance.* Berlin: Springer.

Eysenck, M.W. (2022). *Simply Psychology* (5th edn). Abingdon: Routledge.

Eysenck, M.W., & Derakshan, N. (2011). New perspectives in attentional control theory. *Personality and Individual Differences, 50*, 955–960.

Eysenck, M.W., Derakshan, N., Santos, R., & Calvo, M.G. (2007). Anxiety and cognitive performance: Attentional control theory. *Emotion, 7*, 336–353.

Eysenck, M.W., & Groome, D. (2020). Memory failure and its causes. In M.W. Eysenck & D. Groome (eds), *Forgetting: Explaining Memory Failure*. London: SAGE.

Eysenck, M.W., & Keane, M.T. (2020). *Cognitive Psychology: A Student's Handbook* (8th edn). Abingdon: Psychology Press.

Faes, L., Liu, X., Wagner, S.K., Fu, D.F., Balaskas, K., Sim, D.A., et al. (2020). A clinician's guide to artificial intelligence: How to critically appraise machine learning studies. *Translational Vision Science & Technology, 9*(2), Article No. 7.

Fan, D.-P., Ji, G.P., Sun, G., Cheng, M.-M., Shen, J., & Shao, L. (2020). Camouflaged object detection. *Proceedings of the IEEE/CVF Conference on Computer Vision and Pattern Recognition (CVPR)*, 2777–2787.

Farrar, B.G., & Ostojić, L. (2019). The illusion of science in comparative cognition, 2 October. https://doi.org/10.31234/osf.io/hduyx.

Fawcett, J.M., & Hulbert, J.C. (2020). The many faces of forgetting: Toward a constructive view of forgetting in everyday life. *Journal of Applied Research in Memory and Cognition, 9*, 1–18.

Feinberg, T.E., & Mallatt, J.M. (2016). *The Ancient Origins of Consciousness: How the Brain Created Experience*. Cambridge, MA: MIT Press.

Fernbach, P.M., Light, N., Scott, S.E., Inbar, Y., & Rozin, P. (2019). Extreme opponents of genetically modified foods know the least but think they know the most. *Nature Human Behaviour, 3*, 251–256.

Ferreira, V.S. (2019). A mechanistic framework for explaining audience design in language production. *Annual Review of Psychology, 70*, 29–51.

Festinger, L., Riecken, H., & Schacter, S. (1956). *When Prophecy Fails: A Social and Psychological Study of a Modern Group That Predicted the Destruction of the World*. Minneapolis, MN: University of Minnesota Press.

Fildes, A., Charlton, J., Rudisill, C., Littlejohns, P., Prevost, A.T., & Gulliford, M.C. (2015). Probability of an obese person attaining normal body weight: Cohort study using electronic health records. *American Journal of Public Health, 105*, e54–e59.

Finlayson, S.G., Bowers, J.D., Ito, J., Zittreain, J.L., Beam, A.L., & Kohane, I.S. (2019). Adversarial attacks on medical machine learning. *Science, 363*, 1287–1289.

Firestone, C. (2020). Performance vs competence in human-machine comparisons. *Proceedings of the National Academy of Sciences, 117*, 26562–26571.

Firth, J.R. (1957). A synopsis of linguistic theory, 1930–1955. *Studies in Linguistic Analysis*. In F.R. Palmer (ed.) (1968), *Selected Papers of J.R. Firth 1951–1959*. London: Longman.

Fischer, L., & Läubl, S. (2020). What's the difference between professional human and machine translation? A blind multi-language study on domain-specific MT. arXiv:2006.04781v1 [cs.CL].

Fiske, S.T. (2010). *Social Beings: Core Motives in Social Psychology* (2nd edn). Hoboken, NJ: Wiley.

Fiske, S.T., & Taylor, S.E. (1991). *Social Cognition*. New York: McGraw-Hill.

Flynn, J.R. (1987). Massive IQ gains in 14 nations – What IQ really measures. *Psychological Bulletin, 101,* 171–191.

Formanowicz, M., Goldenberg, A., Saguyc, T., Pietraszkiewicza, A., Walkered, M., & Gross, J.J. (2018). Understanding dehumanisation: The role of agency and communion. *Journal of Experimental Social Psychology, 77,* 102–116.

Formos, P., & Ryan, M. (2020). Making moral machines: Why we need artificial moral agents. *AI & Society*. https://doi.org/10.1007/s00146-020-01089-6.

Fotuhi, O., Fong, G.T., Zanna, M.P., Borland, R., Yong, H.-H., & Cummings, L.M. (2013). Patterns of cognitive dissonance-reducing beliefs among smokers: A longitudinal analysis from the international tobacco control (ITC) four country survey. *Tobacco Control, 22,* 52–58.

Frederick, S. (2005). Cognitive reflection and decision making. *Journal of Economic Perspectives, 19,* 25–42.

Freed, E.M., Hamilton, S.T., & Long, D.L. (2017). Comprehension in proficient readers: The nature of individual variation. *Journal of Memory and Language, 97,* 135–153.

Freeman, J., & Simoncelli, E.P. (2011). Metamers of the ventral stream. *Nature Neuroscience, 14,* 1195–1201.

Friedman, N.P., & Miyake, A. (2017). Unity and diversity of executive functions: Individual differences as a window on cognitive structure. *Cortex, 86,* 186–204.

Funke, C.M., Borowski, J., Stosio, K., Brendel, W., Wallis, T.S.A., & Bethge, M. (2020). Five points to check when comparing visual perception in humans and machines. arXiv:2004.09406v2.

Gao, H., Wang, W., & Fan, Y. (2012). Divide and conquer: An efficient attack on Yahoo! CAPTCHA. *Proceedings of the 2012 IEEE 11th*

International Conference on Trust, Security and Privacy in Computing and Communication, 9–16.

Garrett, B. (2011). *Convicting the Innocent: Where Criminal Prosecutions Go Wrong*. Cambridge, MA: Harvard University Press.

Garson, J. (2015). Connectionism. *Stanford Encyclopedia of Philosophy*. Stanford, CA: Stanford University.

Gibson, E., Tan, C., Futrell, R., Mahowald, K., Konieczny, L., Hemworth, B., & Fedorenko, E. (2017). Don't underestimate the benefits of being misunderstood. *Psychological Science*, *28*, 703–712.

Gigerenzer, G. (2018). The bias bias in behavioral economics. *Review of Behavioral Economics*, *5*, 303–336.

Gilbert, D.T. (2006). *Stumbling on Happiness*. New York: Alfred A. Knopf.

Glas, D.F., Minato, T., Ishi, C.T., Kawahara, T., & Ishiguro, H. (2016). ERICA: The ERATO intelligent conversational android. *25th IEEE International Symposium on Robot and Human Interactive Communication (RO-MAN)*, 26–31 August, Columbia University, NY, USA.

Gleick, J. (1992). *Genius: The Life and Science of Richard Feynman*. New York: Pantheon Books.

Glockner, M., Shwartz, V., & Goldberg, Y. (2018). Breaking NLI systems with sentences that require simple lexical inferences. arXiv:1805.02266v1.

Goel, S., Shroff, R., Skeem, J.L., & Slobogin, C. (2021). The accuracy, equity, and jurisprudence of criminal risk assessment. In R. Vogel (ed.), *Research Handbook on Big Data Law*. Cheltenham: Edward Elgar.

Goertzel, B., Iklé, M., & Wigmore, J. (2012). The architecture of human-like general intelligence. In P. Wang & B. Goertzel (eds), *Theoretical Foundations of Artificial General Intelligence*. Atlantis Thinking Machines, Vol. 4. Paris: Atlantis Press.

Gogoll, J., & Müller, J.F. (2017). Autonomous cars: In favour of a mandatory ethics. *Science and Engineering Ethics*, *23*, 681–700.

Golumbic, E.Z., Cogan, G.B., Schroeder, C.E., & Poeppel, D. (2013). Visual input enhances selective speech envelope tracking in auditory cortex at a "cocktail party". *Journal of Neuroscience*, *33*, 1417–1426.

Goodfellow, I., Pouget-Abadie, J., Mirza, M., Xu, B., Warde-Farley, D., Ozair, S., et al. (2014). Generative adversarial nets. *Advances in Neural Information Processing Systems* (pp. 2672–2680). Cambridge, MA: MIT Press.

Gopnik, A., O'Grady, S., Lucas, C.C., Griffiths, T.L., Wente, A., Bridgers, S., et al. (2017). Changes in cognitive flexibility and hypothesis search across human life history from childhood to adolescence to adulthood. *Proceedings of the National Academy of Sciences, 114*, 7892–7899.

Gordon, S., Todder, D., Deutsch, I., Garbi, D., Alkob, O., Shkedy-Rabani, A., et al. (2020). Effects of neurofeedback and working memory-combined training on executive functions in healthy young adults. *Psychological Research, 84*, 1586–1609.

Graber, M.L. (2013). The incidence of diagnostic error in medicine. *BMJ Quality & Safety, 22*, ii21–ii27.

Grace, K., Salvatier, J., Defoe, A., Zhang, B., & Evans, O. (2018). When will AI exceed human performance? Evidence from experts. *Journal of Artificial Intelligence Research, 62*, 729–754.

Graf, P. (2012). Prospective memory: Faulty brain, flaky person. *Canadian Psychology, 53*, 7–13.

Greene, J.D., Nystrom, L.E., Engell, A.D., Darley, J.M., & Cohen, J.D. (2004). The neural bases of cognitive conflict and control in moral judgement. *Neuron, 44*, 389–400.

Grice, H.P. (1975). Logic and conversation. In P. Cole & J.L. Morgan (eds), *Syntax and Semantics, III: Speech Acts* (pp. 41–58). New York: Academic Press.

Groome, D., Eysenck, M.W., & Law, R. (2020). Motivated forgetting: Forgetting what we want to forget. In M.W. Eysenck & D. Groome (eds), *Forgetting: Explaining Memory Failure* (pp. 147–167). London: SAGE.

Groopman, J. (2007). *How Doctors Think*. New York: Houghton Mifflin.

Grosz, B.J. (2018). Smart enough to talk with us? Foundations and challenges for dialogue-capable AI systems. *Computational Linguistics, 44*, 1–15.

Gruetzemacher, R., Paradice, D., & Bok, L.K. (2020). Forecasting extreme labour displacement: A survey of AI practitioners. *Technological Forecasting and Social Change, 161*, Article No. 120323.

Gu, R., Zhang, S.-X., Xu, Y., Chen, L., Zou, Y., & Yu, D. (2020). Multimodal multi-channel target speech separation. *IEEE Journal of Selected Topics in Signal Processing, 14*, 530–541.

Guizzo, E., & Ackerman, E. (2015). The hard lessons of DARPA's robotics challenge. *IEEE Spectrum, 52*, 11–13.

Hahn, U., & Oaksford, M. (2014). *The Fallacies Explained*. Oxford: Oxford University Press.

Haigh, M., Wood, J.S., & Stewart, A.J. (2016). Slippery slope arguments imply opposition to change. *Memory & Cognition, 44*, 819–836.

Hampson, M., Ruis, S., & Ushiba, J. (2020). Neurofeedback. *NeuroImage, 218*, Article No. 116473.

Harley, T.A. (2010). *Talking the Talk: Language, Psychology and Science.* Hove: Psychology Press.

Hassin, R.R. (2013). Yes it can: On the functional abilities of the human unconscious. *Perspectives on Psychological Science, 8*, 195–207.

Hawkins, A.J. (2020). Waymo pulls back the curtain on 6.1 million miles of self-driving car data in Phoenix. *The Verge*, 30 October.

Hawley-Dolan, A., & Winner, E. (2011). Seeing the mind behind the art: People can distinguish abstract expressionist paintings from highly similar paintings by children, chimps, monkeys, and elephants. *Psychological Science, 22*, 435–441.

Heaven, D. (2019). Deep trouble for deep learning: Artificial-intelligence researchers are trying to fix the flaws of neural networks. *Nature, 574*, 163–166.

Heaven, W.D. (2020). OpenAI's new language generator GPT-3 is shockingly good—And completely mindless. *MIT Technology Review*, 29 July, 1–6. www.technologyreview.com/2020/07/20/1005454/openai-machine-learning-language-generator-gpt-3-nlp/

Heikkinen, H., Patja, K., & Jallinoja, P. (2010). Smokers' accounts on the health risks of smoking: Why is smoking not dangerous for me? *Social Science & Medicine, 71*, 877–883.

Hendrycks, D., Zhao, K., Basart, S., Steinhardt, J., & Song, D. (2021). Natural adversarial examples. arXiv:1907.07174v4 [cs.LG].

Henrich, J. (2016). *The Secret of Our Success: How Culture is Driving Human Evolution, Domesticating Our Species; And Making Us Smarter.* Princeton, NJ: Princeton University Press.

Henrich, J., & Muthukrishna, M. (2021). The origins and psychology of human co-operation. *Annual Review of Psychology, 72*, 207–240.

Herbranson, W.T., & Schroeder, J. (2010). Are birds smarter than mathematicians? Pigeons (*Columba livia*) perform optimally on a version of the Monty Hall Dilemma. *Journal of Comparative Psychology, 124*, 1–13.

Herculano-Houzel, S. (2012). The remarkable, yet not extraordinary, human brain as a scaled-up primate brain and its associated cost. *Proceedings of the National Academy of Sciences, 109* (Supplement 1), 10661–10668.

Hesselmann, G., & Moors, P. (2015). Definitely maybe: Can unconscious processes perform the same functions as conscious processes? *Frontiers in Psychology, 6,* Article No. 584.

Hildt, E. (2019). Multi-person brain-to-brain interfaces: Ethical issues. *Frontiers of Neuroscience, 13,* Article No. 1177.

Hockey, G.R.J. (1997). Compensatory control in the regulation of human performance under stress and high workload: A cognitive-energetical framework. *Biological Psychology, 45,* 73–93.

Hodges, B.H. (2014). Rethinking conformity and imitation: Divergence, convergence, and social understanding. *Frontiers in Psychology, 5,* Article No. 726.

Hofer, F., & Schwaninger, A. (2005). Using threat image projection data for assessing individual screeners performance. *WIT Transactions on the Built Environment, 82,* 417–426.

Hoffrage, U., Hafenbrädle, S., & Marewski, J.N. (2018). The fast-and-frugal heuristics programme. In L.J. Ball & V.A. Thompson (eds), *Routledge International Handbook of Thinking and Reasoning* (pp. 325–345). Abingdon: Routledge.

Hoffrage, U., Lindsey, S., Hertwig, R., & Gigerenzer, G. (2000). Communicating statistical information. *Science, 290,* 2261–2262.

Hofstadter, D.R. (2001): Analogy as the core of cognition. In D. Gentner, K.L., Holyoak, & B.N. Kokinov (eds), *The Analogical Mind: Perspectives from Cognitive Science* (pp. 499–538). Cambridge, MA: MIT Press/A Bradford Book.

Horowitz, M. (2019). When speed kills: Lethal autonomous weapon systems, deterrence and stability. *Journal of Strategic Studies, 42,* 764–788.

Horschler, D.J., MacLean, E.L., & Santos, L.R. (2020). Do non-human primates really represent others' beliefs? *Trends in Cognitive Sciences, 24,* 594–605.

Horton, W.S., & Gerrig, R.J. (2016). Revisiting the memory-based processing approach to common ground. *Topics in Cognitive Science, 8,* 780–795.

Huang, S.G., Yang, J., Fong, S., & Zhao, Q. (2020). Artificial intelligence in cancer diagnosis and prognosis: Opportunities and challenges. *Cancer Letters, 471,* 61–71.

Humberg, S., Dufner, M., Schönbrodt, F.D., Geukes, K., Hutteman, R., Küfner, A.C.P., et al. (2019). Is accurate, positive, or inflated self-perception most advantageous for psychological adjustment? A competitive test of key hypotheses. *Journal of Personality and Social Psychology*, *116*, 835–859.

Huo, J., Herold, C., Gao, Y., Dahimann, L., Khadivi, S., & Ney, H. (2020). Diving deep into context-aware neural machine translation. arXiv:2010.09482v1 [cs.CL].

Ilyas, A., Santurkar, S., Tsipras, D., Engstrom, L., Tran, B., & Ma, A. (2019). Adversarial examples are not bugs, they are features. arXiv:1905.02175. *International Federation of Robotics (IFR)* World Robotics 2019 Edition.

James, W. (1890). *The Principles of Psychology*. New York: H. Holt and Company.

Janssen, E.M., Raoelison, M., & de Neys, W. (2020). "You're wrong!": The impact of accuracy feedback on the bat-and-ball problem. *Acta Psychologica*, *206*, Article No. 103042.

Jara-Ettinger, J. (2019). Theory of mind as inverse reinforcement learning. *Current Opinion in Behavioral Sciences*, *29*, 105–110.

Jaušovec, N. (2019). The neural code of intelligence: From correlation to causation. *Physics of Life Reviews*, *31*, 171–187.

Jeffrey, K. (2015). In our image. In J. Brockman (ed), *What to Think About Machines that Think*. New York: Harper Perennial.

Jia, R., & Liang, P. (2017). Adversarial examples for evaluating reading comprehension systems. arXiv:1707.07328.

Jiang, L.X., Stocco, A., Losey, D.M., Abernethy, J.A., Prat, C.S., & Rao, R.P.N. (2019). BrainNet: A multi-person brain-to-brain interface for direct collaboration between brains. *Scientific Reports*, *9*, Article No. 6115.

Jiang, Z., Xu, F.F., Arak, J., & Neubig, G. (2020). How can we know what language models know? *Transactions of the Association for Computational Linguistics*, *8*, 423–438.

Kac, E. (2000). GFP Bunny. www.ekac.org/gfpbunny.html

Kahan, D.M., Peters, E., Wittlin, M., Slovic, P., Ouellette, L.L., & Braman, D. (2012). The polarising impact of science literacy and numeracy on perceived climate change risks. *Nature Climate Change*, *2*, 732–735.

Kahneman, D. (2011). *Thinking, Fast and Slow*. New York: Farrar, Straus & Giroux.

Kahneman, D., & Tversky, A. (1979). Prospect theory: An analysis of decision under risk. *Econometrica*, *47*, 263–291.

Kahneman, D., & Tversky, A. (1984). Choices, values and frames. *American Psychologist, 39*, 341–350.

Kalra, N., & Paddock, S.M. (2016). *Driving to Safety: How Many Miles of Driving Would it Take to Demonstrate Autonomous Vehicle Reliability?* Santa Monica, CA: RAND Corporation. www.rand.org/pubs/research_reports/RR1478.html

Karimi, H., & Ferreira, F. (2016). Good-enough linguistic representations and online cognitive equilibrium in language processing. *Quarterly Journal of Experimental Psychology, 69*, 1013–1040.

Kellogg, R.T., & Whiteford, A.P. (2012). The development of writing expertise. In E.L. Grigorenko, E. Mambrino, & D.D. Preiss (eds), *Writing: A Mosaic of New Perspectives* (pp. 109–124). Hove: Psychology Press.

Kelly, K. (1995). Singular visionary. *Wired*, 1 June. www.wired.com>article>magazine-3.06

Kemker, R., McClure, M., Abitino, A., Hayes, T., & Kanan, C. (2018). Measuring catastrophic forgetting in neural networks. *Proceedings of the AAAI Conference on Artificial Intelligence, 32*(1), 3390-3398.

Kidd, E., & Donnelly, S. (2020). Individual differences in first language acquisition. *Annual Review of Linguistics, 6*, 319–340.

King, J.-R., Sitt, J.D., Faugeras, F., Rohaut, B., El Karoui, I., Cohen, L., et al. (2013). Information sharing in the brain indexes consciousness in non-communicative patients. *Current Biology, 23*, 1914–1919.

Kitahara, C.M., Flint, M.J., de Gonzalez, A.B., Bernstein, L., Brotzman, M., MacInnis, R.J., et al. (2014). Association between class III obesity (BMI of 40–59 kg/m²) and mortality: A pooled analysis of 20 prospective studies. *PLoS Medicine, 11*, e1001673.

Kleinberg, J., Lakkaraju, H., Leskovec, J., Ludwig, J., & Mullainathan, S. (2017). Human decisions and machine predictions. *Quarterly Journal of Economics, 133*, 237–293.

Kline, M.A., & Boyd, R. (2010). Population size predicts technological complexity in Oceania. *Proceedings of the Royal Society B, 277*, 2559–2564.

Köbis, N., & Mossink, L.D. (2020). Artificial intelligence versus Maya Angelou: Experimental evidence that people cannot differentiate AI-generated from human-written poetry. *Computers in Human Behavior, 114*, 106553.

Koch, C. (2018). Scientists are beginning to unravel a mystery that has long vexed philosophers. *Nature, 557*, 2–5.

Kocijan, V., Cret, A.-M., Camburu, O.-M., Yordanov, Y., & Lukasiewicz, T. (2019). A surprisingly robust trick for the Winograd Schema Challenge. arXiv:1905.06290v2.

Koleva, S.P., Graham, J., Iyer, R., Ditto, P.H., & Haidt, J. (2012). Tracing the threads: How five moral concerns (especially purity) help explain culture war attitudes. *Journal of Research in Personality*, *46*, 184–194.

Konishi, M., & Smallwood, J. (2016). Shadowing the wandering mind: How understanding the mind-wandering state can inform our appreciation of conscious experience. *Wiley Interdisciplinary Reviews – Cognitive Science*, *7*, 233–246.

Koopman, P., Kane, A., & Black, J. (2019). Credible autonomy safety argumentation. *27th Safety-Critical Systems Symposium, Safety-Critical Systems Club*, 5–7 February, Bristol.

Kovacs, K., & Conway, A.R.A. (2016). Process overlap theory: A unified account of the general factor of intelligence. *Psychological Inquiry*, *27*, 151–177.

Kovacs, K., & Conway, A.R.A. (2019). A unified cognitive/differential approach to human intelligence: Implications for IQ testing. *Journal of Applied Research in Memory and Cognition*, *8*, 255–272.

Krause, B., Dresler, M., Loo, C.Y., Sarka, A., & Kadosh, R.C. (2019). Neuroenhancement of high-level cognition: Evidence for homeostatic constraints of non-invasive brain stimulation. *Journal of Cognitive Enhancement*, *3*, 388–395.

Krizhevsky, A., Sutskever, I., & Hinton, G.E. (2012). Imagenet classification with deep convolutional neural networks. *Proceedings of the 25th International Conference on Neural Information Processing Systems*, 1097–1105.

Kruger, J.M., & Dunning, D. (1999). Unskilled and unaware of it: How difficulties in recognising one's own incompetence lead to inflated self-assessments. *Journal of Personality and Social Psychology*, *77*, 1121–1134.

Kurdi, B., Seitchik, A.E., Axt, J.R., Carroll, T.J., Karapetyan, A., Kaushik, N., et al. (2019). Relationship between the implicit association test and intergroup behaviour: A meta-analysis. *American Psychologist*, *74*, 569–586.

Kurzweil, R. (2005). *The Singularity is Near: When Humans Transcend Biology*. New York: Vintage Books.

LaCurts, K. (2002). Criticisms of the Turing Test and why you should ignore (most of) them. Official blog of MIT's course: Philosophy and Theoretical Computer Science. https://people.csail.mit.edu/katrina/papers/6893.pdf

Laird, J.E., Lebiere, C., & Rosenbloom, P.S. (2017). A standard model of the mind: Toward a common computational framework across artificial intelligence, cognitive science, neuroscience, and robotics. *AI Magazine, 38*, 1–19.

Laland, K., & Seed, A. (2021). Understanding human cognitive uniqueness. *Annual Review of Psychology, 72*, 689–716.

Lamme, V.A.F. (2018). Challenges for theories of consciousness: Seeing or knowing, the missing ingredient and how to deal with panpsychism. *Philopsophical Transactions of the Royal Society B, 373*, Article No. 2017.0344.

Lammers, J., Crusius, J., & Gast, A. (2020). Correcting misperceptions of exponential coronavirus growth increases support for social distancing. *Proceedings of the National Academy of Sciences, 117*, 16264–16266.

LawGeex (2018). *Comparing the Performance of Artificial Intelligence to Human Lawyers in the Review of Standard Business Contracts.* February, 1–37. https://images.law.com/contrib/content/uploads/documents/397/5408/lawgeex.pdf

Lee, W.E., Wadsworth, M.E.J., & Hotop, M. (2006). The protective role of trait anxiety: A longitudinal cohort study. *Psychological Medicine, 36*, 345–351.

Lenat, D. (2019). What AI can learn from Romeo & Juliet. *Forbes*, 3 July. www.forbes.com>cognitiveworld>2019/07/03

Lents, N.H. (2018). *Human Errors: A Panorama of Our Glitches, from Pointless Bones to Broken Genes.* London: Weidenfeld & Nicolson.

Levine, M. (1971). Hypothesis theory and non-learning despite ideal S-R reinforcement contingencies. *Psychological Review, 78*, 130–140.

Levinson, J.D., Cai, H., & Young, D. (2010). Guilty by implicit racial bias: The guilty/Not guilty implicit association test. *Ohio State Journal of Criminal Law, 8*, 187–208.

Levinson, J.D., Smith, R.J., & Young, D.M. (2014). Devaluing death: An empirical study of implicit racial bias on jury-eligible citizens in six death penalty states. *New York University Law Review, 89*, 513–581.

Levis, J., & Barriuso, T.A. (2011). Non-native speakers' pronunciation errors in spoken and read English. *Proceedings of Pronunciation in Second Language Learning and Teaching, 3*, 187–194.

Liang, H., Tsui, B., Ni, H., Valentim, C.C.S., Baxter, S.L., Liu, G., et al. (2019). Evaluation and accurate diagnoses of pediatric diseases using artificial intelligence. *Nature Medicine*, *25*, 433–438.

Lichtenstein, S., Slovic, P., Fischhoff, B., Layman, M., & Coombs, J. (1978). Judged frequency of lethal events. *Journal of Experimental Psychology: Human Learning and Memory*, *4*, 551–578.

Lieder, F., & Griffiths, T.L. (2020). Resource-rational analysis: Understanding human cognition as the optimal use of limited computational resources. *Behavioral and Brain Sciences*, *43*, 1–60.

Limpo, T., & Alves, R.A. (2018). Effects of planning strategies on writing dynamics and final texts. *Acta Psychologica*, *188*, 97–109.

Lin, Z., Jung, J., Goel, S., & Skeem, J. (2020). The limits of human predictions of recidivism. *Science Advances*, *6*, Article No. Eaaz0652.

Lindsey, S., Hertwig, R., & Gigerenzer, G. (2003). Communicating statistical DNA evidence. *Jurimetrics*, *43*, 147–163.

Littrell, S., & Fugelsang, J. (2020). A bullshit blind spot? Dunning-Kruger effects in bullshit detection. *Society for Judgment and Decision Making* (poster). www.sjdm.org/presentations/2020-Poster-Littrell-Shane-BullshitDetect-DunningKruger-Blindspot.pdf

Littrell, S., Risko, E.F., & Fugelsang, J.A. (2021). "You can't bullshit a bullshitter" (or can you?): Bullshitting frequency predicts receptivity to various types of misleading information. *British Journal of Social Psychology 60*, 1484–1505.

Liu, F., Shi, Y., & Liu, Y. (2019). Intelligence quotient and intelligence grade of artificial intelligence. *Annals of Data Science*, *4*, 179–191.

Liu, X., Faes, L., Kle, A.U., Wagner, S.K., Fu, D.J., Bruynseels, A., et al. (2019). A comparison of deep learning performance against health-care professionals in detecting diseases from medical imaging: A systematic review and meta-analysis. *Lancet Digital Health*, *1*, e271–297.

Lobera, J., Rodriguez, C.J., & Torres-Albero, C. (2020). Privacy, values and machines: Predicting opposition to artificial intelligence. *Communication Studies*, *71*, 448–465.

Lung, T., Jan, S., Tan, E.J., Killedar, A., & Hayes, A. (2019). Impact of overweight, obesity and severe obesity on life expectancy of Australian adults. *International Journal of Obesity*, *43*, 782–789.

Luria, A.R. (1968). *The Mind of a Mnemonist*. New York: Basic Books.

Ma, W.J., & Woodford, M. (2020). Multiple conceptions of resource rationality. *Behavioral and Brain Sciences*, *43*(e1), 30–31.

Ma, X., Niu, Y., Gu, L., Wang, Y., Zhao, Y., Bailey, J., et al. (2020). Understanding adversarial attacks on deep learning based medical image analysis systems. *Pattern Recognition, 110,* Article No. 107332.

MacCann, C., Jiang, Y.X., Brown, L.E.R., Double, K.S., Bucich, M., & Minbashian, A. (2020). Emotional intelligence predicts academic performance: A meta-analysis. *Psychological Bulletin, 146,* 150–186.

MacNeilage, P.F., Rogers, L.J., & Vallortigara, G. (2009). Evolutionary origins of your right and left brain. *Scientific American, 301,* 60–67.

Mackworth, N.H. (1948). The breakdown of vigilance during prolonged visual search. *Quarterly Journal of Experimental Psychology, 1,* 6–21.

Maetschke, S., Iraeola, D.M., Barnarda, P., Bavania, E.S., Zhonga, P., Xua, Y., et al. (2021). Understanding in artificial intelligence. arXiv:2101.06573v1.

Malanchini, M., Rimfeld, K., Allegrini, A.G., Ritchie, S.J., & Plomin, R. (2020). Cognitive ability and education: How behavioural genetic research has advanced our knowledge and understanding of their association. *Neuroscience and Biobehavioral Reviews, 111,* 229–245.

Malhotra, G., Evans, B.D., & Bowers, J.S. (2020). Hiding a plane with a pixel: Examining shape-bias in CNNs and the benefit of building in biological constraints. *Vision Research, 174,* 57–68.

Malle, B.F. (2020). Moral judgements. *Annual Review of Psychology, 72,* 293–318.

Malle, B.F., Magar, S.T., & Scheutz, M. (2019). AI in the sky: How people morally evaluate human and machine decisions in a lethal strike dilemma. In M.I.A. Ferreira, J.S. Sequeira, G.S. Virk, & E.E. Kadar (eds), *Robotics and Well-Being* (pp. 111–133). Geneva: Springer Nature Switzerland

Malle, B.F., Scheutz, M., Arnold, T., Voiklis, J., & Cusimano, C. (2015). Sacrifice one for the good of many? People apply different moral norms to human and robot agents. *10th ACM/IEEE International Conference on Human-Robot Interaction (HRI),* 2–5 March. Portland, OR, USA, 117–124.

Malle, B.F., Guglielmo, S., & Monroe, A.E. (2014). A theory of blame. *Psychological Inquiry, 25,* 147-186.

Mallpress, D.E.W., Fawcett, T.W., Houston, A.I., & McNamara, J.M. (2015). Risk attitudes in a changing environment: An evolutionary model of the fourfold pattern of risk preferences. *Psychological Bulletin, 122,* 364–375.

Malouff, J.M., Schutte, N.S., & Thorsteinsson, E.B. (2014). Trait emotional intelligence and romantic relationship satisfaction: A meta-analysis. *American Journal of Family Therapy, 42,* 53–66.

Mandelbaum, E. (2019). Troubles with Bayesianism: An introduction to the psychological immune system. *Mind & Language, 34,* 141–157.

Marcus, G. (2008). *Kluge: The Haphazard Evolution of the Human Mind.* Boston, MA: Houghton Mifflin.

Marcus, G. (2018). Deep learning: A critical appraisal. https://arxiv.org/abs/1312.6197.

Marcus, G. (2020). The next decade in AI: Four steps towards robust artificial intelligence. arXiv:2002.06177.

Marcus, G., & Davis, E. (2019). *Rebooting AI: Building Artificial Intelligence We Can Trust.* New York: Pantheon.

Marcus, G., & Davis, E. (2020). GPT-3, Bloviator: Open AI's language generator has no idea what it's talking about. *MIT Technology Review,* 8 August, 1–4. www.technologyreview.com

Marsh, A. (2018). Elektro the moto-man had the biggest brain at the 1939 World's Fair. *IEEE,* 28 September. https://spectrum.ieee.org>elektro-the-moto-man-had-the-biggest-brain-at-the-1939-world's-fair

Marsh, R.L., Hicks, J.L., & Landau, J.D. (1998). An investigation of everyday prospective memory. *Memory & Cognition, 26,* 633–643.

Marshall, A. (2017). My herky-jerky ride in General Motors' ultra cautious self-driving car. *Wired,* 29 November. www.wired.com/story/ride-general-motors-self-driving-car/

Massimini, M., Ferrarelli, F., Huber, R., Esser, S.K., Singh, H., & Tononi, G. (2005). Breakdown of cortical effective connectivity during sleep. *Science, 309,* 2228–2232.

Mathur, M.B., Reichling, D.B., Lunardini, F., Geminiani, A., Antonietti, A., Ruijten, P.A.M., et al. (2020). Uncanny but not confusing: Multi-site study of perceptual category confusion in the uncanny valley. *Computers in Human Behavior, 103,* 21–30.

Mazzone, M., & Elgammal, A. (2019). Art, creativity, and the potential of artificial intelligence. *Arts, 8*(26), 1–9.

McCarthy, J., Minsky, M., Rochester, N., & Shannon, C.E. (1955). A proposal for the Dartmouth summer research project on artificial intelligence. www.formal.stanford.edu/jmc/history/dartmouth/dartmouth.html

McCoy, R.T., Pavlick, E., & Linzen, T. (2019). Right for the wrong reasons: Diagnosing syntactic heuristics in natural language inference. *Proceedings of the 57th Annual Meeting of the Association for Computational Linguistics*, 3328–3448.

McDermott, D. (2007) Artificial intelligence and consciousness, in P. Zelazo, M. Moscovitch, & E. Thompson, E. (eds), *Cambridge Handbook of Consciousness* (pp. 117–150). Cambridge: Cambridge University Press.

McDermott, R., Fowler, J.H., & Smirnov, O. (2008). On the evolutionary origin of prospect theory preferences. *Journal of Politics*, *70*, 335–350.

McGurk, H., & MacDonald, J. (1976). Hearing lips and seeing voices. *Nature*, *264*, 746–748.

McKinney, S.M., Sieniek, M., Godbole, V., Godwin, J., Antropova, N., Ashrafian, H., et al. (2020). International evaluation of an AI system for breast cancer screening. *Nature*, *577*, 89–113.

Mendel, R., Traut-Mattausch, E., Leucht, S., Kane, J.M., Maino, K., Kissling, W., et al. (2011). Why psychiatrists stick to wrong preliminary diagnoses. *Psychological Medicine*, *41*, 2651–2659.

Mercier, H., & Sperber, D. (2017). *The Enigma of Reason*. Cambridge, MA: Harvard University Press.

Michotte, A. (1946/1963). *The Perception of Causality*. New York: Basic Books (translated by T. Miles & E. Miles; original work published 1946).

Mikhalevich, I., Powell, R., & Logan, C. (2017). Is behavioural flexibility evidence of cognitive complexity? How evolution can inform comparative cognition. *Interface Focus*, 7, Article No. 20160121.

Mikhaylovskiy, N. (2020). How do you test the strength of AI?. In B. Goertzel, A. Panov, A. Potapov, & R. Yampolskiy (eds), *Artificial General Intelligence. AGI 2020. Lecture Notes in Computer Science*, Vol. 12177. Springer, Cham.

Minsky, M. (1986). *The Society of Mind*. New York: Simon & Schuster.

Michie, D. (1973). Machines and the theory of intelligence. *Nature*, *241*, 507–512.

Mitroff, S.R., & Biggs, A.T. (2014). The ultra-rare-item effect: Visual search for exceedingly rare items is highly susceptible to error. *Psychological Science*, *25*, 284–289.

Monroe, A.E., Dillon, K.D., & Malle, B.F. (2014). Bringing free will down to Earth: People's psychological concept of free will and its role in moral judgement. *Consciousness and Cognition, 27,* 100–108.

Montoya, R.M., Horton, R.S., & Kirchner, J. (2008). Is actual similarity necessary for attraction? A meta-analysis of actual and perceived similarity. *Journal of Social and Personal Relationships, 25,* 889–922.

Moor, J.H. (2006). The nature, importance, and difficulty of machine ethics. *IEEE Intelligent Systems, 21,* 18–21.

Moore, G.E. (1965). Cramming more components onto integrated circuits. *Electronics, 38,* 114–117.

Moore, G.E. (2015). The man whose name means progress, the visionary engineer reflects on 50 years of Moore's Law. *IEEE Spectrum: Special Report:* 50 years of Moore's Law (interview with Rachel Courtland). *IEEE Spectrum,* 30 March. http://spectrum.ieee.org/computing/hardware/gordon-moore-the-man-whose-name-means-progress

Moors, A. (2016). Automaticity: Componential, causal, and mechanistic explanations. *Annual Review of Psychology, 67,* 263–287.

Moravec, H. (1988). *Mind Children.* Harvard, MA: Harvard University Press.

Moravčík, M., Schmid, M., Burch, N., Lisy, V., Morrill, D., Bard, N., et al. (2017). Deepstack: Expert-level artificial intelligence in heads-up no-limit poker. *Science, 356,* 508–513.

Morgan, C.L. (1903). *An Introduction to Comparative Psychology.* London: W. Scott.

Morgenroth, E., Saviola, F., Gilleen, J., Allen, B., Luhrs, M., Eysenck, M.W., & Allen, P. (2020). Using connectivity-based real-time fMRI neurofeedback to modulate attentional and resting state networks in people with high trait anxiety. *NeuroImage-Clinical, 25,* Article No. 102191.

Mori, M. (1970). The uncanny valley. *Energy, 7*(4), 33–35.

Morse, S.C. (2019). When robots make legal mistakes. *Oklahoma Law Review, 72,* 214–230.

Motta, M., Callaghan, T., & Sylvester, S. (2018). Knowing less but presuming more: Dunning-Kruger effects and the endorsement of anti-vaccine policy attitudes. *Social Science & Medicine, 211,* 274–281.

Mueller, S.T. (2020). Cognitive anthropomorphism of AI: How humans and computers classify images. *Ergonomics in Design: The Quarterly of Human Factors Applications, 28*(3), 12–19.

Müller,V.C. (2020). Ethics of artificial intelligence and robotics. *Stanford Encylopedia of Philosophy*. Palo Alto, CA: Stanford University.

Müller,V.C., & Bostrom, N. (2016), Future progress in artificial intelligence: A survey of expert opinion. In V.C. Müller (ed.), *Fundamental Issues of Artificial Intelligence* (pp. 553–571). Berlin: Springer.

Muthukrishna, M., Doebeli, M., Chudek, M., & Henrich, J. (2018). The cultural brain hypothesis: How culture drives brain expansion, sociality, and life history. *PLoS Computational Biology, 11*, e1006504.

Nachar, R.A., Inaty, E., Bonnin, P.J., & Alayli, Y. (2015). Breaking down captcha using edge corners and fuzzy logic segmentation/recognition technique. *Security and Communication Networks, 8*, 3995–4012.

Nairne, J.S. (2015). The three "Ws" of episodic memory: What, when, and where. *American Journal of Psychology, 128*, 267–279.

Nangia, N., & Bowman, S.R. (2019). Human vs muppet: A conservative estimate of human performance on the GLUE benchmark. *Proceedings of the Association of Computational Linguistics (ACL)*, 28 July–2 August, Florence, Italy, 4566–4575.

National Academies of Sciences and Medicine (2017). *Human Genome Editing: Science, Ethics, and Governance*. Washington, DC: National Academies Press.

National Center for Statistics and Analysis (2019). Alcohol-impaired driving: 2018 data. *(Traffic Safety Facts. Report No. DOT HS 812 864)*. Washington, D.C: National Highway Traffic Safety Administration.

Navarrete-Dechent, C., Dusza, S.W., Liopyris, K., Marghoob, A.A., Halpen, A.C., & Marchetti, M.A. (2018). Automated dermatological diagnosis: Hype or reality? *Journal of Investigative Dermatology, 138*, 2277–2279.

Nelson, B., Thompson, A., & Yung, A.R. (2012). Basic self-disturbance predicts psychosis onset in the ultra high risk for psychosis "prodromal" population. *Schizophrenia Bulletin, 38*, 1277–1287.

Newell, A., Shaw, J.C., & Simon, H.A. (1958). Elements of a theory of human problem solving. *Psychological Review, 65*, 151–166.

Ng, N.F., Schafer, R.J., Simone, C.M., & Osman, A.M. (2020). Perceptions of brain training: Public expectations of cognitive benefits from popular activities. *Frontiers of Human Neuroscience, 14*, Article No. 15.

Niiler, E. (2019). Can AI be a fair judge in court? Estonia thinks so. *Wired*, 25 March. www.wired.com/story/can-ai-be-fair-judge-court-estonia-thinks-so/

Nobandegani, A.S., da Silva, K., O'Donnell, T.J., & Shultz, T.R. (2019). On robustness: An undervalued dimension of human rationality. *Proceedings of the 17th International Conference on Modelling*, 19–22 July, Montreal, QC, Canada.

Norby, S. (2015). Why forget? On the adaptive value of memory loss. *Perspectives on Psychological Science*, *10*, 551–578.

Norris, D., & Kinoshita, S. (2012). Reading through a noisy channel: Why there's nothing special about the perception of orthography. *Psychological Review*, *119*, 517–545.

Novack, M.A., & Waxman, S. (2020). Becoming human: Human infants link language and cognition, but what about the other great apes? *Philosophical Transactions of the Royal Society B*, *375*, Article No. 20180408.

Nurullah, A.S. (2015). Cell phone conversation while driving. In Z. Yan (ed.), *Encylopaedia of Mobile Phone Behaviour*, Vol. III (pp. 1328–1339). Hershey, PA: IGI Global.

Nyholm, S. (2018). The ethics of crashes with self-driving cars: A roadmap, 1. *Philosophy Compass*, *13*, Article No. e12507.

O'Boyle, E.H., Humphrey, R.H., Pollack, J.M., Hawver, T.H., & Story, P.A. (2011). The relation between emotional intelligence and job performance: A meta-analysis. *Journal of Organizational Behavior*, *32*, 788–818.

Ogunleye, O.O., Mabiala, M., & Anderson, R. (2019). Accuracy of self-reported weight compared to measured BMI among rural middle school students in Michigan. *Journal of Public Health: From Theory to Practice*, *27*, 603, 612.

Olah, C., Satyanarayan, A., Johnson, I., Carter, S., Schubert, L., Ye, K., et al. (2018). The building blocks of interpretability. *Distill*, *3*, Article No. e10.

Onishi, K.H., & Baillargeon, R. (2005). Do 15-month-old infants understand false beliefs? *Science*, *308*, 255–258.

O'Reilly, R.C., Wyatte, D., Herd, S., Mingus, B., & Jilk, D.J. (2013). Recurrent processing during object recognition. *Frontiers in Psychology*, *4*, Article No. 124.

Orne, M.T. (1962). On the social psychology of the psychological experiment: With particular reference to demand characteristics and their implications. *American Psychologist*, *17*, 776–783.

Pachet, F. (2002). Playing with virtual musicians: The Continuator in practice. *Journées d'Informatique Musicale*, May, 185–190.

Pais-Vieira, M., Chiuffa, G., Lebedev, M., Yada, A., & Nicolelis, M.A.L. (2015). Building an organic computing device with multiple interconnected brains. *Scientific Reports*, *5*, Article No. 11869.

Palomäki, J., Laakasyi, M., Cowley, B.U., & Lapp, O. (2020). Poker as a domain of expertise. *Journal of Expertise*, *3*, 603–612.

Papazova, I., Strube, W., Wienert, A., Henning, B., Schwippel, T., Fallgatter, A.J., et al. (2020). Effects of 1 mA and 2 mA transcranial direct current stimulation on working memory performance in healthy participants. *Consciousness and Cognition*, *83*, Article No. 102959.

Parker, D.A., Summerfield, L.J., Walmsley, C., O'Byrne, R., Dave, H.P., & Crane, G. (2021). Trait emotional intelligence and interpersonal relationships: Results from a 15-year longitudinal study. *Personality and Individual Differences*, 169, Article No. 110013.

Parthasarathi, S.H.K., Sivakrishnan, N., Ladkat, P., & Strom, N. (2019). Realising petabyte scale acoustic modelling. *Journal on Emerging and Selected Topics in Circuits and Systems*, *9*, 422–432.

Patrick, J.R. (1934a). Studies in rational behaviour and emotional excitement: I. Rational behaviour in human subjects. *Journal of Comparative Psychology*, *18*, 1–22.

Patrick, J.R. (1934b). Studies in rational behaviour and emotional excitement: II. The effect of emotional excitement on rational behaviour in human subjects. *Journal of Comparative Psychology*, *18*, 153–195.

Paxton, R., & Hampton, R.R. (2009). Tests of planning and the Bischof-Köhler hypothesis in rhesus monkeys (*Macaca mulatta*). *Behavior Processes*, *80*, 238–246.

Pelegrin-Borondo, J., Arias-Oliva, M., Murata, K., & Souto-Romero, M. (2020). Does ethical judgement determine the decision to become a cyborg? Influence of ethical judgement on the cyborg market. *Journal of Business Ethics*, *161*, 5–17.

Peng, P., Barnes, M., Wang, C., Wang, W., Li, S., & Swanson, H.L. (2018). A meta-analysis on the relation between reading and working memory. *Psychological Bulletin*, *144*, 48–76.

Pennartz, C.M.A. (2018). Consciousness, representation, action: The importance of being goal-directed. *Trends in Cognitive Sciences*, *22*, 137–153.

Pennartz, C.M.A., Farisco, M., & Evers, K. (2019). Indicators and criteria of consciousness in animals and intelligent machines: An inside-out approach. *Frontiers in Systems Neuroscience, 13*, Article No. 25.

Peretti-Watel, P., Constance, J., Guilbert, P., Gautier, A., Beck, F., & Moatti, J.-P. (2007). Smoking too few cigarettes to be at risk? Smokers' perceptions of risk and risk denial, a French survey. *Tobacco Control, 16*, 351–356.

Petrović, D., Mijailović, R., & Pešić, D. (2020). Traffic accidents with autonomous vehicles: Type of collisions, manoeuvres and errors of conventional vehicles' drivers. *Transportation Research Procedia, 45*, 161–168.

Pfungst, O. (1911). *Clever Hans (The Horse of Von Osten)* (translated by C.L. Rahm). New York: Henry Holt & Co.

Pinker, S. (1997). *How the Mind Works*. New York: W.W. Norton.

Plebe, A., & Grasso, G. (2019). The unbearable shallow understanding of deep learning. *Minds and Machines, 29*, 515–553.

Pope, D.G., & Schweitzer, M.E. (2011). Is Tiger Woods loss averse? Persistent bias in the face of experience, competition, and high stakes. *American Economic Review, 101*, 129–157.

Pope, J.W. (2014). False uniqueness effect. In K.D. Keith (ed), *The Encyclopedia of Cross-Cultural Psychology*. Oxford: Wiley Blackwell.

Pope, S.M., Meguerditchian, A., & Hopkins, W.D. (2015). Baboons (*Papio Papio*), but not humans, break cognitive set in a visuo-motor task. *Animal Cognition, 18*, 1339–1346.

Popel, M., Tomkova, M., Tomek, J., Kaiser, L., Uszkoreit, J., Bojar, O., et al. (2020). Transforming machine translation: A deep learning system reaches news translation quality comparable to human professionals. *Nature Communications, 11*, Article No. 4381.

Porot, N., & Mandelbaum, E. (2020). The science of belief: A progress report. *WIREs Cognitive Science, 11*, e1539, 1–17.

Posner, M.I., & Barbey, A.K. (2020). General intelligence in the age of neuroimaging. *Trends in Neuroscience and Education, 18*, Article No. 100126.

Proudfoot, D. (2011). Anthropomorphism and AI: Turing's much misunderstood imitation game. *Artificial Intelligence, 175*, 950–957.

Pulsifer, M.B., Brandt, J., Salorio, C.F., Vining, E.P.G., Carson, B.S., & Freeman, J.M. (2004). The cognitive outcome of hemispherectomy in 71 children. *Epilepsia, 45*, 243–254.

Puri, A. (2020). Moral imitation: Can an algorithm really be ethical? *Rutgers Law Record.* http://lawrecord.com/files/48_Rutgers_L_Rec_47.pdf

Rabinowitz, N., Perbet, F., Song, F., Zhang, C., Eslami, S.M.A., & Botvinick, M. (2018). Machine theory of mind. *Proceedings of the 35th International Conference on Machine Learning, 80,* 4218–4227.

Radford, A., Wu, J., Child, R., Luan, D., Arnold, D., & Sutskever, I. (2019). Language models are unsupervised multi-task learners. *OpenAI blog,* 14 February. https://openai.com/blog/better-language-models/

Raichle, M.E. (2010). Two views of brain function. *Trends in Cognitive Sciences, 14,* 180–190.

Raichle, M.E. (2015). The brain's default mode network. *Annual Review in Neuroscience, 38,* 433–447.

Ramnerö, J., Molander, O., Lindner, P., & Carlbring, P. (2019). What can be learned about gambling from a learning perspective? A narrative review. *Nordic Psychology, 71,* 303–322.

Raoult, A., & Yampolskiy, R. (2015). Reviewing tests for machine consciousness. www.researchgate.net/publication/284859013_DRAFT_Reviewing_Tests_for_Mach ine_Consciousness

Raven, J.C. (1936). *Mental Tests Used in Genetic Studies: The Performance of Related Individuals on Tests Mainly Educative and Mainly Reproductive.* M.Sc. thesis, University of London.

Reggia, J.A., Huang, D.-W., & Karz, G. (2015). Beliefs concerning the nature of consciousness. *Journal of Consciousness Studies, 22,* 146–171.

Regier, T., & Xu, Y. (2017). The Sapir-Whorf hypothesis and inference under uncertainty. *Wiley Interdisciplinary Reviews – Cognitive Science, 8,* Article No. UNSP e1440.

Remez, R.E., Ferro, D.F., Dubowski, K.R., Meer, J., Broder, R.S., & Davids, M.L. (2010). Is desynchrony tolerance adaptable in the perceptual organisation of speech? *Attention, Perception & Psychophysics, 72,* 2054–2058.

Ricci, M., Cadène, R., & Serre, T. (2021). Same-different conceptualisation: A machine vision perspective. *Current Opinion in Behavioral Sciences, 37,* 47–55.

Richards, B.A., & Frankland, P.W. (2017). The persistence and transience of memory. *Neuron, 94,* 1071–1084.

Richens, J.G., Lee, C.M., & Johri, S. (2020). Improving the accuracy of medical diagnosis with causal machine learning. *Nature Communications, 11,* Article No. 3923.

Richerson, P.J., & Boyd, R. (2005). *Not by Genes Alone: How Culture Transformed Human Evolution.* Chicago, IL: The University of Chicago Press.

Ricker, T. (2016). Elon Musk: We're already cyborgs. *The Verge*, 2 June. www.theverge.com/2016/6/2/11837854/neural-lace-cyborgs-elon-musk

Rindermann, H., Flores-Mendoza, C., & Mansur, M. (2010). Reciprocal effects between fluid and crystallized intelligence and their dependence on parents' socio-economic status and education. *Learning and Individual Differences*, *20*, 544–548.

Rini, R. (2020). The digital zeitgeist ponders our obsolescence. *Daily Nous, Philosophers on GPT-3 (updated with replies by GPT-3)*, 30 July. https://dailynous.com/2020/07/30/philosophers-gpt-3/#rini

Ritchie, S.J., & Tucker-Drob, E.M. (2018). How much does education improve intelligence? A meta-analysis. *Psychological Science*, *29*, 1358–1369.

Roberts, P., & Stewart, B.A. (2019). Defining the "generalist specialist" niche for pleistocene *Homo sapiens*. *Nature Human Behaviour*, *2*, 542–550.

Robison, M.K., Miller, A.L., & Unsworth, N. (2020). A multi-faceted approach to understanding individual differences in mind-wandering. *Cognition*, *198*, Article No. 104078.

Roff, H.M., & Danks, D. (2018). Trust but verify. *Journal of Military Ethics*, *17*, 2–20.

Rogers, A., Kovaleva, O., & Rumshisky, A. (2020). A primer in BERTology: What we know about how BERT works. *Transactions of the Association for Computational Linguistics*, *8*, 842–866.

Ross, L.D., Amabile, T.M., & Steinmetz, J.L. (1977). Social roles, social control, and biases in social-perception processes. *Journal of Personality and Social Psychology*, *35*, 485–494.

Russakovsky, O., Deng, J., Su, H., Krause, J., Satheesh, S., Ma, S., et al. (2015). ImageNet large scale visual recognition challenge. *International Journal of Computer Vision*, *115*, 211–252.

Rumelhart, D.E., & Ortony, A. (1977). The representation of knowledge in memory. In R.C. Anderson, R.J. Spiro, & W.E. Montague (eds), *Schooling and the Acquisition of Knowledge* (pp. 99–135). Hillsdale, NJ: Lawrence Erlbaum Associates.

Ryskin, R., Futrell, R., Kiran, S., & Gibson, E. (2018). Comprehenders model the nature of noise in the environment. *Cognition*, *181*, 141–150.

Šabanović, S., Bennett, C.C., & Lee, H.R. (2014). Towards culturally robust robots: A critical social perspective on robotics and culture. *Proceedings of the Workshop on Culturally Aware Robots. 9th International*

Conference on Human-Robot Interaction, 3–6 March, Bielefeld, Germany.

Sakata, R., McGale, P., Grant, E.J., Ozasa, K., Peto, R., & Darby, S.C. (2012). Impact of smoking on mortality and life expectancy in Japanese smokers: A prospective cohort study. *BMJ, 345*, e7093.

Sala, G., & Gobet, F. (2017). Does far transfer exist? Negative evidence from chess, music, and working memory training. *Current Directions in Psychological Science, 26*, 515–520.

Sala, G., & Gobet, F. (2020). Cognitive and academic benefits of music training with children: A multi-level meta-analysis. *Memory & Cognition, 48*, 1429–1441.

Salles, A., Evers, K., & Farisco, M. (2020). Anthropomorphism in AI. *AJOB Neuroscience, 11*, 88–95.

Samhita, L., & Gross, H.J. (2013). The "Clever Hans Phenomenon" revisited. *Communicative & Integrative Biology, 6*, e27122.

Sanbonmatsu, D.M., Strayer, D.L., Biondi, F., Behrends, A.A., Ward, N., & Watson, J.M. (2016). Why drivers use cell phones and support legislation to restrict this practice. *Accident Analysis and Prevention, 92*, 22–33.

Sandberg, A. (2013) Feasibility of whole brain emulation. In V. Müller (ed), *Philosophy and Theory of Artificial Intelligence. Studies in Applied Philosophy, Epistemology and Rational Ethics*, Vol. 5 (pp. 251–264). Berlin: Springer.

Saon, G., Kurata, G., Sercu, T., Audhkhasi, K., Thomas, S., Dimitriadis, D., et al. (2017). English conversational telephone speech recognition by humans and machines. *Eighteenth Annual Conference of the International Speech Communication Association (Interspeech 2017)*, 20–24 August, Stockholm, Sweden; Vols 1–6: *Situated Interaction*, 132–136.

Sauce, B., & Matzel, L.D. (2018). The paradox of intelligence: Heritability and malleability co-exist in hidden gene-environment interplay. *Psychological Bulletin, 144*, 26–47.

Savage, J.E., Jansen, P.R., Stringer, S., Watanabe, K., Bryois, J., de Leeuw, C.A., et al. (2018). Genome-wide association meta-analysis in 269,867 individuals identifies new genetic and functional links to intelligence. *Nature Genetics, 50*, 912–919.

Schacter, D.L., & Addis, D.R. (2007). The cognitive neuroscience of constructive memory: Remembering the past and imagining the future. *Philosophical Transactions of the Royal Society B: Biological Sciences, 362*, 773–786.

Schacter, D.L., & Madore, K.P. (2016). Remembering the past and imagining the future: Identifying and enhancing the contribution of episodic memory. *Memory Studies, 9*, 245–255.

Schild, C., Stern, J., Penke, L., & Zettler, I. (2020). Voice pitch - A valid indicator of one's unfaithfulness in committed relationships? *Adaptive Human Behavior and Physiology*. doi:10.1007/s40750-020-00154-0.

Schmidhuber, J. (2015). Deep learning in neural networks: An overview. *Neural Networks, 61*, 85–117.

Schnell, A.K., Amodio, P., Boeckle, M., & Clayton, N.S. (2021). How intelligent is a cephalopod? Lessons from comparative cognition. *Biological Reviews, 96*, 162–178.

Schönherr, L., Kohls, K., Zeiler, S., Holz, T., & Kolossa, D. (2018). Adversarial attacks against automatic speech recognition systems via psychoacoustic hiding. arXiv:1808.05665.

Schooler, J.W. (2002). Re-representing consciousness: Dissociations between experience and meta-consciousness. *Trends in Cognitive Science, 6*, 339–344.

Schooler, J.W., Reichle, E.D., & Halpern, D.V. (2005). Zoning-out during reading: Evidence for dissociations between experience and meta-consciousness. In D.T. Levin (ed), *Thinking and Seeing: Visual Meta-Cognition in Adults and Children* (pp. 204–226). Cambridge, MA: MIT Press.

Schrittwieser, J., Antonoglou, I., Hubert, T., Simonyan, K., Sifre, L., Schmitt, S., et al. (2020). Mastering Atari, Go, chess and shogi by planning with a learned model. *Nature, 388*, 604–609.

Schwark, J., Sandry, J., MacDonald, J., & Dolgov, I. (2012). False feedback increases detection of low-prevalence targets in visual search. *Attention, Perception & Psychophysics, 74*, 1583–1589.

Schwartz, B., Ward, A., Monterosso, J., Lyubormirsky, S., White, K., & Lehman, D.R. (2002). Maximising versus satisficing: Happiness is a matter of choice. *Journal of Personality and Social Psychology, 83*, 1178–1197.

Searle, J. (1980). Minds, brains and programs. *Behavioral and Brain Sciences, 3*, 417–457.

Searle, J. (2010). Why dualism (and materialism) fail to account for consciousness. In R.E. Lee (ed), *Questioning Nineteenth Century Assumptions about Knowledge (III: Dualism)*. New York: SUNY Press.

Searle, J.R. (2014). What your computer can't know. *The New York Review of Books*, 9 October, 1–7. www.nybooks.com/articles/2014/10/09/what-your-computer-cant-know

Serre, T., Oliva, A., & Poggio, T. (2007). A feedforward architecture accounts for rapid categorisation. *Proceedings of the National Academy of Sciences U.S.A., 104*, 6424–6429.

Shah, H., Warwick, K., Bland, I., Chapman, C.D., & Allen, M.J. (2012). Turing's I imitation game: Role of error-making in intelligent thought. *Turing in Context II*, 10–12 October, Brussels, 31–32.

Shah, S.S.H. (2019). The perils of AI for nuclear deterrence. *CISS Insight Journal, 7*, 1–16.

Shamma, S.A., Elhilali, M., & Micheyl, C. (2011). Temporal coherence and attention in auditory scene analysis. *Trends in Neurosciences, 34*, 114–123.

Shanahan, M., Crosby, M., Beyrer, B., & Clarke, L. (2020). Artificial intelligence and the common sense of animals. *Trends in Cognitive Sciences, 24*, 862–872.

Shank, D.B., & DeSanti, A. (2018). Attributions of morality and mind to artificial intelligence after real-world moral violations. *Computers in Human Behavior, 86*, 401–411.

Shank, D.B., DeSanti, A., & Maninger, T. (2019a). When are artificial intelligence versus human agents faulted for wrongdoing? Moral attributions after individual and joint decisions. *Information, Communication & Society, 22*, 648–663.

Shank, D.B., Graves, C., Gotta, A., Gamez, P., & Rodriguez, S. (2019b). Feeling our way to machine minds: People's emotions when perceiving mind in artificial intelligence. *Computers in Human Behavior, 98*, 256–266.

Shariff, A.F., Greene, J.D., Karremans, J.C., Luguri, J.B., Clark, C.J., Schooler, J.W., et al. (2014). Free will and punishment: A mechanistic view of human nature reduces retribution. *Psychological Science, 25*, 1563–1570.

Sharkey, N. (2012). The inevitability of autonomous robot warfare. *International Review of the Red Cross, 94*, 787–799.

Sharot, T. (2010). The optimism bias. *Current Biology, 21*, R941–R945

Sheetz, K.H., Claflin, J., & Dimick, J.B. (2020). Trends in the adoption of robotic surgery for common surgical procedures. *JAMA Network Open, 3*, e1918911.

Shereena, E.A., Gupta, R.K., Bennett, C.N., Sagar, K.J.V., & Rajeswaran, J. (2019). EEG neurofeedback training in children with attention deficit/hyperactivity disorder: A cognitive and behavioural outcome study. *Clinical EEG and Neuroscience, 50*, 242–255.

Shevlin, H. (2021). Rethinking creative intelligence: Comparative psychology and the concept of creativity. *European Journal for Philosophy of Science, 11*, Article No. 16.

Silver, D., Hubert, T., Schrittwieser, J., Antonoglkou, I., Lai, M., Lanctot, M., et al. (2018). A general reinforcement learning algorithm that masters chess, shogi, and go through self-play. *Science, 362*, 1140–1144.

Silver, D., Schrittwieser, J., Simonyan, K., Antonoglou, I., Huang, A., Guez, A., et al. (2017). Mastering the game of go without human knowledge. *Nature, 550*, 354–362.

Simon, H.A. (1957). *Models of Man: Social and Rational*. New York: Wiley.

Simon, H.A. (1960). *The New Science of Management Decision*. New York: Harper & Row.

Simon, H.A. (1990). Invariants of human behaviour. *Annual Review of Psychology, 41*, 1–19.

Simons, D.J., Boot, W.R., Charness, N., Gathercole, S.E., Chabris, C.F., Hambrick, D.Z., et al. (2016). Do "brain-training" programs work? *Psychological Science in the Public Interest, 17*, 103–186.

Simons, D.J., & Chabris, C.F. (2011). What people believe about how memory works: A representative survey of the US population. *PLoS ONE, 6*, Article No. e22757.

Simonson, I., & Staw, B.M. (1992). De-escalation strategies: A comparison of techniques for reducing commitment to losing courses of action. *Journal of Applied Psychology, 77*, 419–426.

Simonton, D.K. (2015). On praising convergent thinking: Creativity as blind variation and selective retention. *Creativity Research Journal, 27*, 262–270.

Singh, J.S. (2015). Critical reasons for crashes investigated in the national motor vehicle crash causation survey, Washington, DC, USA, Tech. Rep. DOT HS 812 115.

Skinner, B.F. (1938). *The Behaviour of Organisms: An Experimental Analysis*. New York: Appleton-Century-Crofts.

Skipper, J.I., Devlin, J.T., & Lametti, D.R. (2017). The hearing ear is always found close to the speaking tongue: Review of the role of the motor system in speech perception. *Brain & Language, 164*, 77–105.

Sloan, N.P., Byrne, L.K., Enticott, P.G., & Lum, J.A.G. (2021). Non-invasive brain stimulation does not improve working memory in schizophrenia: A meta-analysis of randomised controlled trials. *Neuropsychology Review, 31,* 115–138.

Smith, B.C. (2019). *The Promise of Artificial Intelligence: Reckoning and Judgement.* Cambridge, MA: MIT Press.

Society of Automotive Engineers (2016). Taxonomy and definitions for terms related to driving automation systems for on-road motor vehicles. *SAE Tech,* Paper J3016_201806.

Spearman, C. (1904). General intelligence, objectively determined and measured. *American Journal of Psychology, 15,* 201–293.

Spearman, C. (1927). *The Abilities of Man.* London: Macmillan.

Spille, C., & Meyer, B.T. (2014). Identifying the human-machine differences in complex binaural scenes: What can be learned from our auditory system. *15th Annual Conference of the International Speech Communication Association (Interspeech 2014),* Singapore, 14–18 September; Vols 1–4, 626–630.

Spratley, S., Ehinger, K., & Miller, T. (2020). A closer look at generalisation in RAVEN. ecva.net.

Šprogar, M. (2018). A ladder to human-comparable intelligence: An empirical metric. *Journal of Experimental & Theoretical Artificial Intelligence, 30,* 1037-1050.

Staddon, J.E.R. (2014). *The New Behaviourism* (2nd edn). New York: Psychology Press.

Stango, V., & Zinman, J. (2009). Exponential growth bias and household finance. *Journal of Finance, 64,* 2807–2849.

Stanovich, K.E. (2018). Miserliness in human cognition: The interaction of detection, override and mindware. *Thinking & Reasoning, 24,* 423–444.

Stanovich, K.E., West, R.F., & Toplak, M.E. (2013). Myside bias, rational thinking, and intelligence. *Current Directions in Psychological Science, 22,* 259–264.

Staufenbiel, S.M., Brouwer, A.-M., Keizer, A.W., & van Wouwe, N.C. (2014). Effect of beta and gamma neurofeedback on memory and intelligence in the elderly. *Biological Psychology, 95,* 74–85.

Sternberg, R.J. (2019). A theory of adaptive intelligence and its relation to general intelligence. *Journal of Intelligence, 7,* Article No. 23.

Sternberg, R.J., & Powell, J.S. (1983). Comprehending verbal comprehension. *American Psychologist, 36,* 878–893.

Stramaccia, D.F., Meyer, A.-K., Rischer, K.M., Fawcett, J.M., & Benoit, R.G. (2020). Memory suppression and its deficiency in psychological disorders: A focused meta-analysis. *Journal of Experimental Psychology: General, 150*, 828-850.

Strayer, D.L., & Fisher, D.L. (2016). SPIDER: A framework for understanding driver distraction. *Human Factors, 58*, 5–12.

Süssenbach, P., Sarah Niemeier, S., & Glock, S. (2013). Effects of and attention to graphic warning labels on cigarette packages. *Psychology & Health, 28*, 1192–1206.

Symmonds, M., Emmanuel, J.J., Drew, M.E., Batterham, R.L., & Dolan, R.J. (2010). Metabolic state alters economic decision making under risk in humans. *PLoS ONE, 5*, e11090.

Szegedy, C., Zaremba, W., Sutskever, I., Bruna, J., Erhan, D., Goofellow, I., et al. (2014). Intriguing properties of neural networks. arXiv: 1312.6199v1.

Tajfel, H., & Turner, J.C. (1979). An integrative theory of intergroup conflict. In W.G. Austin & S. Worchel (eds), *The Social Psychology of Intergroup Relations* (pp. 33–47). Monterey, CA: Brooks/Cole.

Tan, K.H., & Lim, B.P. (2018). The artificial intelligence renaissance: Deep learning and the road to human-level machine intelligence. *APSIPA Transactions on Signal and Information Processing, 7*, e6.

Taub, G.E., & McGrew, K.S. (2014). The Woodcock–Johnson tests of cognitive abilities III's cognitive performance model. *Journal of Psychoeducational Assessment, 32*, 187–201.

Taylor, S.E., & Brown, J.D. (1988). Illusion and well-being: A social psychological perspective on mental health. *Psychological Bulletin, 103*, 193–210.

Tegmark, M. (2018). *Life 3.0: Being Human in the Age of Artificial Intelligence*. London: Penguin.

Tennie, C., Call, J., & Tomasello, M. (2009). Ratcheting up the ratchet: On the evolution of cumulative culture. *Proceedings of the Royal Society B, 364*, 2405–2415.

Tetlock, P.E. (2002). Social functionalist frameworks for judgment and choice: Intuitive politicians, theologians, and prosecutors. *Psychological Review, 109*, 451–471.

Thorndike, E.L., & Woodworth, R.S. (1901). The influence of improvement in one mental function upon the efficiency of other functions (i). *Psychological Review, 8*, 384–395.

Tian, Y., Pei, K., Jana, S., & Ray, B. (2018). Deep Test: Automated testing of deep-neural-network-driven autonomous cars. *Proceedings of the 40th International Conference on Software Engineering (ICSE)*, 303–314.

Todd, P.M., & Miller, G.F. (1999). From pride and prejudice to persuasion: Satisficing in mate search. In G. Gigerenzer, P.M. Todd, and the ABC Group (eds), *Simple Heuristics That Make Us Smart* (pp. 287–308). Oxford: Oxford University Press.

Tolstoy, L. (1897/1995). *What Is Art?* (translated by Richard Pevear and Larissa Volokhonsky). London: Penguin.

Tomasello, M. (1999). *The Cultural Origins of Human Cognition*. Cambridge, MA: Harvard University Press.

Tononi, G. (2008). Consciousness as integrated information: A provisional manifesto. *Biological Bulletin, 215*, 216–242.

Tononi, G., Boly, M., Massimini, M., & Koch, C. (2016). Integrated information theory: From consciousness to its physical substrate. *Nature Reviews Neuroscience, 17*, 450–461.

Tononi, G., & Koch, C. (2015). Consciousness: Here, there and everywhere? *Philosophical Transactions of the Royal Society B, 370*, 20140167.

Toral, A., & Way, A. (2018). What level of quality can neural machine translation attain on literary text? In J. Moorkens, S. Castilho, F. Gaspari, & S. Doherty (eds), *Translation Quality Assessment, Machine Translation: Technologies and Applications*, Vol. 1 (pp. 263–287). Berlin: Springer.

Trahan, L.H., Stuebing, K.K., Fletcher, J.M., & Hiscock, M. (2014). The flynn effect: A meta-analysis. *Psychological Bulletin, 140*, 1332–1360.

Trickett, S.B., & Trafton, J.G. (2007). "What if…?": The use of conceptual simulations in scientific reasoning. *Cognitive Science, 31*, 843–875.

Truesdale, K.P., & Stevens, J. (2008). Do the obese know they are obese? *North Carolina Medical Journal, 69*, 188–194.

Tsimenidis, S. (2020). Limitations of deep neural networks: A discussion of G. Marcus' critical appraisal of deep learning. arXiv:2012.15754 [cs.AI].

Turchin, A., & Denkenberger, D. (2020). Classification of global catastrophic risks connected with artificial intelligence. *AI & Society, 35*, 147–163.

Turing, A.M. (1937). On computable numbers, with an application to the Entscheidungsproblem. *Proceedings of the London Mathematical Society, s2–42*, 230–265.

Turing, A. (1992 [1948]). Intelligent machinery. Technical report, National Physical Laboratory, London. In D.C. Ince (ed.) *Collected Works of A.M. Turing: Mechanical Intelligence.* Amsterdam: Elsevier.

Turing, A.M. (1950). Computing machinery and intelligence. *Mind, 40,* 433–460.

Tversky, A., & Kahneman, D. (1974). Judgement under uncertainty: Heuristics and biases. *Science, 185,* 1124–1130.

Tversky, A., & Kahneman, D. (1983). Extensional versus intuitive reasoning: The conjunction fallacy in probability judgement. *Psychological Review, 91,* 293–315.

Tversky, A., & Shafir, E. (1992). The disjunction effect in choice under uncertainty. *Psychological Science, 3,* 305–309.

Twenge, J.M., & Im, C. (2007). Changes in the need for social approval, 1958-2001. *Journal of Research in Personality, 41,* 171–189.

United States Department of Health and Human Services (2014). *The Health Consequences of Smoking—50 Years of Progress. A Report of the Surgeon General.* Atlanta, GA: U.S. Department of Health and Human Services, Centers for Disease Control and Prevention, National Center for Chronic Disease Prevention and Health Promotion, Office on Smoking and Health.

Utrera, F., Kravitz, E., Erichson, N.B., Khanna, R., Mahoney, M.W., Van den Brink, D., et al. (2020). Adversarially-trained deep nets transfer better. arXiv:2007.05869v1.

Van Bavel, J.J., Reinero, D.A., Harris, E., Robertson, C.E., & Pärnamets, P. (2020). Breaking groupthink: Why scientific identity and norms mitigate ideological epistemology. *Psychological Inquiry, 31,* 66–72.

van den Berg, R., & Ma, W.J. (2018). A resource-rational theory of set size effects in human visual working memory. *ELife, 7,* e34963.

Van den Brink, D., Van Berkum, J.J.A., Bastiaansen, M.C.M., Tesink, C.M.J.Y., Kos, M., Buitelaar, J.K., et al. (2012). Empathy matters: ERP evidence for inter-individual differences in social language processing. *Social Cognitive and Affective Neuroscience, 7,* 173–183.

van der Linden, D., Pekaar, K.A., Bakker, A.B., Schermer, J.A., Vernon, P.A., Dunkel, C.S., et al. (2017). Overlap between the general factor of personality and emotional intelligence: A meta-analysis. *Psychological Bulletin, 43,* 36–52.

van der Woerdt, S., & Haselager, P. (2019). When robots appear to have a mind: The human perception of machine agency and responsibility. *New Ideas in Psychology*, *54*, 93–100.

van Dyke, J.A., Johns, C.L., & Kukona, A. (2014). Low working memory capacity is only spuriously related to poor reading comprehension. *Cognition*, *131*, 373–403.

Van Gerven, M., & Bohte, S. (2017). Editorial: Artificial neural networks as models of neural information processing. *Frontiers in Computational Neuroscience*, *11*, Article No. 114.

Vanlancker-Sidtis, D. (2004). When only the right hemisphere is left: Studies in language and communication. *Brain and Language*, *91*, 199–211.

van Schaik, C.P., & Burkart, J.M. (2011). Social learning and evolution: The cultural intelligence hypothesis. *Philosophical Transactions of the Royal Society B*, *366*, 1008–1016.

Vanschoren, J. (2018). Meta-learning: A survey. http://arXiv.org/abs/arXiv:1810.03548.

van Wynsberghe, A., & Robbins, S. (2019). Critiquing the reasons for making artificial moral agents. *Science and Engineering Ethics*, *25*, 719–735.

Vinge, V. (1993). The coming technological singularity: How to survive in the post-human era. In *Vision 21: Interdisciplinary Science and Engineering in the Era of Cyberspace*. (pp. 11–22). Cleveland, OH: National Aeronautics and Space Administration, Office of Management, Scientific and Technical Information Program.

von Frisch, K. (1967). *The Dance Language and Orientation of Bees*. Cambridge, MA: Harvard University Press.

Voss, P. (2016). On intelligence. *Medium*, 10 October. https://medium.com/@petervoss/on-intelligence-1714ef5693ef

Wagenaar, W.A., & Sagaria, S.D. (1975). Misperception of exponential growth. *Perception & Psychophysics*, *18*, 416–422.

Walker, N.K., & Burkhardt, J.F. (1965). The combat effectiveness of various human operator controlled systems. *Proceedings of the 17th Military Operations Research Symposium*, 58–66.

Wallach, W.V., & Allen, C. (2009). *Moral Machines: Teaching Robots Right From Wrong*. OxfordSuperGLUE: A stickier benchmark for general-purpose language understanding systems. arXiv preprint 1905.00537.

Wang, A., Singh, A., Michael, J., Hill, F., Levy, O., & Bowman, S.R. (2019). GLUE: A multi-task benchmark and analysis platform for natural language understanding. *Proceedings of the 2018 EMNLP Workshop BlackboxNLP: Analysing and Interpreting Neural Networks for NLP* (pp. 353–355). Brussels: Association for Computational Linguistics. https://aclanthology.org/W18-54

Wang, J.X. (2021). Meta-learning in natural and artificial intelligence. *Current Opinion in Behavioral Sciences, 38*, 90–95.

Ward, T.B., & Sifonis, C.M. (1997). Task demands of generative thinking: What changes and what remains the same? *Journal of Creative Behavior, 31*, 245–259.

Ward, T.B., Smith, S.M., & Finke, R.A. (1995). *The Creative Cognition Approach*. Cambridge, MA: MIT Press.

Warnell, K.R., & Redcay, E. (2019). Minimal coherence among varied theory of mind measures in childhood and adulthood. *Cognition, 191*, Article No. 103997.

Warwick, K., & Shah, M. (2016). Can machines think? A report on Turing Test experiments at the Royal Society. *Journal of Experimental & Theoretical Artificial Intelligence, 28*, 989–1007.

Watson, D. (2019). The rhetoric and reality of anthropomorphism in artificial intelligence. *Minds and Machines, 29*, 417–440.

Watson, J.B. (1913). Psychology as the behaviourist sees it. *Psychological Review, 20*, 158–177.

Waytz, A., Heafner, J., & Epley, N. (2014). The mind in the machine: Anthropomorphism increases trust in an autonomous vehicle. *Journal of Experimental Social Psychology, 52*, 113–117.

Webb, T.W., & Graziano, M.S.A. (2015). The attention schema theory: A mechanistic account of subjective awareness. *Frontiers in Psychology, 6*, Article No. 500.

Wee, Y., Kuo, L.-Y., & Ngu, C.-Y. (2020). A systematic review of the true benefit of robotic surgery. *Ergonomics, 16*, e2113.

Wegner, D.M., & Gray, K. (2017). *The Mind Club: Who Thinks, What Feels, and Why it Matters*. London: Penguin.

Weiner, B. (1995). *Judgements of Responsibility: A Foundation for a Theory of Social Conduct*. New York: Guilford Press.

Weissenborn, D., Wiese, G., & Seiffe, L. (2017). Making neural QA as simple as possible but not simpler. *Proceedings of the 21st Conference on Computational Natural Language Learning (CoNLL)*, 271–280.

Wendel, W.B. (2019). The promise and limitations of artificial intelligence in the practice of law. *Okalahoma Law Review, 72*, 21–49.

Wheeler, G. (2018). Bounded rationality. *Stanford Encylopedia of Philosophy*. Palo Alto, CA: Stanford University.

Wild, C., Davis, M.H., & Johnsrude, J.S. (2012). The perceptual clarity of speech modulates activity in primary auditory cortex: fMRI evidence of interactive processes in speech perception. *NeuroImage, 60,* 1490–1502.

Wixted, J.T., & Wells, G.L. (2017). The relationship between eyewitness confidence and identification accuracy: A new synthesis. Psychological Science in the Public Interest, 18, 10-65.

Woollett, K., & Maguire, E.A. (2011). Acquiring "The Knowledge" of London's layout drives structural brain changes. *Current Biology, 21,* 2109–2114.

Xiong, W., Droppo, J., Huang, X., Seide, F., Seltzer, M., Stolcke, A., et al. (2017a). The Microsoft 2016 conversational speech recognition system. *2017 IEEE International Conference on Acoustics, Speech and Signal Processing (ICASSP)* 5–9 March, New Orleans, LA, USA, 5255–5259.

Xiong, W., Droppo, J., Huang, X.D., Seide, F., Seltzer, M.L., Stolcke, A., et al. (2017b). Toward human parity in conversational speech recognition. *IEEE-ACM Transactions on Audio Speech and Language Processing, 25,* 2410–2423.

Xiong, Wu, L., Alleva, F., Droppo, J., Huang, X., & Stolcke, A. (2018). The Microsoft 2017 conversational speech recognition system. *2018 IEEE International Conference on Acoustics, Speech and Signal Processing (ICASSP),* Calgary, AB, Canada, 15–20 April, 5934–5938.

Xue, A. (2021). End-to-end Chinese landscape painting creation using generative adversarial networks. *Proceedings of the IEEE/CVF Winter Conference on Applications of Computer Vision (WACV),* 3863–3871.

Yang, Z., Dai, Z., Yang, Y., Carbonell, J., Salakhutdinov, R., Quoc, V., & Le, Q.V. (2019). XLNet: Generalized autoregressive pretraining for language understanding. *Advances in Neural Information Processing Systems (NeurIPS), Vol. 32* (eds H. Wallach, H. Larochelle, A. Beygelzimer, F. d'Alché-Buc, F., E. Fox, & R. Garnett), 5754–5764.

Ye, J., Yeung, D.Y., Liu, E.S.C., & Rochelle, T.L. (2019). Sequential mediating effects of provided and received social support on trait emotional intelligence and subjective happiness: A longitudinal examination in Hong Kong Chinese University students. *International Journal of Psychology, 54,* 478–486.

Yin, D. & Kaiser, M. (2021). Understanding neural flexibility from a multi-faceted definition. NeuroImage, 235, 118027.

Yin, D., Liu, W., Zeljic, K., Wang, Z., Lv, Q., Fan, M., Cheng, W., et al. (2016). Dissociable changes of frontal and parietal cortices in inherent functional flexibility across the human life span. *Journal of Neuroscience, 36*, 10060–10074.

Yong, J.C., Li, N.P., & Kanazawa, S. (2021). Not so much rational but rationalising: Humans evolved as coherence-seeking, fiction-making animals. *American Psychologist.* doi:10.1037/amp0000674.

Yurtsever, E., Lambert, J., Carballo, A., & Takeda, K. (2020). A survey of autonomous driving: Common practices and emerging technologies. *IEEE Access, 8*. doi:10.1109/ACCESS.2020.2983149.

Zador, A.M. (2019). A critique of pure learning and what artificial neural networks can learn from animal brains. *Nature Communications, 10*, Article No. 3770.

Zamir, E., & Teichman, D. (2021). Mathematics, psychology, and law: The legal ramifications of the exponential growth bias.

Zamir, E. and Teichman, D. (2021). Mathematics, psychology, and law: The legal ramifications of the exponential growth bias. Hebrew University of Jerusalem Legal Research Paper No. 21-11, 14 March. https://ssrn.com/abstract=3804329.

Zell, E., Strickhouser, J.E., Sedikides, C., & Alicke, M.D. (2020). The better-than-average effect in comparative self-evaluation: A comprehensive review and meta-analysis. *Psychological Bulletin, 146*, 118–149.

Zhang, C., Gao, F., Jia, B., Zhu, Y., & Zhu, S.-C. (2019). RAVEN: A dataset for Relational and Analogical Visual rEasoNing. arXiv:1903.02741 [cs.CV].

Index

Abrams, D. 167
Addis, D.R. 81
ad hominem fallacy 164
Adiwardana, D. 113, 116
AICAN (creative adversarial
  network) 130
AI developments: effects,
  on society 278–280;
  massive transforming
  changes 270–276; minor
  transforming changes
  276–277; non-transforming
  changes 276–277
AI strengths: anthropocentrism
  and anthropofabulation
  261–265; underestimating
  261–265
Alba 292
ALBERT (A Lite BERT) 39
Alexa 10
algorithms 8–9
Al-Jazari, Ismail 13
AlphaFold 2 57
AlphaGo 25–27
AlphaGo Zero 27–28, 295
AlphaZero 135
Alter, Harrison 152
Alves, R.A. 110
American Civil War 180

animals: *vs* artificial
  intelligence 121–126;
  cognitive abilities of 123–124;
  intelligence *vs* artificial
  intelligence 121–126; tests
  of intelligence 125–126
anthropocentrism 261–265
anthropofabulation 261–265
anthropormorphism 235–240
anxiety 182–183
Apocalypse 279–280
Appel, M. 205
Apple 45
Arcade Learning
  Environment 28
Aristotle 162
Arnold, T. 214
artificial general intelligence
  100, 134–135, 227–229
artificial intelligence (AI) 4–5;
  vs animals' intelligence
  121–126; anthropormorphism
  235–240; artificial general
  intelligence 227–229;
  "biological plausibility" 6;
  bounded rationality 259–261;
  and careers of people 44–58;
  classifying images 219–222;
  complex games 21–35;

conclusions 229–230; consciousness 230–235; creativity 127–133; deep learning 9–13, 240–241; defined 5; developing 269–278; dominance 19–59; facilitating drug discovery 56–57; Generative Pre-Trained Transformer 3 (GPT-3) 227–229; having moral agency 205–208; history of 7–9; humans, limitations of 246–257; humans, strengths of 242–245; humans responding to 280–286; and intelligence 101; language ability 35–44; language limitations 223–227; limitations 218–241; massive transforming changes 270–276; and medicine 51–57; minor, non-transforming changes 276–277; and moral responsibility 211–213; neural networks 6–7; neurofeedback 284–286; non-invasive brain stimulation 280–284; overall conclusions 242; overview 5–7; perceived as morally responsible 208–211; strengths 216–218; task specificity 222–223; tests of intelligence 125–126; (un)intelligence of 95–136
artificial narrow intelligence 100
Asch, Solomon 166–168
atari 27–29
audience design 77–78
automatic speech recognition systems 36, 105–107

"Automaton" 21
autonomous vehicles 184–195; conclusions 192; ethical issues 192–195; findings 187–190; programming of 190–191
autonomous weapons systems 195–200
Awad, E. 184, 194

Baddeley, A.D. 74
Baidu 102
Baumeister, R.F. 174, 209
Bentham, Jeremy 193
Berra, Yogi 269
BERT (Bi-directional Encoder Representation from Transformers) 39–40, 108, 218, 225
biases: cognitive 152–164; exponential growth 253–256; human limitations 164–170; prone to 164–170
Binsted, L. 127
Bischof-Köhler hypothesis 83
black-box attacks 106
Boden, M.A. 127
Bolt, Usain 35
Bonnefon, J.-F. 193–194
Booch, G. 242
Booth, R.W. 180
Bostrum, N. 205
Botnik 111
bounded rationality 170–172, 259–261
Boyd, R. 64, 246
Braga, A. 278
brain-machine interfaces 289–291
BrainNet 287–288
brain-to-brain interfaces 287–289
Broadbent 181

Brogaard, B. 233
Brooks, R. 96–97, 98
Brown, Joshua 187
Buckner, C. 261, 264
Bullmore, E. 65–66
Burdett, B.R.D. 141
Burkhardt, J.F. 180
Byron De La Beckwith 46

Cai, C.J. 54
Campbell, D.T. 179
Capek, Karel 13
CAPTCHA (Completely
    Automated Turing test to
    tell Computers and Humans
    Apart) 95, *96*
Cattell, R.B. 92
Chabris, C.F 81
Chalmers, D. 277
chatbots 117–118
Chen, Y. 106
chess: artificial intelligence
    21–24; "Automaton" 21;
    complex games 21–24; and
    deep learning 23
children 244–245
Chinese Room argument
    212, 223
Chomsky, N. 75–77
Chou, Jimmy 30
Chung-Jen Tan 3
Cleverbot 113–114
cobots (collaborative robots)
    17–18
"cognitive anthropomorphism"
    236
cognitive biases 152–164; and
    irrational humans 156–157;
    limitations due to 152–164
"cognitive dissonance" 176
cognitive misers 247–248
Cognitive Reflection Test 247
Cole, D. 224

Colman, Andrew 5
combinatorial creativity 127
communication: and language
    64; and social brain 63
COMPAS (Correctional
    Offender Management
    Profiling for Alternative
    Sanctions) 47–51
complex games: artificial
    intelligence 21–35; chess
    21–24; Go 24–27; Jeopardy!
    33–35; poker 29–33; shogi
    and atari 27–29
conformity 166–168
Connectome 65–68, *66*
consciousness 71–74, 230–235;
    external awareness 72;
    human *vs* other species 73;
    internal awareness 72
convergent thinking 126
conversation 38
convolution 11
Conway, A.R.A. 93
Cook, Alastair 239
Corbett-Davies, S. 50
Corner, A. 163
Cotton, Ronald 146
Coulborn, S. 282
Covid-19 180, 255, 257, 275
creativity: art 128–133;
    artificial intelligence systems
    vs human abilities 126–134;
    human limitations 178–180;
    types of 127
Critical Assessment for Structure
    Prediction (CASP) 56–57
Croskerry, Pat 153–154
CUBBITT 41
cultural brain hypothesis
    63–65
cultural intelligence 62
Cunningham, W.A. 46
cyborgs 289–291

Danks, D. 200
Darwin, Charles 2, 72
da Vinci, Leonardo 14
Davis, E. 228
The Day a Computer Writes a Novel 111
Deep Blue 3–4, *4*, 6, 22
deep learning 9–13, 240–241; and chess 23; and medicine 51
Dehaene, S. 230
Demertzi, A. 71–72
depression 182–183
DeSanti, A. 206
Devalla, S.K. 54
Discriminator 129–130
Dismukes, R.K. 144
divergent thinking 126–127
DNA: *vs* genes 2; human 2; pseudogenes 3
Dressel, J. 48, 49
dual-inheritance theory 63–65
Dufner, M. 174
Dunbar, R.I.M. 62
Duncan, J. 93
Dunning-Kruger effect 169
Dutta, A. 289
Dyson, Sir James 179

Earth: human dominance 1–5; scientific discoveries on importance of 1
ecological intelligence 61
Edison, Thomas 179
Eil, D. 33, 159
Elektro (robot) 14, *15*
Elgammal, A. 130
Elias, Darren 31
Elmo 27
emotional intelligence 100
emotional states: limitations due to 180–183
emotions, negative 182–183

employment/careers: and artificial intelligence (AI) 44–58; legal profession 45–47
Erica (robot) 15–16, *17*
ethical issues and autonomous vehicles 192–195
Eugene Goostman (chatbot) 38, 115
Evers, Medgar 46
evolutionary history 246–247
exploratory creativity 127
exponential growth bias 253–256
Eysenck, M.W. 181, 284

Farid, H. 48, 49
"far transfer" 147
Fawcett, J.M. 145
Feinberg, T.E. 73
Ferguson, Chris 31, *32*
Ferreira, V.S. 78
Festinger, L. 175, 176
Feynman, Richard 2
Fildes, A. 252
Fischer, L. 41
Fiske, S.T. 173
flexibility, of human brain 68–70, *69*
fluid intelligence 93
Flynn effect 149
forgetting 141–147
Formula Medicine 141
forward modelling approach 78
Frankenstein (Shelley) 14
Frederick, S. 247
Fugaku 138, 258

Galton, Sir Francis 291
Garrett, B. 145
Gates, Bill 5
Geminoid-DK 14–15

Geneplore theory 178
General Language
    Understanding Evaluation
    (GLUE) test 218
General Problem Solver 5–6
Generative Pre-Trained
    Transformer 3 (GPT-3) 12,
    42–44, 112–113, 227–229
Generator 129
genes: described 2; *vs* DNA 2;
    human 2
genetic engineering 291–294
Gilbert, D.T. 176
GLUE (General Language
    Understanding Evaluation) 39
Go: artificial intelligence
    24–27; complex games 24–27
Goel, S. 50
GOFAI (Good Old-Fashioned
    Artificial Intelligence) 22
Good Old-Fashioned AI
    (GOFAI) 97
Google 39
Google Search 10
Google Translate 40
Gopnik, Alison 245
Grace, K. 275, 279
Griess test 155
Griffiths, T.L. 260
Gruetzemacher, R. 275
Guardian 4

Haigh, M. 164
Harris, Sam 23
Hawking, Stephen 279
Heaven, D. 229
Hemingway, Ernest 192
Hendrycks, D. 219–220
Henrich, J. 64
Hephaestus (Greek God) 13
Herzberg, Elaine 187–188
high-level machine intelligence
    (HLMI) 275

Hitch, G.J. 74
Hockey, G.R.J. 181
Hodges, B.H. 167
Hoffrage, U. 172
Hofstadter, Doug 5
Homo habilis 60
Homo sapiens 60, 243
Horowitz, M. 196
Houdebine, Louis-Marie 292
Huang, S.G. 54
Hulbert, J.C. 145
human brain 60–70;
    brain-machine interfaces
    289–291; brain-to-brain
    interfaces 287–289; caveats
    and a broader perspective
    84–89; Connectome 65–68;
    cultural brain hypothesis
    63–65; cyborgs 289–291;
    dual-inheritance theory
    63–65; episodic simulation
    82; and evolution 60–63;
    flexibility 68–70, *69*; genetic
    engineering 291–294;
    making more effective
    286–294; memory storage
    capacity 68; *vs* other species
    70–89; size *61*; theory
    of mind 83–84; working
    memory and attentional
    control 74–75
Human Connectome Project
    65–68
human intelligence 100
human limitations: anxiety and
    depression 182–183; bounded
    rationality 171–172; cognitive
    biases and irrationality
    156–157; conformity
    166–168; creativity 178–180;
    due to cognitive biases and
    "irrationality" 152–164; due
    to emotional states 180–183;

due to limited capacity
138–151; forgetting 141–147;
logical reasoning 162–164;
loss aversion 158–162;
mental set 149–151; negative
emotions 182–183; prone
to biases and irrationality
164–170; rational humans
170–178; self-deception
and self-enhancement
173–177; self-enhancement
and self-esteem 169–170;
social factors 166–168; social
identity 172–173; stress
effects 180–182; sustained
attention 139–141; transfer
of learning 147–149
humans: children 244–245;
cognitive misers 247–248;
evolutionary history
246–247; exponential growth
bias 253–256; how rational
are 170–178; killing ourselves
250–253; limitations 246–257;
mathematics 253–256; obesity
251–253; prioritisation among
multiple goals 248–250;
smoking 250–251; species,
flourishing 243–244; speed-
accuracy trade-off 247–248;
strengths 242–245
human species: Darwin on
2; and Earth 1–5; language
ability 35
human strengths: human
brain 60–70; humans *vs*
other species 70–89; inter-
dependent abilities 89–93;
underestimating 265–267
Humberg, S. 174

images, classifying 219–222
Implicit Association Test 47

intelligence: artificial
general 100; and artificial
intelligence 101; artificial
narrow 100; defined 98–99;
general 99–100; high, and
humans 99; human 100;
narrow 100; tests 101–104
intelligence tests (IQ tests) 100;
of AI 102
Intelligent Conversational
Android 15
inter-dependent abilities:
human strengths 89–93;
intelligence 92–93
irrationality: human limitations
164–170; limitations due to
152–164; prone to 164–170

Jape 127
Jeffrey, K. 267
Jennings, Ken 34
Jeopardy! 33–35
Jia, R. 109
Jiang, Z. 287–288
Joyce, James 119
junk DNA 2

Kac, Edouardo 292
Kahneman, D. 152–153, 156–158
Kant, Immanuel 193
Kardashian, Kim 221–222
Kasparov, Garry 3–4, 6,
21–22, 29
Keech, Marian 175–176
Kellogg, R.T. 110
Kelly, Kevin 274
killer robots 195–200;
conclusions 200;
moral issues 198–200
Kim, Dong 30
King, J.-R. 231
Kleinberg, J. 48
Kline, M.A. 64

Köbis, N. 42
Koch, C. 234
Ko Ju-yeon 26
Konishi, M. 280
Koopman, P. 191
Kovacs, K. 93
Krause, B. 283
Krizhevsky, A. 11
Kurdi, B. 47
Kurzweil, Ray 4–5

Laland, K. 81
language: and communication 64; and cultural brain hypothesis 64; flexibility and human brain 77–81
language ability: artificial intelligence 35–44; conversation 38; and human brain 75–77; and human intelligence 35; speech recognition 35–38; text comprehension 38–40; text generation 42–44; translation 40–42
language limitations: artificial intelligence 223–227; general issues 223–227
language skills: and AI 104; general language abilities 112–113; and intelligence 104–121; limitations 117–118; speech recognition 104–107; text comprehension 107–110; text generation 110–112; translation 119–120; Turing test 113–117
Läubl, S. 41
LawGeex 45
learning: deep 240–241; transfer of 147–149
Leela Chess Zero 12, 23
Lee Sedol 27

legal profession, and AI 45–47
Les, Jason 30, 31
Levine, M. 150
Levinson, J.D. 47
Liang, P. 109
Libratus (AI) 30–31, 33
Lieder, F. 260
Lien, J.W. 33, 159
limited capacity, limitations due to 138–151
Limpo, T. 110
Lin, Z. 49
Lindsey, S. 156
Liu, F. 101–102
Liu, X. 53
Logan, R.K. 278
logical reasoning 162–164
"Lord of the Rings" 203
loss aversion 158–162
Lovelace, Ada 7
Lubat, Bernard 128
Lung, T. 251

Maetschke, S. 239–240
Mallatt, J.M. 73
Malle, B.F. 199, 210
Manet, Édouard 127
Marcus, G. 228, 240, 246
Markowitz, Harry 157
marriage of AI and humans 294–295
Marsh, R.L. 145
Massimini, M. 233
massive transforming changes 270–276
mathematics 253–256
Mathur, M.B. 204
Mazzone, M. 130–131
McAulay, Daniel 30
McCarthy, J. 7
McDermott, D. 230
McDermott, R. 161

McGurk effect 105
McKinley, Evan 153–154
medicine: and artificial intelligence 51–57; and deep learning 51; diagnosis 51–55; facilitating drug discovery 56–57; surgical robots 55–56
memory storage capacity, of human brain 68
mental set 149–151
meta-consciousness 72–73
Miller, G.F. 171
minor transforming changes 276–277
Minsky, M. 96
Monet, Claude 127
Moore, Gordon 270
moral agency and AI 205–208
moral agents, producing 213–215
morality: killer robots 198–200; and robots 184–215
Moravec, Hans 95
Moravec's paradox 95–98, 100
Morgenroth, E. 284
Mori, M. 203
Mossink, L.D. 42
Musk, Elon 279, 291
MuZero algorithm 28, 135

Nachar, R.A. 96
Nairne, J.S. 81
National Academies of Sciences and Medicine 293
National Institutes of Health 65
"near transfer" 147
negative emotions 182–183; anxiety and depression 182–183
Nestelbacher, Reinhard 292
neural machine translation 41
neural networks 6–7; and deep learning 10–11

neurofeedback 284–286
Newell, Allen 6
Ng, N.F. 147
non-invasive brain stimulation 280–284
non-transforming changes 276–277
Nowinski, J.L. 144

obesity 251–253
Ogunleye, O.O. 252
The Origin of Species (Darwin) 2
Ortony, A. 80
Oxford Dictionary of Psychology (Colman) 5

Pachet, F. 128
Pais-Vieira, M. 287
Patrick, J.R. 180
Pennartz, C.M.A. 72
Pfungst, Oskar 224
Piaget-MacGuyver Room test 126
Pinker, S. 71
Pluribus (AI) 31, 33
poker: and artificial intelligence 29–33; complex games 29–33
Pope, D.G. 160
Pope, J.W. 150
Popel, M. 41
"Portrait of Edmond de Belamy" 128–129, 129
predation 63
principle of cost control 65
principle of efficiency 65
prioritisation among multiple goals 248–250
The Promise of Artificial Intelligence: Reckoning and Judgement (Smith) 135
prospective-memory failures 145
pseudogenes 3

Raichle, M.E. 67
RAND Corporation 187
"ratchet effect" 65
Raven's Progressive Matrices
    102–103
Realpolitik 200
Renoir, Auguste 127
"rich club" 68
Richens, J.G. 51
Richerby, David 259
Richerson, P.J. 246
Ritchie, S.J. 149
RoBERTA 39
robots 13–18, 200–213;
    autonomous vehicles 184–195;
    autonomous weapons systems
    195–200; in car production
    57–58; "killer robots"
    195–200; and morality
    184–215; producing moral
    agents 213–215; programming
    of 205; robots 200–213; treating
    202–204; warfare 195–200
Roff, H.M. 200
Rogers, Carl 174
Rubik's cube 19–20
Rumelhart, D.E. 80
Russell, Bertrand 169
Rutter, Brad 34

Sagaria, S.D. 253–254
Samsung 45
Sandberg, A. 271
Saon, G. 37
"saying-is believing" effect 143
Schacter, D.L. 81
Schärfe, Henrik 15, *16*
Scheutz, M. 214
Schooler, J.W. 71
Schrittwieser, J. 28
Schwark, J. 139
Schweitzer, M.E. 160
scurvy 3

Searle, John 276–277
Second World War 139
Seed, A. 81
segmentation 36
self-deception 173–176
self-enhancement 169–170,
    173–176
self-esteem 169–170
Shafir, E. 158
Shank, D.B. 206, 207
Shariff, A.F. 209
Shaw, John 6
Sheetz, K.H. 55
Shelley, Mary 14, 33
Shereshevskii, Solomon 142
shogi 27–29
Sifonis, C.M. 179
Silver, D. 27
Simon, Herb 6, 7, 44, 170–171,
    260
Simon, Herbert 98
Simons, D.J. 81, 148
Simonson, I. 160
Simonton, D.K. 179
Siri 10, 102
Smallwood, J. 280
SMILY (Similar Medical
    Images Like Yours) 54–55
Smith, Brian Cantwell 135
smoking 250–251
social brain hypothesis 62–63
social factors and human
    limitations 166–168
social identity 172–173
social intelligence 61
society, and AI developments
    278–280
Spearman, Charles 92
species, flourishing 243–244
speech recognition 35–38; AI
    systems 104–107; automatic
    36, 105–107; and human
    listeners 105; segmentation 36

speech-recognition models 36–37
speed-accuracy trade-off
    247–248
Sporns, O. 65–66
Spratley, S. 103
Star Trek 289
Star Wars 289
Staw, B.M. 160
Stockfish 27–28
Stramaccia, D.F. 143
stress effects 180–182
Sunway TaihuLight
    supercomputer 20
supercomputers 20–21
SuperGLUE 108
SuperVision 11–12
surgical robots 55–56
sustained attention 139–141

Taiwanese Ing Foundation 24
task specificity 222–223
Tegmark 46, 259
Terminator 2 195
text comprehension, and AI
    38–40
theory of mind 83–84
Thompson, Jennifer 146
Thorndike, E.L. 148
Todd, P.M. 171
Tononi, G. 234
Toral, A. 119
transcranial direct current
    stimulation (tDCS) 281–284
transfer of learning 147–149
transformational creativity 127
translation, and AI 40–42
Tsimenidis, S. 242
Tucker-Drob, E.M. 149
Turing, Alan 7–8, 38, 236,
    262, 271
Turing test 38, 113–117
Tversky, A. 152, 153, 156,
    157, 158

Ulysses (Joyce) 119

Vanschoren, J. 218
vehicles, autonomous
    184–195
Velsberg, Ott 46
Vinge, Vernor 273–274,
    276
Vohs, K.D. 174
Voss, P. 99

Wagenaar, W.A. 253–254
Walker, N.K. 180
Wang, A. 39
Ward, T.B. 178
warfare: autonomous
    weapons systems
    195–200; "killer robots"
    195–200
Watson (AI) 34–35
Watson, Thomas 34
Way, A. 119
Weiner, B. 209
white-box attacks 106
Whiteford, A.P. 110
*Who Wants to be
    a Millionaire* 160
Wikipedia 34
Winograd Schema Challenge
    109–110
Wittgenstein, Ludwig 104
Woodworth, R.S. 148
working memory 74–75, 282
Wozniak, Steve 125–126

Xiaofa (robot) 46
Xiong, W. 37

Yusheng Du 19

Zador, A.M. 97
Zell, E. 169
Zhang, C. 103